PAL Series
Program-Assisted Learning

Dennis P. Curtin
Cathleen Morin
Kim Foley
Kunal Sen

Windows® 95 PAL

Microsoft® Word for Windows® 95 (Version 7.0) PAL

Microsoft® Excel for Windows® 95 (Version 7.0) PAL

Microsoft® Access for Windows® 95 (Version 7.0) PAL

MICROSOFT® ACCESS FOR WINDOWS® 95 PAL:
PROGRAM-ASSISTED LEARNING

VERSION 7.0

Dennis P. Curtin

Kunal Sen

Kim Foley

Prentice Hall, Upper Saddle River, New Jersey 07458

Library of Congress Cataloging-in-Publication Data:
Curtin, Dennis P.
    Microsoft Access for Windows 95 PAL [computer file] : program-
assisted learning [for] version 7.0 / Dennis P. Curtin, Kunal Sen,
Kim Foley.
    1 computer laser optical disc : sd., col. : 4¾ in. + 1 manual.
    Computer program.
    System requirements: 486 PC or better: 12MB RAM (16MB recommended);
Windows 95; Microsoft Access for Windows 95; SVGA with 256 colors
(640x480 minimum, 800x600 recommended); sound card and speakers
(optional); printer (optional); hard drive with 10MB free; 3½ in.
high density floppy disk drive; mouse; CD-ROM player.
    Title from manual t.p.
    Summary: Program-assisted instruction program for learning
Microsoft Access for Windows 95 (version 7.0). Displays interactive
animations, graphics, movies, and step-by-step instructions.
Includes concepts, tutorials, and drills.
    ISBN 0-13-237025-5
    1. Microsoft Access—Computer-assisted instruction—Software.
2. Relational databases—Software. 3. Database management—
Software. I. Sen, Kunal. II. Foley, Kim. III. Title.

QA76.8.D3 <1997 00469> <MRC>
005.75—DC12   96-12215
                                                        CIP

Microsoft and Windows are registered trademarks of Microsoft Corporation
in the USA and other countries.

Acquisitions editor: Carolyn Henderson
Marketing manager: Nancy Evans
Director of production and manufacturing: Joanne Jay
Production manager: Lorraine Patsco
Illustrator: Warren Fischbach
Design director: Patricia Wosczyk
Senior manufacturing supervisor: Paul Smolenski
Editorial assistant: Lori Cardillo
Production coordinator: Renée Pelletier
Project manager: Cecil Yarbrough

Interior design by Kenny Beck
Additional design by Christy Mahon
Cover art by Marjory Dressler
Cover design by Ginidir Marshall
Screen shots by Cathleen Morin

© 1997 by Prentice-Hall, Inc.
A Simon & Schuster Company
Upper Saddle River, NJ 07458

ISBN 0-13-237025-5

Printed in the United States of America
9 8 7 6 5 4 3 2 1

Prentice-Hall International (UK) Limited, *London*
Prentice-Hall of Australia Pty. Limited, *Sydney*
Prentice-Hall of Canada Inc., *Toronto*
Prentice-Hall Hispanoamericana, S.A., *Mexico*
Prentice-Hall of India Private Limited, *New Delhi*
Prentice-Hall of Japan, Inc., *Tokyo*
Simon & Schuster Asia Ptd. Ltd., *Singapore*
Editora Prentice-Hall do Brasil, Ltda., *Rio de Janeiro*

CONTENTS

QUICKSTEPS BOXES

P R E F A C E

Databases are one of the most common application of computers because they provide such an efficient way to store and manage data. Once you have stored data in a program such as Access, you can use it to answer questions you might have such as "Which 1988 models are still in stock?" or "Whose bill is more than 90 days overdue?" You can also use the same information to print labels, reports, invoices, and other frequently used documents. The applications of a program such as Access are almost endless, ranging from tasks that can be done with a card file index, such as keeping track of a baseball card collection, to those that aren't anywhere near as easy without the power of a computer. For example, you can automate an entire college course sign-up process.

This text, *Microsoft Access for Windows 95 (Version 7.0) PAL: Program-Assisted Learning,* is an outline and guide to the accompanying interactive multimedia program *PAL,* our system of *Program-Assisted Learning.* This learning system assumes only basic Windows experience such as pointing, clicking, and dragging. Everything else you need to know to become a proficient user of Microsoft Access for Windows 95 is presented here.

PAL—PROGRAM-ASSISTED LEARNING

PAL—*Program-Assisted Learning*—is designed to guide you through learning Microsoft Access for Windows 95 while you use the actual program. It does this by displaying interactive animations, graphics, movies, and step-by-step instructions on top of the Access screen display. PAL is an intuitive, easy-to-use system that makes learning Access not only more efficient, but more enjoyable. When you use it with this text, it lets you master the most frequently used Access features more quickly.

The PAL System. The PAL system uses on-screen interactive multimedia and printed text material working together: (1) the PAL CD; (2) the PAL window on top of the Access screen; (3) the PAL text.

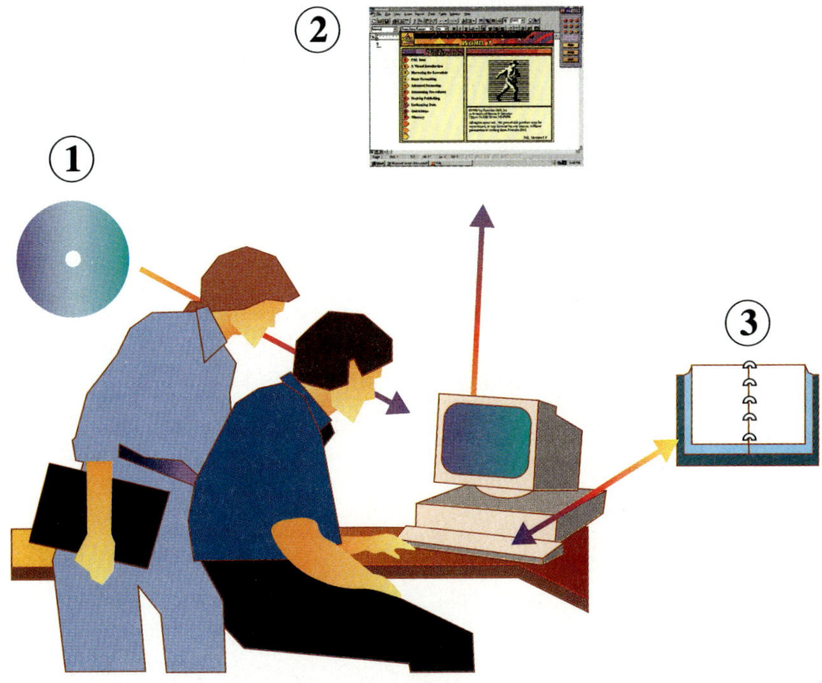

1. PAL's setup procedure copies to your computer's hard drive the PAL program and a database containing the program's text components. The graphic, movie, and sound files on the PAL CD are not copied to the hard drive, so you must have the CD in your computer's CD-ROM drive when you use the program. The PAL CD also contains the files you copy to your own 3.5-inch floppy disks when you make your *Access Student Resource Disks,* described later in this preface.

2. When you start PAL, an interactive multimedia window opens on top of the Access screen to guide you through interactive concepts, tutorials, drills, and review questions. As you study Access, you have immediate on-line access to illustrated glossary terms, demonstration videos, and step-by-step procedures.

3. This book, a guide to using the PAL system, provides the context for your studies with concepts, examples, exercises, reference material, and a checklist of on-line activities.

TIP

Also Available at a Computer Screen Near You

Microsoft Access for Windows 95 PAL (Version 7.0): Program-Assisted Learning is one of a series of texts that use a highly visual, interactive multimedia approach to learning Windows 95 and its application programs. Similar texts are available on Windows 95 itself and on the Microsoft Office applications Word and Excel.

PAL—The Advantages of Its Approach

There is a big difference between a static textbook and a dynamic, interactive multimedia presentation. Here are just some of the advantages of using PAL:

▶ Basic concepts are presented interactively so they are more interesting and understandable than those presented in a text.

▶ You do not have to refer back and forth between the book and screen. Many resources are just a mouse click away, ready for instant access. Click a blue word or phrase to see an illustrated definition. Click a **QuickSteps** button for a step-by-step guide to a procedure. Click a **Graphic** button for an illustration. Click a **Demo** button to see a movie of a key step demonstrated on screen. Click a **Loudspeaker** button to hear a word pronounced.

▶ The on-screen instructions and animations of concepts are immediate and understandable demonstrations of the computer's usefulness that will help motivate you to learn.

▶ Review questions—both multiple choice and true-false—are more interactive than in a textbook. They provide immediate feedback and directions. You are immediately told if you answered correctly or incorrectly and, if incorrect, you are directed back to the section where the material was covered.

LAB ACTIVITIES—FIVE STEPS TO MASTERY

Learning operating systems and application programs takes time and practice. There really aren't any shortcuts. This text recognizes that no one masters procedures the first time through. It takes repetition and practice—and yes, even mistakes. Our approach uses five steps to mastery: concepts, tutorials, drills, exercises, and projects. As you proceed through these five steps in the order shown, you are given less and less guidance and have more and more room to make mistakes. You are also required to use more and more procedures to perform combined tasks.

1. *On-line concepts* provide you with a step-by-step interactive introduction to, and a walk-through of, the procedure you are studying. Your actions are controlled so you cannot make a mistake.

2. *On-line tutorials* provide you with step-by-step guidance as you explore a procedure for the first time using the actual Access for Windows program. If you follow the steps, you can't go wrong.

3. *On-line drills*, which you complete after finishing a matching tutorial, are very narrow in focus and drill you on a single procedure. The purpose of these drills is to allow you to repeat a procedure until you have mastered it. For example, you may create several queries for a database table instead of the one you created in the tutorial.

4. *Text-based exercises*, which you complete after the drills, are more challenging than drills and usually require an understanding of more than one procedure. Procedures are not spelled out for you. You either have to recall them or look them up. These activities are much like the real world, where you are told what to do but not how to do it.

5. *Text-based projects* state a problem or provide a situation and tell you what should be done about it but provide no instructions on how to do it.

ACCESS FOR WINDOWS 95 PAL'S ORGANIZATION

Access for Windows 95 PAL is organized into pictorial tutorials called *PicTorials*.

PicTorial T takes you on a simulated tour of PAL and its elements. You'll see how to explore concepts, complete tutorials and drills, and answer review questions.

PicTorial 1 introduces Access and shows you how to get around the program's screens. You open an existing database, view its tables, queries, and reports, and explore Access's extensive Help system.

In PicTorial 2 you create your own database and learn how to design, modify, and print tables.

PicTorial 3 shows you how to use uses the Find command, filters, and queries to harness the real power of a database.

PicTorial 4 teaches you how to design forms to enter data and reports to print out just what you need to see.

PicTorial 5 explains one-to-many relationships, and gives you practice in relating tables to create complex queries and reports

PAL—WHAT'S NEEDED TO USE IT

The complete PAL learning system contains the following components:

▶ This text is your guide to using PAL. It contains conceptual and reference material, an outline of your on-line activities, exercises, and projects.

▶ Inside the back cover of the book is packaged the CD which contains the entire PAL program. Printed on the flap of the back cover are instructions for installing PAL on your system and for making the *Access Student Resource Disks*.

▶ The *Access Student Resource Disks* contains all of the files needed to complete the computer activities in this text. You cannot run PAL past PicTorial 1 without having the first disk in the floppy drive of your computer (though you can view the PAL Tour and PicTorial 1 without it). To make these disks, you will need three blank, formatted 3.5-inch high-density (1.44MB capacity) floppy disks and the PAL Identification Number (PIN) printed on the outside of the CD package. Note that it is illegal to use the PAL Identification Number from a book unless you are the rightful owner of the book/CD package.

Supplements

The following supplements to this text have been made available by the publisher:

▶ An *Instructor's Manual with Tests* contains suggested course outlines for a variety of course lengths and formats, teaching tips and a list of competencies to be attained for each PicTorial, solutions and answers to all computer activities, and a complete test bank of over 200 questions.

▶ A Windows-based computerized testing program, *Prentice Hall Custom Test*, features user-friendly test creation as well as the ability to administer tests traditionally or on-line, evaluate and track students' results, and analyze the success of each exam—all with a simple click of the mouse.

Sending Your Opinions and Feedback

We are happy to hear from users or potential users of this program. It's through such exchanges that improvements are made. If you have any comments or questions, send them to one of us at the Internet e-mail address listed at the end of this preface.

Acknowledgments

We would like to thank all of those people who have worked hard to make this the best possible program.

On the academic end have been the following reviewers of the text or the PAL program:

- Kathryn M. Baalman, St. Charles Community College
- Susan Blackman, Fort Lewis College
- Kate Crawford, Edison Community College
- Edward Eill, Delaware County Community College
- Michael A. Feiler, Merritt College
- Lisa E. Gueldenzoph, Bowling Green State University
- Matthew Hightower, Bakersfield College
- Robert A. Hogue, Youngstown State University
- Lester W. Horn, Pensacola Junior College
- Barbara Hotta, Leeward Community College
- Rajeev Kaula, Southwest Missouri State University
- William Kornegay, Miami-Date Community College
- Hao Lou, Ohio University
- Philip McCauley, ITT Technical Institute
- Mike Miller, Kansas State University
- Lou Price, DeVry Institute of Technology (Columbus, Ohio)
- Fred M. Schwartz, Business Solutions Unlimited
- Dennis D. Shafer, Cuyahoga Community College
- Randy Stolze, Marist College
- Frederick L. Wells, DeKalb College
- Donald C. Westlake, Computer Learning Center (Los Angeles)
- Marlys Willard, Iowa Western Community College, Council Bluffs

At the publisher's end Cecil Yarbrough continued with his efforts to improve our texts. His guidance and leadership are always most welcome. Supporting the production at the publisher have been Suzanne Behnke, Warren Fischbach, Joanne Jay, Christy Mahon, John Nestor, Lorraine Patsco, Paul Smolenski, and Patricia Wosczyk.

All of these people, each and every one, took a personal interest in this text, and that interest shows in the work you are now holding. Any shortcomings that remain are our responsibility.

DENNIS P. CURTIN	Dennis_Curtin@msn.com
KUNAL SEN	76625,2444@compuserve.com
KIM FOLEY	74071,2240@compuserve.com
CATHLEEN MORIN	102662,237@compuserve.com

MICROSOFT® ACCESS FOR WINDOWS® 95 PAL: PROGRAM-ASSISTED LEARNING

Version 7.0

A PAL TOUR

PAL stands for *Program-Assisted Learning*; it is an interactive multimedia series consisting of textbooks and accompanying computer programs. PAL guides you through learning Windows 95 and its Microsoft Office application programs by displaying animations, graphics, and step-by-step instructions on top of each program's own screen display. You'll find that PAL is an intuitive, easy-to-use system that makes learning Windows 95 and its applications more efficient and more enjoyable. ▶

Installing PAL and Making the Student Resource Disks

The PAL program must be installed on your computer or network before you can run it, and to do more than view the PAL Tour and the first PicTorial you must also have made your own *Student Resource Disks* using the *MakeSRD* program that comes on the CD, together with the PAL Identification Number, or PIN, that is included on the inside back cover of your book/CD package. Instructions for these steps are included on the back cover flap of this book.

Once PAL is installed on your system, you are ready to learn how to start it—also called *opening*, *running*, or *launching* it—and how to close or exit it. To use PAL you first turn on your computer to start Windows 95. Then follow the steps in the QuickSteps box "Starting PAL." (If you will be running PAL on a network, your lab instructor may give you special instructions for starting PAL.)

QUICKSTEPS

Starting PAL

1. Insert the CD into your computer's CD-ROM drive.

2. Insert the *Student Resource Disk* with the PAL Identification Number, or PIN, into your computer's floppy drive.

3. With Windows on the screen, use the mouse to point to the **Start** button at the left of the taskbar at the bottom of the Windows screen, and click the left mouse button to display the Start menu.

4. Using the mouse, point to the word **Programs** on the menu to display a submenu listing the programs on your system.

5. Point to the words **PAL Systems** on the menu to display another submenu listing the PAL programs on your system.

6. Click the name of the PAL program you are studying. PAL opens with an animation, and then the *Contents* window appears.

COMMON WRONG TURNS

No Student Resource Disk?

If you start PAL without the proper *Student Resource Disk* in your computer's floppy drive, a dialog box will appear asking you to insert the disk.

▶ If you have the disk, insert it into your floppy drive, then click the drop-down arrow in the lower-left corner of the window to display a list of the drives on your system. Click the drive into which you inserted the disk, then click the **OK** button to continue.

▶ If you don't have a disk, click the **Demo** button and you can explore the PAL Tour and PicTorial 1. Or click the **Cancel** button to leave PAL.

The PAL *Contents* window is much like the table of contents in a book. When you select a PicTorial (chapter) from the list on the left, the sections in that PicTorial are displayed on the right. Just by selecting one PicTorial after another you can easily scan the entire contents of the program. When you select one of the sections on the right, the *Section Introduction* window appears. From this window you can explore the section's concepts or begin a step-by-step tutorial or drill. And PAL's Remote Control is always available to help you move around in the program. The illustration "PAL's Organization" shows a sample of each of these screens.

PAL's Organization. PAL Is organized into a series of related windows, each of which is described in this introduction.

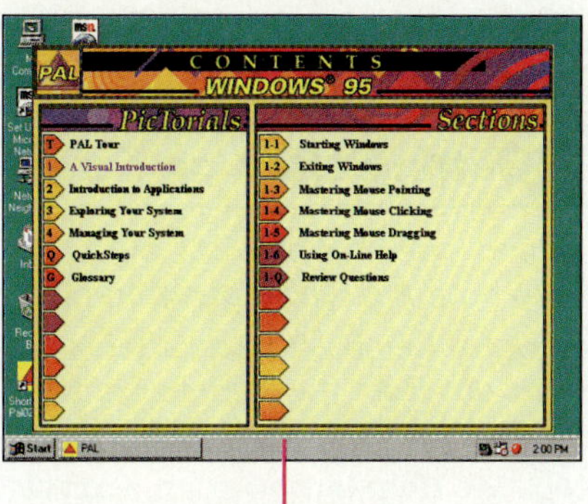

The *Contents* Window

When you start PAL, the *Contents* window appears. Clicking a PicTorial on the left side of the window displays a list of its sections on the right side.

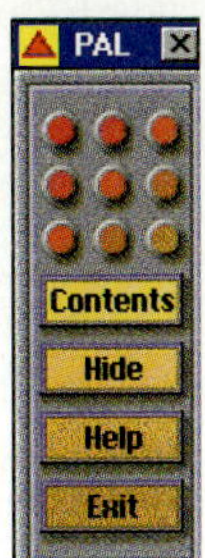

The Remote Control. The Remote Control is always on the screen when PAL is open.

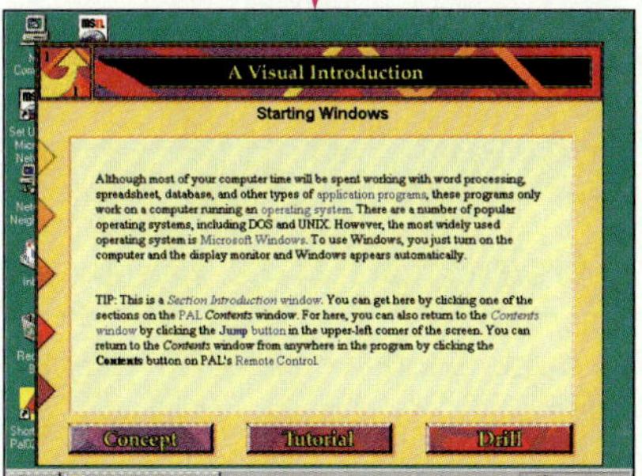

The *Section Introduction* Window

Clicking one of the sections on the *Contents window* displays the *Section Introduction* window. This window is your gateway to learning about a topic by exploring concepts, a tutorial, and a drill step by step.

The *Concepts* Window

Clicking the **Concept** button on the *Section Introduction* window displays a step-by-step introduction to the topic you are studying.

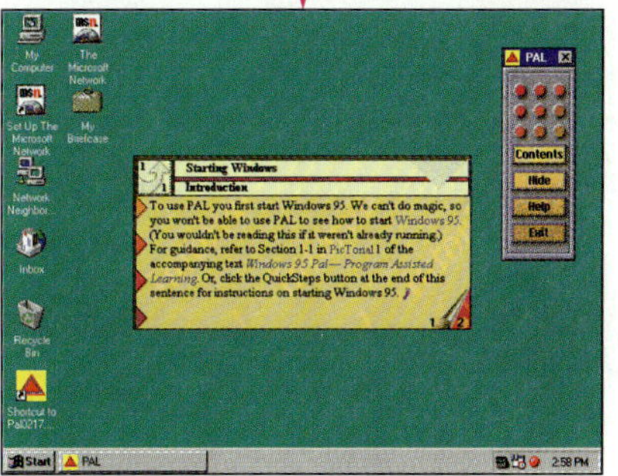

The *Tutorial* Window

Clicking the **Tutorial** button on the *Section Introduction* window displays a smaller *Tutorial* window that leads you step by step through a procedure.

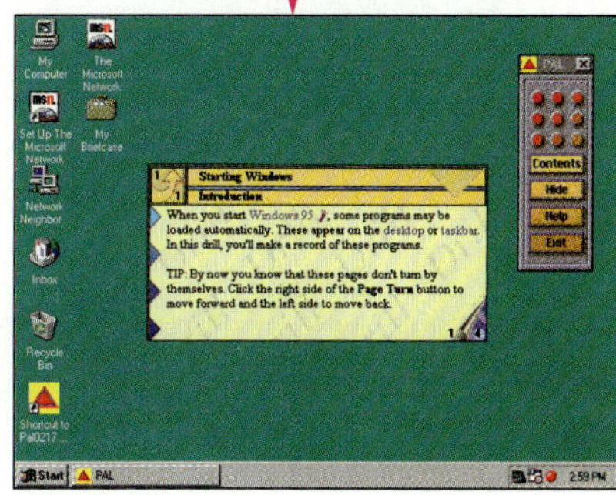

The *Drill* Window

Clicking the **Drill** button on the *Section Introduction* window displays a smaller *Drill* window that leads you through a procedure so you can master it.

T I P

Stopping the Opening Animation

PAL begins with an opening animation. If you don't want to watch it, you can click anywhere in this animation with the left mouse button and go directly to the PAL *Contents* window.

Getting On-Line Help

You can use the **Help** button on PAL's Remote Control to display Help at any time. Clicking it once with the left mouse button displays help on things you point to. Clicking it twice takes you into the on-line Help system.

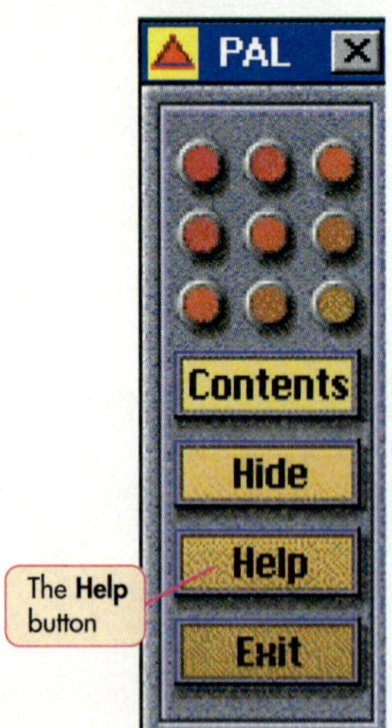

The Help Button. Clicking the **Help** button on the Remote Control adds a question mark to the mouse pointer. When you then point to any PAL object on the screen, a description of that object is displayed.

QUICKSTEPS

Getting Help on Screen Objects

1. To find out what any PAL button, window, or other object does, click the **Help** button to add a question mark to the mouse pointer.
2. Point to the object in question to display its description in a window that slides out from the Remote Control.
3. To close the Help window and remove the question mark from the pointer, click the **Help** button again. (You can also click anywhere on a clear area of PAL, but be careful. Clicking buttons or glossary terms activates them.)

QUICKSTEPS

Using On-Line Help

1. For more extensive Help, double-click the **Help** button to enter PAL's Help system.
2. Click any Help topic button on the left side of the Help window to display Help on that topic on the right.
3. Use the scroll bar to scroll through Help text on the right, or click the **Done** button to close Help. Within any Help text, you can also click a **Graphic** button (⌷) to display a pop-up graphic, a **Demo** button (⌷) to display an animated demonstration, or a **Loudspeaker** button to hear a word pronounced.

Hiding and Restoring PAL

If a PAL window or the Remote Control covers a part of the screen you want to see, or if you want to put PAL away for awhile, you can hide it by clicking the **Hide** button on the Remote Control. This reduces the PAL program ("minimizes it") to a button on Windows' taskbar. It is still running but not taking up space on your screen. When you want to see it again, click the PAL button on the taskbar to restore it. (If you cannot see the Remote Control, clicking the PAL button on the taskbar moves it in front of all other windows.)

Closing PAL

When finished with PAL, you can close it. This removes it from your computer's memory and the screen. To use it again, you have to restart it from Windows' Start menu. To close PAL, you would normally use the left mouse button to click the **Exit** button on PAL's Remote Control, but you can use any of the procedures listed in the QuickSteps box "Closing PAL and Setting a Bookmark."

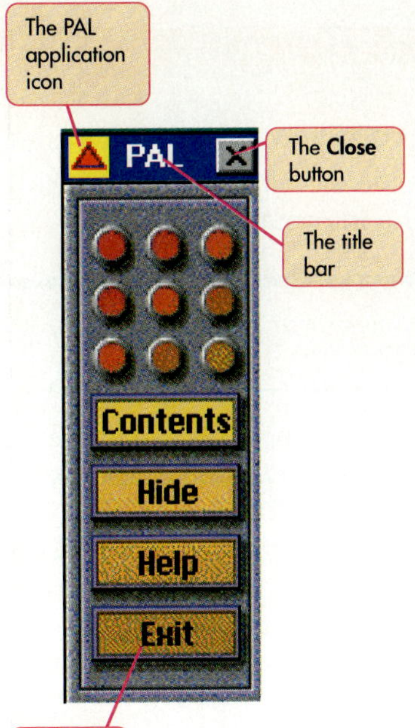

Closing PAL. One of the quickest ways to close PAL is to click the **Exit** button on the Remote Control.

Closing PAL and Setting a Bookmark

To close PAL and display the PAL Bookmark dialog box:

▶ With the left mouse button, click the **Exit** button on PAL's Remote Control.

You can also do any of the following:

▶ With the left mouse button click the **Close** button (⊠) on the Remote Control's title bar.

▶ With the left mouse button, click the PAL application icon on the Remote Control's title bar to display a shortcut menu, then use the left mouse button to click the shortcut menu's **Close** command.

▶ With the right mouse button, click the Remote Control's title bar to display a shortcut menu, then use the left mouse button to click the shortcut menu's **Close** command.

▶ With the right mouse button, click PAL's button on the taskbar (at the bottom of the Windows screen), then click the shortcut menu's **Close** command.

When the PAL Bookmark dialog box asks whether you want to mark your place:

▶ Click the **Yes** button, and the next time you start PAL, the PicTorial and section that you have just finished will be highlighted in the Contents window..

▶ Click the **No** button to close PAL without setting a bookmark.

PAL ACTIVITIES CHECKLIST

☐**T-1 PAL TOUR.** In this section, you begin to explore the PAL system of learning.

1. Follow the steps listed in the text-based tutorial that follows to display PAL's *Contents* window.

2. Click the **Exit** button on PAL's Remote Control to close PAL. (If you can't see the Remote Control, click the PAL button on Windows' taskbar.)

☐**TOURING PAL ON YOUR OWN.** In this section, you explore starting and closing PAL on your own.

1. Start PAL and this time click anywhere on the opening animation to stop it before it finishes.

2. Click the **Help** button on the Remote Control and then point to objects on the screen to see what they do. (If you can't see the Remote Control, click the PAL button on Windows' taskbar.) When finished, click the **Help** button again to turn off Help.

3. Double-click the **Help** button on the Remote Control (that is, click it twice very rapidly) to display the Help window. Click Help topics on the left and read about them. When finished, click the **Done** button.

4. Close PAL using any of the procedures described in the QuickSteps box "Closing PAL."

5. Start PAL again and continue to the next section.

In this tutorial you turn on your system so it starts Windows 95 and then start PAL. On some systems, additional steps may be required. If this is the case with your system, your instructor will supply you with the information you need.

LOOKING AHEAD
Pointing and Clicking

To perform many actions with the computer, you use the mouse to move the mouse pointer on the screen so that it points to a button or a menu command, and then you press and release the left mouse button. This is called pointing and clicking, and you will become expert at it as you use PAL. Here is a tip in advance: Always hold the mouse so that it is perpendicular to the face of the monitor. That way, when you move the mouse left or right, the mouse pointer will move in the same direction on the screen. When the mouse pointer is over the button you want to click, press the left mouse button gently so you don't move the mouse at the same time.

Getting Ready

1. Open the door to floppy drive A or eject any disk from that drive.

Starting Windows 95

2. To start Windows, turn on the computer and the display monitor. If you can't find the on/off switches, ask someone where they are. When you turn on the computer, the computer first runs a diagnostic program to be sure the system is operating correctly. Then the Windows loading sequence begins. At some point in the process, you may be prompted to log onto Windows or a network.

3. When the Windows desktop and taskbar are displayed, you can begin work. If a *Welcome to Windows 95* screen appears on the desktop, point to the **Close** button in the lower-right corner of its window and click the left mouse button. There also may be other windows that appear on your screen automatically.

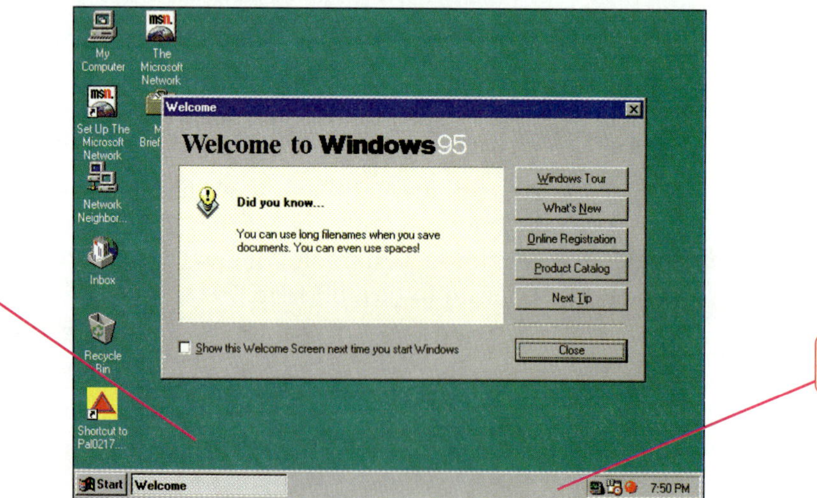

The Windows desktop

The taskbar

Starting PAL

4. Insert the CD into your computer's CD-ROM drive.

5. Insert the *Student Resource Disk* with the PAL Identification Number (PIN) into one of your computer's floppy drives.

6. Using the mouse, point to the **Start** button on the taskbar and click the left mouse button to display the Start menu. (Your menu may look different from the one shown here.)

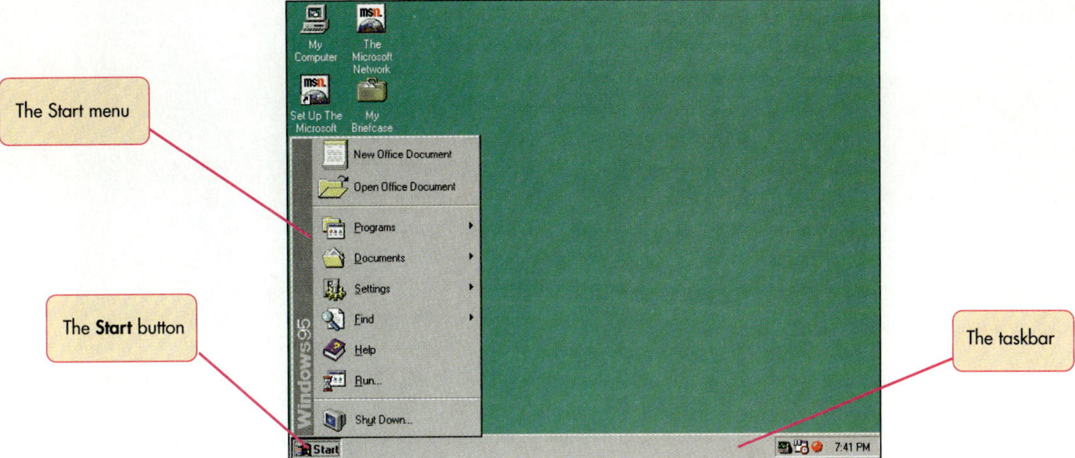

7. Point to the menu's **Programs** folder so it cascades and displays a submenu. (Your submenu may look different from the one shown here.)

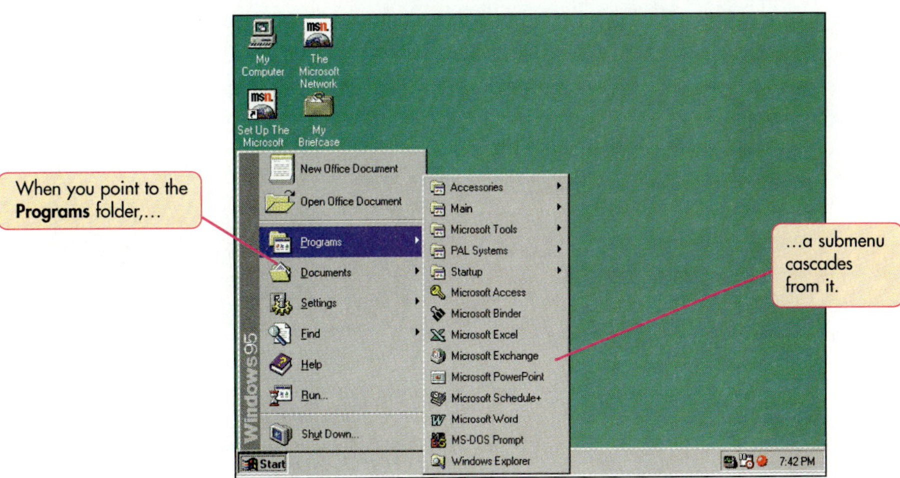

8. Point to the menu's **PAL Systems** folder so it cascades and displays a list of the PAL programs on your system. (Your submenu may look different from the one shown here.)

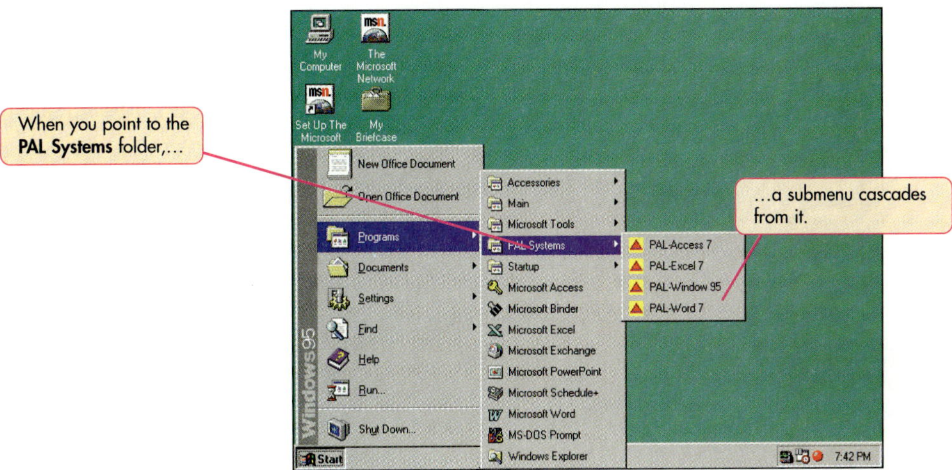

9. On the PAL submenu, click the name of the PAL program you are studying. This starts PAL and displays an opening screen and an animation.

10. With the left mouse button, click anywhere in the animation screen, or just wait for the animation to end, and the *Contents* windows appears, listing the PicTorials (chapters) in the course. Notice how a button for PAL appears on the taskbar (at the bottom of the Windows screen) and the PAL Remote Control appears at the top right of the screen.

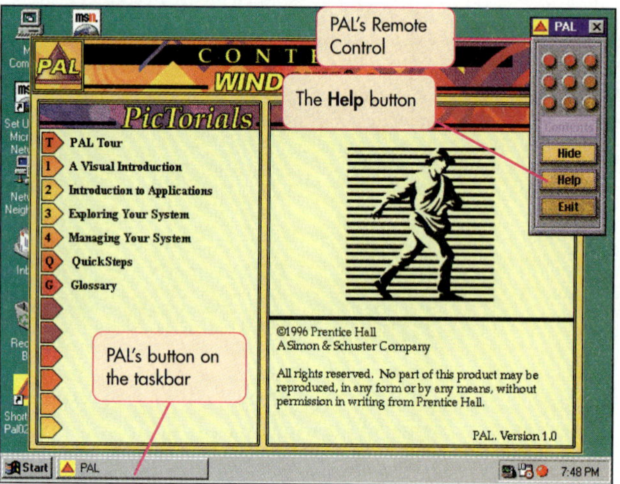

Exploring Help

11. Click the **Help** button on the Remote Control to add a question mark to the mouse pointer. (If the Remote Control is hidden, just click the PAL button on the taskbar to move it on top of other windows.)

12. Point to PAL objects on the screen to display a description of them in a window that slides out from the Remote Control. When finished, click any clear area of a PAL window to close the Help window. (To avoid clicking command buttons and activating them by mistake, just click the **Help** button on the Remote Control again.)

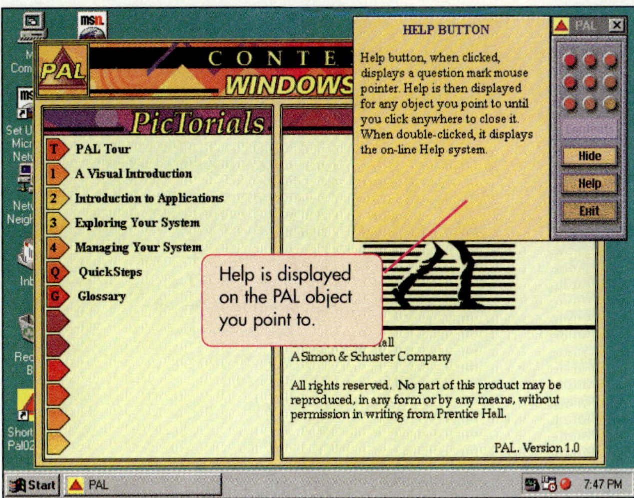

13. Double-click the **Help** button on the Remote Control to open the main Help window.

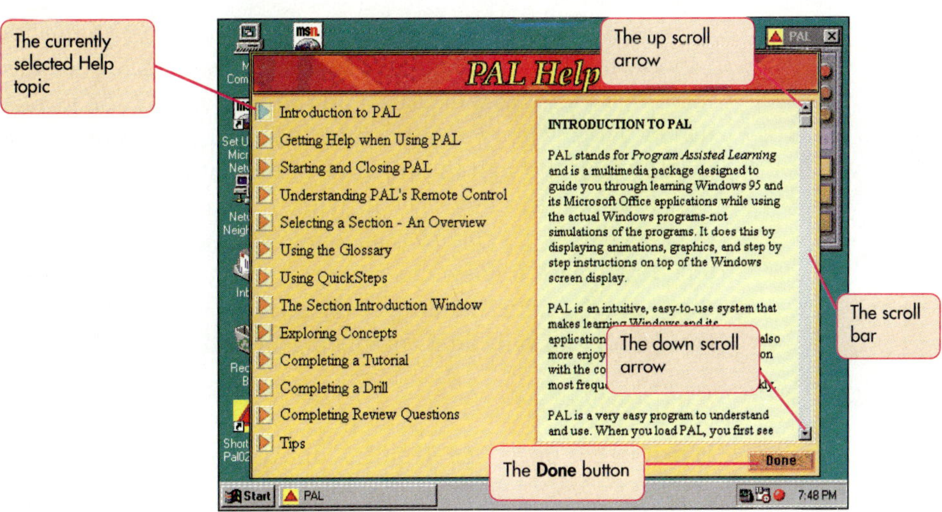

14. Click any Help button or topic on the left side of the window to display Help on that topic. Sometimes, the Help text on the right side of the screen is too long to fit on one screen. To scroll through it, click the up and down scroll arrows on the scroll bar.

15. When finished exploring Help, click the Help window's **Done** button.

Finishing Up

16. Continue to the next section to learn more about PAL. If you have to quit now, click the **Exit** button on the Remote Control to close PAL. (If the Remote Control is hidden, click the PAL button on Windows' taskbar to move it in front of other open windows.)

T-2 PAL—GETTING STARTED

Starting PAL displays its *Contents* window and Remote Control. Both of these are used extensively when navigating and studying with PAL.

PAL'S Contents Window

When you start PAL, the first window you see after the animation is the *Contents* window, which is organized like the table of contents in a book.

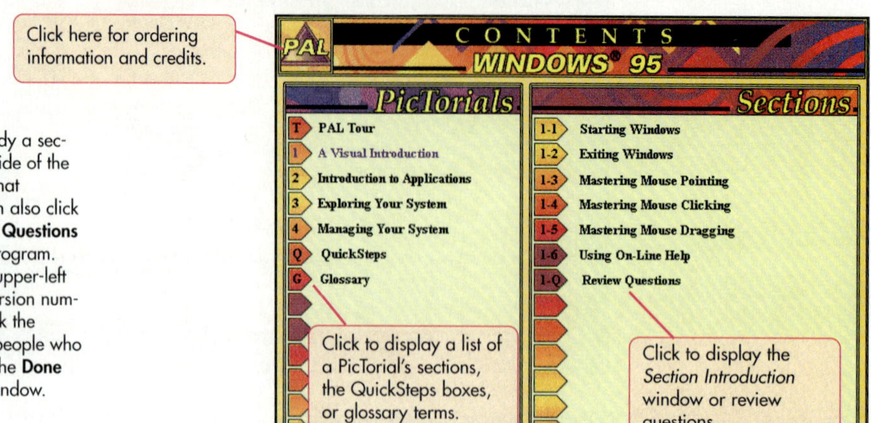

The PAL *Contents* Window. To study a section click the PicTorial on the left side of the window and then click a section that appears on the right side. You can also click **Glossary**, **QuickSteps**, or **Review Questions** to move to those sections of the program. You can click the PAL logo in the upper-left corner to display ordering and version number information. You can then click the **Credits** button to see a list of the people who developed this program, or click the **Done** button to return to the *Contents* window.

To begin study, first select a PicTorial from the list on the left side of the *Contents* window by clicking its name or number. When you do so, a list of sections or topics in that PicTorial is displayed on the right side of the window. (Sections are hidden by a logo when you first load PAL.) You can click one PicTorial after another to quickly skim through the contents of the entire program. When you find the section you want to study, click its name or number on the right side of the window to display its *Section Introduction* window. When finished with all of the sections in a PicTorial, click **Review Questions** on the *Sections* list to display a set of questions that test your understanding of the selected PicTorial. You would normally answer these questions only after completing all of the sections in the PicTorial.

PAL'S Remote Control

When PAL is open, the Remote Control is always on the screen. Like the remote control for your television or stereo, the buttons on PAL's Remote Control enable you to control the PAL program. If the Remote Control gets hidden by other PAL windows, click the PAL button on Windows' taskbar to bring it to the front. If it gets in your way, you can drag it to a new position.

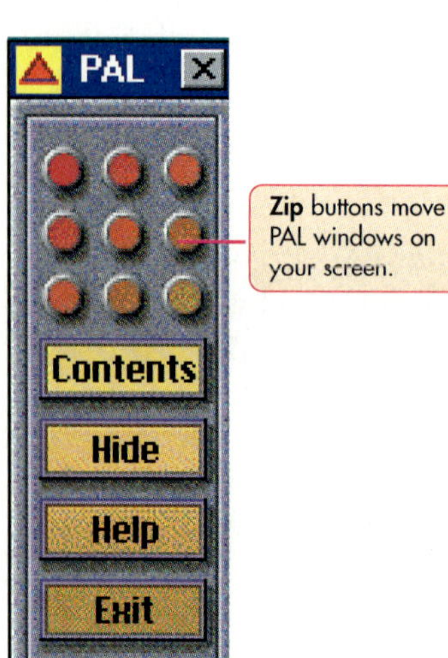

Zip buttons move PAL windows on your screen.

The Remote Control. The Remote Control is always on the screen when PAL is open.

LOOKING AHEAD
Dragging

If the Remote Control gets in your way, you can move it to a new position. Point to a clear area of its title bar, hold down the left mouse button, and move the mouse in the direction you want to move the Remote Control. As you do so, an outline of the Remote Control moves on the screen. Release the mouse button, and the Remote Control moves to fill the outline. This is called dragging, and you will become expert at it as you proceed through this PAL.

▶ **Zip** buttons, arranged in a grid, immediately move any PAL window to one of nine preset positions on the screen to get the window out of your way. For example, if you click the upper-right **Zip** button, the PAL window will zip to the upper-right corner of the screen. You'll find these buttons a quick way to see what's under the PAL window.

- ▸ **Contents** button returns you to the opening *Contents* window where you can select a new PicTorial or section to study, display questions for any PicTorial, or display lists of QuickSteps and glossary terms. The PicTorial and section that you last worked on are highlighted when you return.

- ▸ **Hide** button acts like a Windows **Minimize** button. Clicking it reduces PAL and all open PAL windows to just a button on the taskbar. This is useful whenever any of PAL's windows get in your way. To display PAL again, click the PAL button on the taskbar.

- ▸ **Help** button displays Help on the PAL program. Clicking it once lets you point to PAL objects to display a brief description of them. Clicking the **Help** button again turns pointer help off. Double-clicking the **Help** button displays the full Help system.

- ▸ **Exit** button closes PAL and removes it from your system's memory. To use it again, you have to restart it from Windows' Start menu.

Like all Windows applications, the Remote Control has a title bar. You can point to a clear area on this title bar, hold down the left mouse button, and drag it to a new position on the screen.

- ▸ **Application icon** at the left end of the title bar displays a shortcut menu when you click it.

- ▸ **Close** button (⊠) at the right end of the title bar is the standard Windows 95 button used to close an application. Clicking this button removes PAL from your computer's memory and the screen. To use it again, you have to restart if from Windows' Start menu.

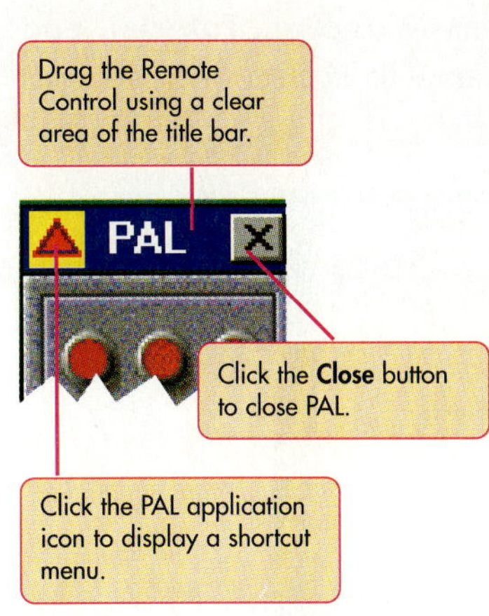

The Remote Control's Title Bar. The Remote Control's title bar can be used to drag the Remote Control, display a shortcut menu, or close PAL.

P A L   A C T I V I T I E S   C H E C K L I S T

☐ **T-2 PAL TOUR.** In this section, you start PAL and use it to explore PAL's Remote Control and a few basic ways to navigate through the PAL program.

1. Start PAL or click the **Contents** button on the Remote Control to return to the *Contents* window.

2. On the *PicTorials* list, click the letter **T** or the name **PAL Tour**. This displays a list of the sections in the tour.

3. On the *Sections* list, click **T-2, PAL—Getting Started** to display the first screen of the tour.

4. Follow the instructions that appear on the screen. If nothing seems to happen, click the **Page Turn** button in the lower-right corner of PAL's window. Clicking the left side of this button moves you back one step and clicking the right side moves you forward.

☐ **TOURING PAL ON YOUR OWN.** In this section, you explore PAL's Remote Control and a few basic ways to navigate through the PAL program.

1. Click each of the PicTorials on the *PicTorials* list to see their sections in the *Sections* list. Don't click **QuickSteps** or **Glossary** yet. If you do, click the **Done** button in the windows that appears to return to the *Contents* window.

2. Click PAL's button on the taskbar to move the Remote Control in front of other windows.

3. Practice clicking the **Hide** button on the Remote Control, then clicking PAL's button on the taskbar. Repeat this until you understand exactly what is happening.

Selecting a PicTorial on the *Contents* window displays a list of the sections in that PicTorial on the right side of the *Contents* window. Clicking any of those sections (other than **Review Questions**) displays the *Section Introduction* window. This window contains a brief introduction to the section and it is your gateway to exploring a procedure. The window displays three buttons—**Concept**, **Tutorial**, and **Drill**—which you would normally click in that sequence to explore the concepts and procedures covered in the section.

The *Section Introduction* Window. The *Section Introduction* window introduces a procedure and allows you to display an interactive concept, a step-by-step tutorial, or a procedure-mastery drill.

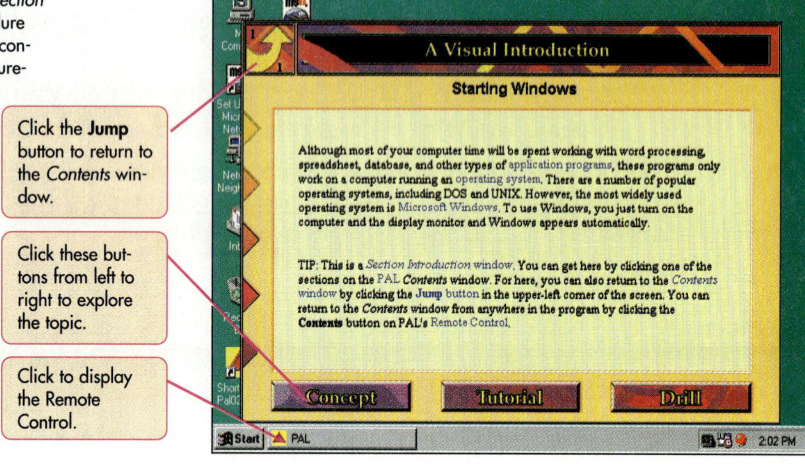

Click the **Jump** button to return to the *Contents* window.

Click these buttons from left to right to explore the topic.

Click to display the Remote Control.

UNDERSTANDING
Hot Spots—Items to Click for More Information

While working with PAL there are many clickable "hot spots" in the windows that display additional information.

▸ Click any term highlighted in blue to display a pop-up glossary definition, many of which are illustrated. After reading the definition, click the pop-up's **Done** button to close it. If you display a glossary term, and then click a glossary term within it, click the **Back** button to return to the previously displayed glossary term.

▸ Click a **Graphic** button (📷) in any of the steps or glossary windows to display a pop-up graphic of the procedure described in that step. When finished looking at the graphic, click the **Done** button.

▸ Click a **Demo** button (🖵) in any of the steps or glossary windows to display an animated demonstration of the procedure described in that step.

▸ Click a **QuickSteps** button (🏃) to display the *QuickSteps* window. (These buttons appear primarily in drills.) This window lists the steps that you follow to complete the procedure. To move through the sequence of steps, use the scroll bar. When finished, click the **Done** button to return to where you were.

▸ Click a **Loudspeaker** button to hear a word pronounced.

Understanding Navigation

To navigate PAL, you click buttons in the windows on the screen.

▸ The **Jump** button in the upper-left corner of many windows has two numbers on it. The left number indicates the PicTorial you are in and the right number indicates the section within that PicTorial. Clicking the button backs you up one level. For example, if the *Section Introduction* window is on the screen, clicking it returns you to the *Contents* window. If a *Tutorial* or *Drill* window is on the screen, clicking it returns you to the *Section Introduction* window. One of the fastest ways to navigate the system is to click other buttons to move forward and then click this one to move back.

▶ The **Page Turn** button in the lower-right corner of many windows moves you forward and back through the steps or pages. This button also has two numbers on it. The left number indicates the step you are currently on. The right number indicates the total number of steps in the concept, tutorial, or drill.

▶ When you display the last step in a concept, tutorial, or drill, a window tells you that you have finished. You can then click any of the listed *jump terms* to go to the indicated places. (You can also click the **Jump** button one or more times to back up and go down another branch.)

Exploring Concepts

Clicking the **Concept** button on the *Section Introduction* window displays a section illustrating and describing the key concepts underlying the procedures you are studying in the section. To move through the concepts, follow the instructions that appear in the window or click the right or left side of the **Page Turn** button to move forward or back.

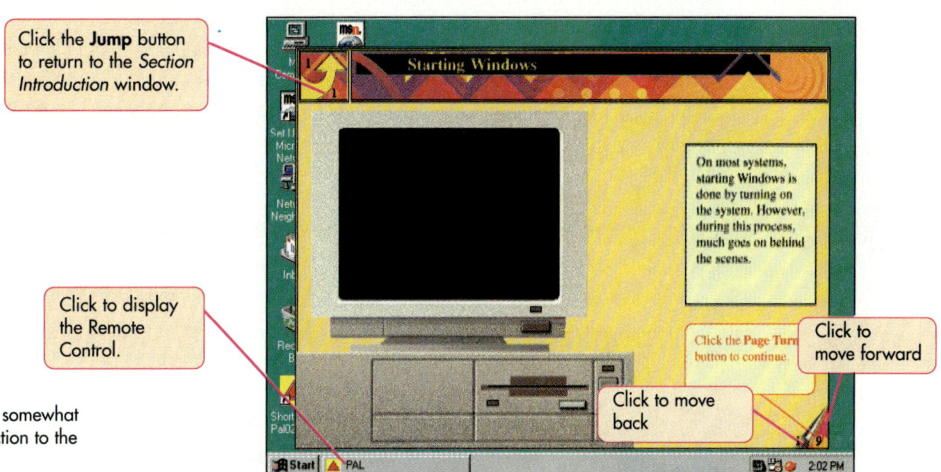

Concepts. *Concept* windows vary somewhat but display an interactive introduction to the procedure you are studying.

Completing a Tutorial

Tutorials are designed to guide you step by step through specific procedures using the actual Windows program that you are studying. When you click the **Tutorial** button on the *Section Introduction* window, a smaller *Tutorial* window appears with an introduction to the tutorial. As you proceed through the steps, you are told what to do with the actual program you are studying. For example, a step may tell you to pull down a menu and click a command. If you carefully follow the instructions, you will be introduced to the actual procedure without ever getting lost.

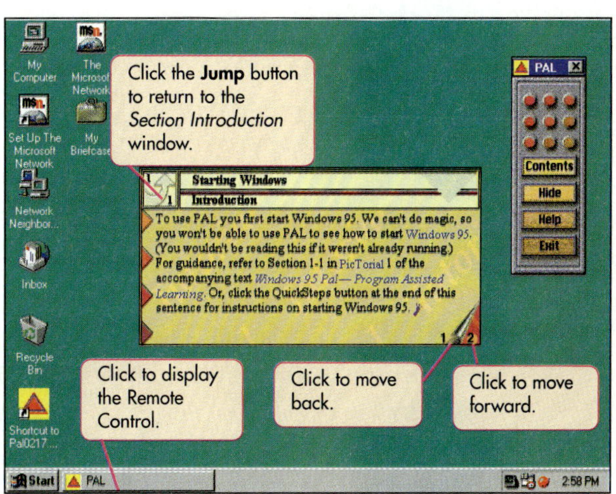

The *Tutorial* Window. The *Tutorial* window displays the steps that you follow to complete a tutorial. Clicking the **Page Turn** buttons in the lower-right corner move you forward and back through the steps. Clicking the **Jump** button in the upper-left corner returns you to the *Section Introduction* window.

Completing a Drill

Drills are designed to let you practice the procedures to which you were introduced in the tutorial. They reinforce your understanding of these procedures and improve your skill in implementing them.

When you click the **Drill** button on the *Section Introduction* window, a smaller *Drill* window appears with an introduction to the drill. This window is identical to the *Tutorial* window.

☐ **T-3 PAL TOUR.** In this section, you explore the sequence you follow to explore a section—first the concept, then the tutorial, then the drill.

1. Start PAL or click the **Contents** button on the Remote Control to return to the *Contents* window.

2. On the *PicTorials* list, click the letter **T** or the name **PAL Tour**. This displays a list of the sections in the tour.

3. On the *Sections* list, click **T-3, Exploring a Section** to display the first screen of the tour.

4. Follow the instructions that appear on the screen. If nothing seems to happen, click the **Page Turn** button in the lower-right corner of the window. Clicking the left side of this button moves you back one step and clicking the right side moves you forward.

☐ **TOURING PAL ON YOUR OWN.** In this section, you explore PAL's organization until you become familiar with it.

1. Click any PicTorial on the *PicTorials* list (other than **QuickSteps** or **Glossary**) and then click any section in the *Sections* list (other than *Review Questions*). This displays a *Section Introduction* window.

2. Click each of the three buttons at the bottom of the *Section Introduction* window to see what happens. When a new window appears, click the **Page Turn** buttons in its lower-right corner to see how they work. Click the **Jump** button in the upper-left corner of the window to return to the *Section Introduction* window.

3. Repeat Steps 1 and 2 until you feel comfortable navigating through the program. If you get lost at any time, click PAL's button on the taskbar to move the Remote Control in front, then click its **Contents** button.

T-4 COMPLETING REVIEW QUESTIONS

Review questions are designed to test your understanding of the procedures discussed in the PicTorial.

Displaying Questions

There are two ways to display questions. At any time, you can click the **Contents** button on the Remote Control to display the PAL *Contents* window. You can then select the PicTorial on which you want to be tested. Click the **Review Questions** button at the bottom of the *Sections* list on the right side of PAL's *Contents* window to display the *Review Questions* window. Also, as you complete a PicTorial, the last window in the last drill lets you jump directly to the *Review Questions* window.

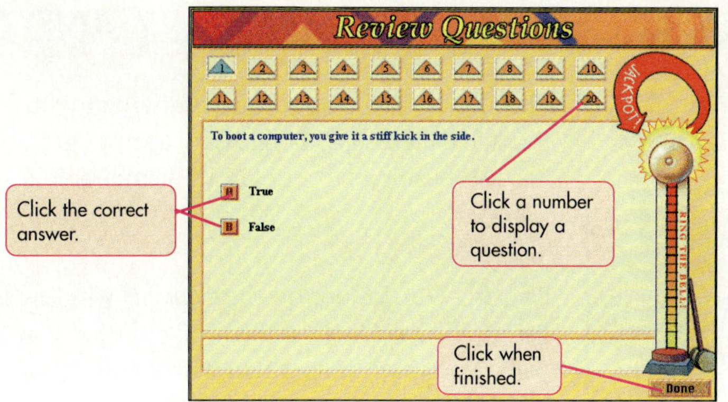

The *Review Questions* Window. The *Review Questions* window allows you to test your understanding of the material you covered in the PicTorial. Clicking any numbered button on one of the two rows of buttons at the top of the window displays a question.

Answering Questions

With the *Review Questions* window displayed, click any numbered **Question** button to display a question and then click to answer it. When you answer a question, you are told immediately whenever you got it right and your current score is indicated on the score meter.

When finished answering all questions, click the **Done** button to display the *Question Summary* window. Here your results are summarized and for those questions you got wrong, you are referred to sections in the accompanying text for more study. You can click the **Print** button to print the summary, click the **Continue** button to return to the questions (if you haven't finished answering them all), or click the **Done** button to exit questions and return to the *Contents* window.

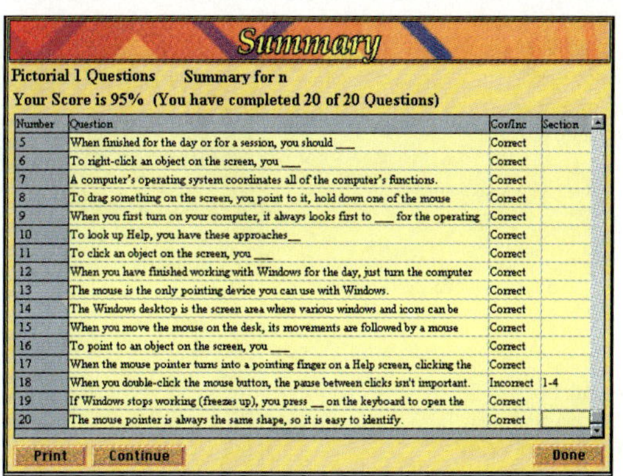

Summary

Pictorial 1 Questions   Summary for n
Your Score is 95% (You have completed 20 of 20 Questions)

Number	Question	Cor/Inc	Section
5	When finished for the day or for a session, you should ___	Correct	
6	To right-click an object on the screen, you ___	Correct	
7	A computer's operating system coordinates all of the computer's functions.	Correct	
8	To drag something on the screen, you point to it, hold down one of the mouse	Correct	
9	When you first turn on your computer, it always looks first to ___ for the operating	Correct	
10	To look up Help, you have these approaches ___	Correct	
11	To click an object on the screen, you ___	Correct	
12	When you have finished working with Windows for the day, just turn the computer	Correct	
13	The mouse is the only pointing device you can use with Windows.	Correct	
14	The Windows desktop is the screen area where various windows and icons can be	Correct	
15	When you move the mouse on the desk, its movements are followed by a mouse	Correct	
16	To point to an object on the screen, you ___	Correct	
17	When the mouse pointer turns into a pointing finger on a Help screen, clicking the	Correct	
18	When you double-click the mouse button, the pause between clicks isn't important.	Incorrect	1-4
19	If Windows stops working (freezes up), you press ___ on the keyboard to open the	Correct	
20	The mouse pointer is always the same shape, so it is easy to identify.	Correct	

Print   Continue   Done

The *Question Summary* Window. The *Question Summary* window displays your results and suggests what to review in the text for those questions that you answered incorrectly.

PAL ON-LINE ACTIVITIES CHECKLIST

☐ **T-4 PAL TOUR.** In this section, you explore PAL's review questions.

1. Start PAL or click the **Contents** button on the Remote Control to return to the *Contents* window.

2. On the *PicTorials* list, click the letter **T** or the name **PAL Tour**. This displays a list of the sections in the tour.

3. On the *Sections* list, click **T-4, Completing Review Questions** to display the first screen of the tour.

4. Follow the instructions that appear on the screen. If nothing seems to happen, click the **Page Turn** button in the lower-right corner of the window. Clicking the left side of this button moves you back one step and clicking the right side moves you forward.

Throughout PAL you will encounter many items that are accessible in context. These include QuickSteps and glossary terms. On the *Contents* window's *PicTorials* list, there are also headings for these two elements that let you access them directly.

QUICKSTEPS

Clicking **QuickSteps** on the *Contents* window's *PicTorials* list displays an alphabetical list of all QuickSteps pulled together for you in one place. This is especially useful when you want to use them when working on your own documents. You can use the scroll bar to locate any procedure, and click it to display the steps you follow to complete it. You can even click the **Print** button to print it out for future reference. When finished with a QuickStep, click the **Done** button to close the QuickSteps window.

GLOSSARY

Clicking **Glossary** on the *Contents* window's *PicTorials* list displays an alphabetical list of all glossary terms. Each of the terms on this list can be accessed in context by clicking highlighted words or phrases in other PAL windows, but here the entire glossary is pulled together for you in one place. You can use the scroll bar to locate any term, and click it to display a definition. When you are finished reading a definition, click the **Done** button to close the definition window and return to where you were. However, if you click a glossary term within a glossary definition, first click the **Back** button to return to the previously displayed glossary term.

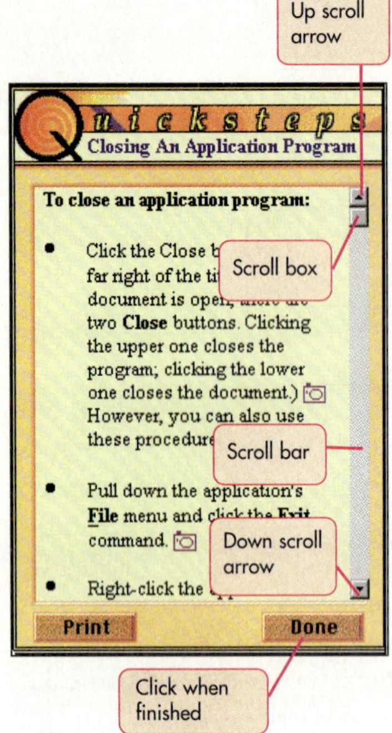

The *QuickSteps* Window. The *QuickSteps* window lists the steps you follow for a procedure. The scroll bar allows you to scroll through the steps if they don't all fit in the window. To use the scroll bar to scroll through the text, click the up and down scroll arrows or drag the scroll box.

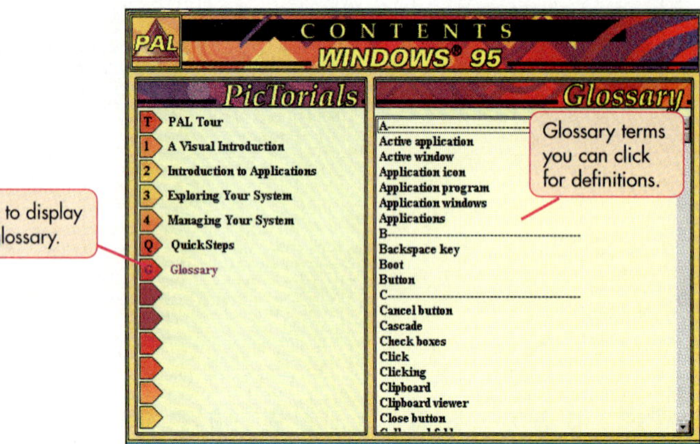

The *Glossary* Window. Clicking the **Glossary** choice on the PAL *Contents* window displays an alphabetical list of glossary terms. Use the scroll bar to locate any term, click it to display a definition, then click the **Done** button to close the definition window.

PAL ON-LINE ACTIVITIES CHECKLIST

☐ **T-5 PAL TOUR.** In this section, you explore the direct-access listings of QuickSteps and glossary terms from the *Contents* window.

1. Start PAL or click the **Contents** button on the Remote Control to return to the *Contents* window.

2. On the *PicTorials* list, click the letter **T** or the name **PAL Tour**. This displays a list of the sections in the tour.

3. On the *Sections* list, click T-5, **Directly Accessing Embedded Items** to display the first screen of the tour.

4. Follow the instructions that appear on the screen. If nothing seems to happen, click the **Page Turn** button in the lower-right corner of the window. Clicking the left side of this button moves you back one step and clicking the right side moves you forward.

A VISUAL INTRODUCTION

After completing this PicTorial, you will be able to:

- **Explain the basic concept of a database**
- **Describe the differences between fields and records**
- **Start the Access application**
- **Open an existing database**
- **View the database tables using Design, Datasheet, and Form views**
- **Query the database**
- **Print tables and use reports**
- **Close databases and exit Access**
- **Use on-line Help**
- **Manage database files on the disk**

COMPUTERS are used for many applications, but the management of databases is probably the most important of them all. And it's an application that has a significant bearing on your daily life. Databases throughout government, business, and academia store information about your birth and death; your employment, credit, and medical history; your driver's license; your Social Security number; and just about every other aspect of your life. For example:

▶ When you step up to an automated teller machine (ATM) and insert your card, information about you is immediately looked up in the bank's database. Any transaction you make is instantly recorded.

▶ When you make a reservation with an airline, your name and address are entered into its database, and a seat on a specific flight is reserved for you in the same database. Should you call later and give your name, the airline can locate your assigned seat by searching the database.

▶ When you make a credit card charge, your card is scanned, a computer is dialed up, and information about you is looked up and new information recorded.

▶ When you call some mail-order catalog companies to place an order, their computers capture your phone number, look you up in the database, and display information about you on the operator's screen even before he or she says "hello."

▶ When you file a tax return, computers compare information in it against a database from your employer to see if the information matches.

▶ When you apply for insurance or file a claim for health benefits, this data is all recorded in insurance company databases.

With this much data being stored on you, how it's done and how the data is used should be of more than just passing interest. In this text we'll explore some of these concepts and applications.

Other than the people who collect data on you, very few people use databases as often as they use word processors and spreadsheets. It takes a lot of work to design and create a useful database. Why, then, are databases important? First, almost all corporate and government data is stored in databases. If you want access to this data, it helps to understand databases. Second, you would be amazed to know how often database programs are at the core of other applications. For example, all accounting, inventory management, and scheduling programs are basically databases in which data is stored and manipulated. The same is true for many CD-ROM reference titles, and even the computerized card catalog at your college or local library. Almost all word processing and spreadsheet applications have database features built into them.

What Is a Database?

A *database* is simply an organized body of information. Word processing and spreadsheet applications also store words and numbers in an organized way. What are the differences between a database and a word processing or spreadsheet application? And why would you use a database instead of one of the other tools? The key difference is in how tightly organized the data is. You would use a database instead of one of the other tools because of the way you can access, view, and output the data.

A word processing
document

In a word processing program, the only organization is that which you give the document when you enter and edit it. The structure is grammatical in that the document is built up from words, phrases, sentences, and paragraphs.

When working with a word processing application, you can pretty much type whatever you want. The only structure in the document is the grammatical structure that you give to the words, sentences, and paragraphs as you enter and edit them. The only output is the document itself.

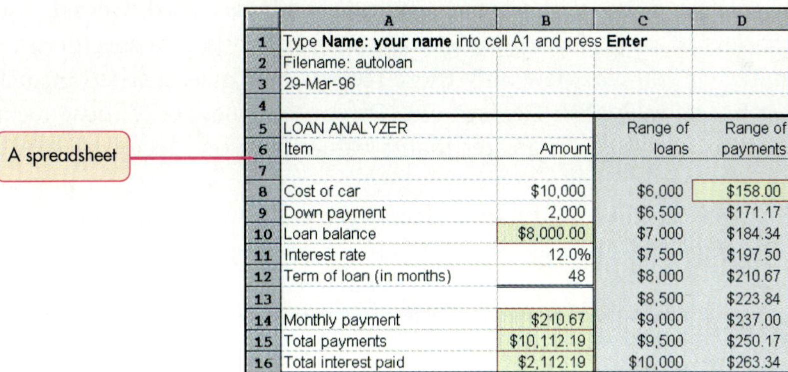

	A	B	C	D
1	Type **Name: your name** into cell A1 and press **Enter**			
2	Filename: autoloan			
3	29-Mar-96			
4				
5	LOAN ANALYZER		Range of	Range of
6	Item	Amount	loans	payments
7				
8	Cost of car	$10,000	$6,000	$158.00
9	Down payment	2,000	$6,500	$171.17
10	Loan balance	$8,000.00	$7,000	$184.34
11	Interest rate	12.0%	$7,500	$197.50
12	Term of loan (in months)	48	$8,000	$210.67
13			$8,500	$223.84
14	Monthly payment	$210.67	$9,000	$237.00
15	Total payments	$10,112.19	$9,500	$250.17
16	Total interest paid	$2,112.19	$10,000	$263.34

A spreadsheet

When working with a spreadsheet, you can enter data only in cells—at the intersection of rows and columns. This is a fairly rigid structure; however, it's flexible in that you can enter text, numbers, or formulas into cells anywhere on the worksheet. The structure is rigid, but the data doesn't have to be.

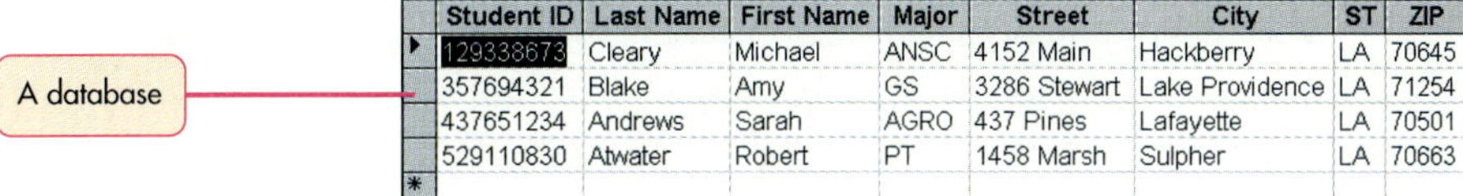

Student ID	Last Name	First Name	Major	Street	City	ST	ZIP
129338673	Cleary	Michael	ANSC	4152 Main	Hackberry	LA	70645
357694321	Blake	Amy	GS	3286 Stewart	Lake Providence	LA	71254
437651234	Andrews	Sarah	AGRO	437 Pines	Lafayette	LA	70501
529110830	Atwater	Robert	PT	1458 Marsh	Sulpher	LA	70663

A database

When working with a database, you enter information into rows and columns in a table that looks much like a spreadsheet. But in a database, each column is defined for a specific type of data. If a column is defined to hold currency, you can't enter text into it. This is the most rigid structure of the three basic types of applications.

Fields and Records

A database table's columns and rows are called fields and records.

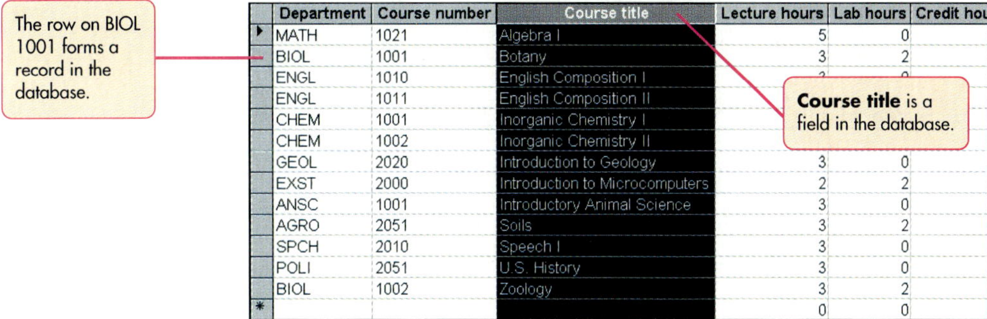

Department	Course number	Course title	Lecture hours	Lab hours	Credit hou
MATH	1021	Algebra I	5	0	
BIOL	1001	Botany	3	2	
ENGL	1010	English Composition I	2	0	
ENGL	1011	English Composition II			
CHEM	1001	Inorganic Chemistry I			
CHEM	1002	Inorganic Chemistry II			
GEOL	2020	Introduction to Geology	3	0	
EXST	2000	Introduction to Microcomputers	2	2	
ANSC	1001	Introductory Animal Science	3	0	
AGRO	2051	Soils	3	2	
SPCH	2010	Speech I	3	0	
POLI	2051	U.S. History	3	0	
BIOL	1002	Zoology	3	2	
			0	0	

The row on BIOL 1001 forms a record in the database.

Course title is a field in the database.

Fields and records

▶ A *field* (column) is one item of the description stored in a record. In the figure "Fields and records," the fields are *Department*, *Course number*, *Course title*, *Lecture hours*, *Lab hours*, and *Credit hours*. A field holds a specific category of data—for example, the name of a course or its number of credit hours.

▶ A *record* (row) is a collection of fields containing data about a single entity— such as a person, thing, or activity. In the figure "Fields and records," a record is the complete description of the Biology 1001 course. Each record contains the same set of fields, and each field contains the same type of data in each record. For example, the field containing a course's credit hours in one record must contain credit hours in all.

Because of the data's organization, it can be accessed, viewed, and printed in a variety of ways. For example, you can go directly to a specific record for John Smith. Or you can view only those records that meet a criterion such as records just from the English Department. Or you can view only those records that are equal to, less than, or greater than a value that you specify, such as credit hours greater than 4. Finally, you can print the data in a variety of formats. The data in this table could be used to print a college catalog or enrollment cards. Tables with other data could be used to print mailing labels or even checks.

TIP
Spelling and Usage

When reading about databases, you may find the term spelled as *database* or *data base*. There is no difference between the two terms. Also, until recently it was common to use *data* as a plural and *datum* as a singular. However, the term *data* is now used as both a singular and plural. Where one used to say "The data **are** stored in the database," it is now general practice to say "The data **is** stored in the database."

Database Management Programs

To create, maintain, and use a database, you use a *database management application* such as Microsoft Access. Such programs allow you to store information, retrieve it when you need it, and update it when necessary. For example, you can:

▶ Add and delete data or update data that has changed.

▶ Find specific data by asking questions called *queries*.

▶ Arrange the data in a specified order.

▶ Print reports containing all or some of the information.

▶ Combine the data in more than one table so it doesn't have to be repeated in each table.

1-1 STARTING AND CLOSING ACCESS

To use an application program such as Access, you must first know how to start it—variously called *starting*, *opening*, *running*, or *launching* it—and how to exit or close it.

Starting Access

There are a number of ways to start Windows 95 programs, but the most common is using the Start menu. When you use the mouse to click the **Start** button on the taskbar at the bottom of the Windows 95 screen, the *Start menu* appears. When you highlight any name on this menu with an arrowhead next to it (▶), and pause or click, a submenu cascades out from the first menu. Once you locate the icon and name of the program you want to run, you click it to start it.

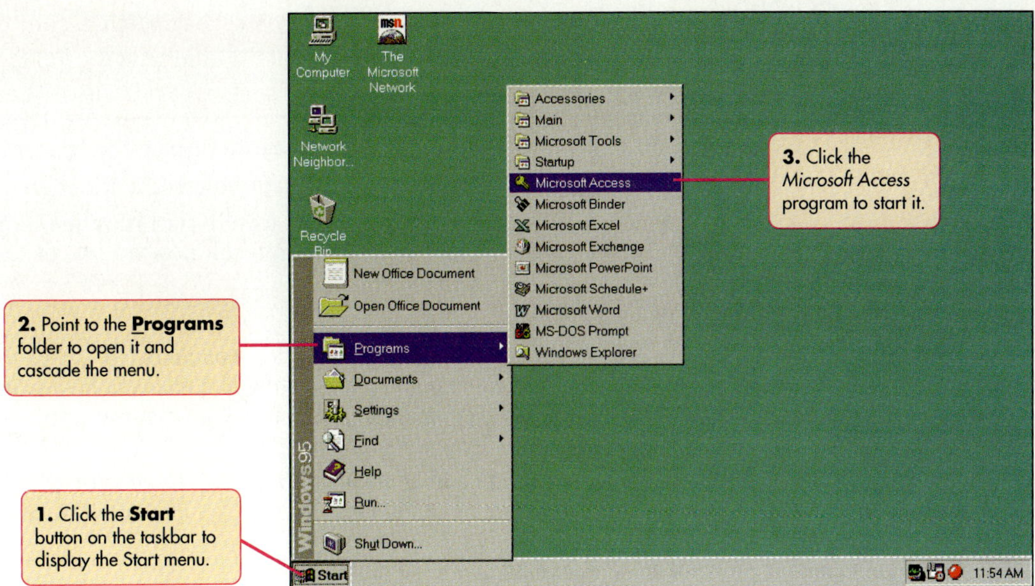

When you start a program, its button is displayed on the taskbar. When more than one program is running at the same time, you can quickly switch between them by clicking the taskbar button of the one you want to use.

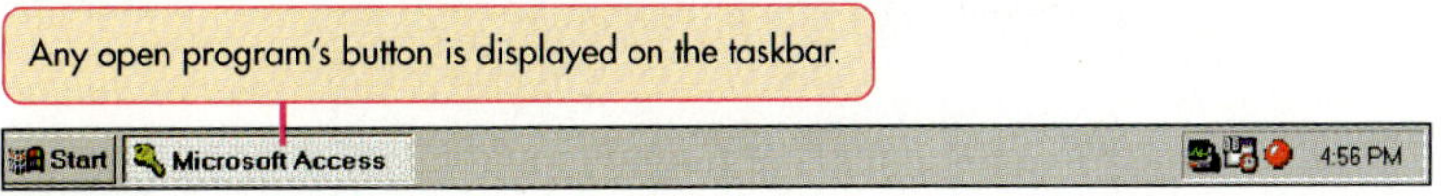

TIP
QuickSteps Boxes

QuickSteps boxes summarize the steps you follow to complete Access procedures. These boxes can be found throughout this text and serve two purposes:

▶ On your first pass through a section, they give you an advance look at the steps you must follow to complete the procedure. Don't actually execute the commands this time around. If you do so, you may not know how to recover from any mistakes you might make.

▶ Later on, when you want to refresh your memory about a procedure, they make it easy to find and review the steps you must follow. At this later stage, you can use them as a quick reference guide.

Starting Access

1. Click the **Start** button on the Windows taskbar to display the Start menu.

2. Point to the **Programs** folder on the Start menu to cascade the menu.

3. Click the **Microsoft Access** program name or icon to start it. When it opens, it displays the Microsoft Access dialog box. You can now do one of the following:

   ▶ Click the **Cancel** button to close the dialog box.

   ▶ With the **Open an Existing Database** option button on (◉), click one of the listed databases to open it, or click the *More Files* choice to display the Open dialog box discussed in Section 1-2, "Opening and Closing Databases."

   ▶ Click the **Blank Database** or **Database Wizard** option button to create a new database as described in PicTorial 2 and then click the **OK** button.

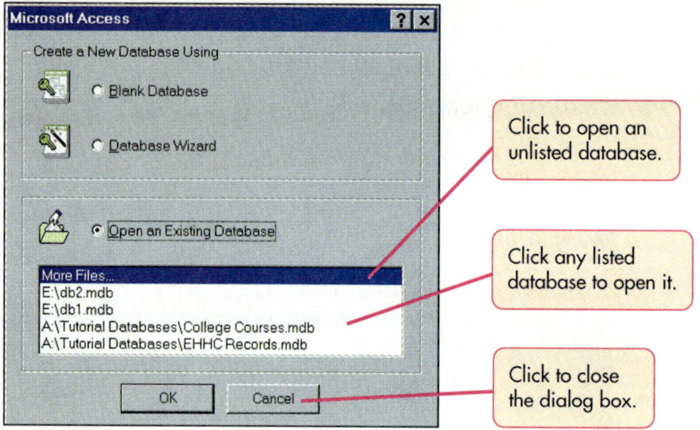

Closing Access

When you are finished with a program such as Access, you exit or close it. This removes it from the computer's memory and removes its window from the desktop and its button from the taskbar.

It is important to quit Access using the commands designed for this purpose. Access creates temporary files on the disk while you are working, and these are deleted only if you exit correctly. If you quit incorrectly, your database may be left damaged.

You can close almost any window simply by clicking its **Close** button. This and other methods are described in the QuickSteps box "Closing Access."

Closing Access

To close Access:

▶ Click the **Close** button at the far right of Access's title bar. (If a database is open, there are two **Close** buttons. Clicking the upper one closes the program; clicking the lower one on the Database window closes the database.)

You can also use these procedures:

▶ Pull down Access's **File** menu and click the **Exit** command.

▶ Right-click Access's button on the taskbar to display a shortcut menu, and click the **Close** command.

▶ Double-click Access's icon at the left of the title bar, or click the icon to display a shortcut menu, and then click the **Close** command.

▶ Right-click the title bar to display a shortcut menu, and then click the **Close** command.

▶ Hold down [Alt] and press [F4] when Access is the active window.

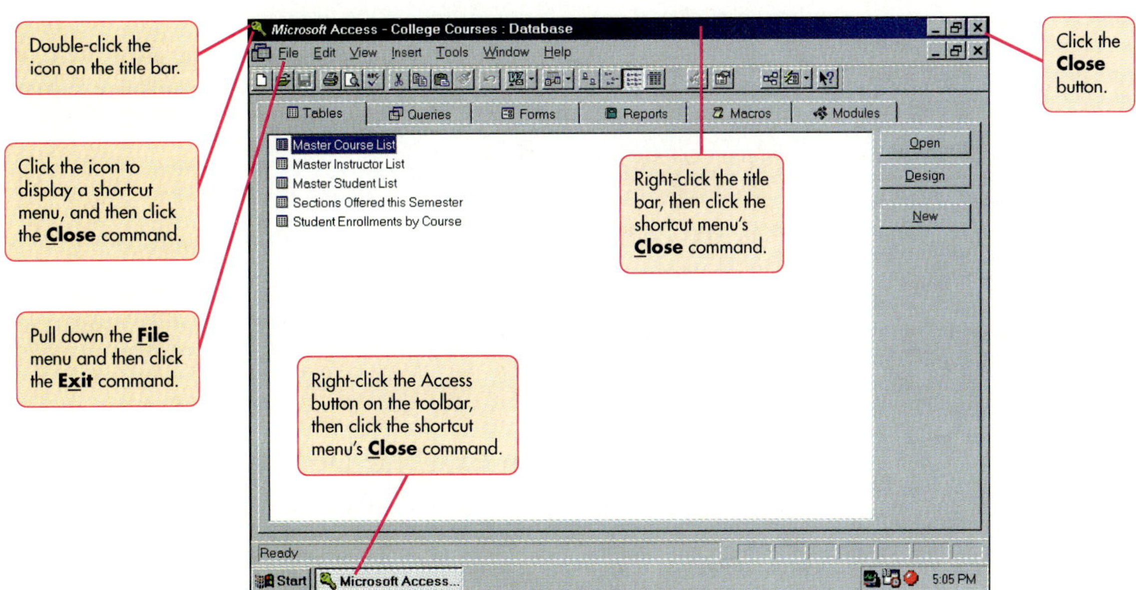

COMMON WRONG TURNS
Not Saving Changes

Although changes to databases are saved automatically, if you close Access without saving changes to some elements, a dialog box asks if you want to save the current changes.

▶ To save the changes, click the **Yes** button.

▶ To abandon the changes, click the **No** button.

▶ To cancel the command and return to the database instead of closing it, click the **Cancel** button.

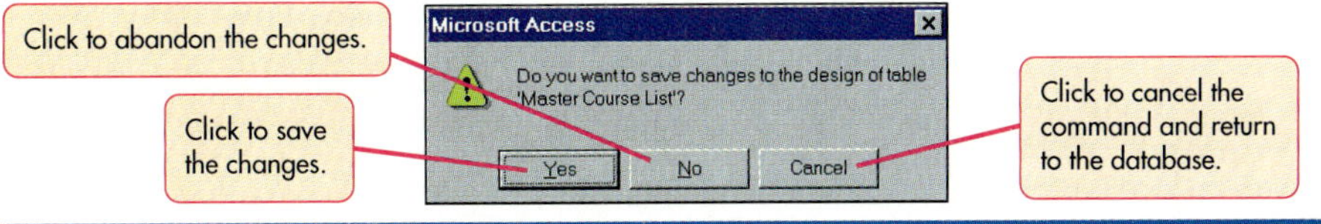

☐ **1-1 CONCEPTS.** To do any useful work on a computer you must first start an application program. In this on-line concepts section, you are introduced to starting Access using the **Start** button and the Start menu. The concepts you learn here apply to all Windows applications.

☐ **1-1 TUTORIAL.** In this tutorial you start and close Access. When you open Access, it displays a dialog box that allows you to create a new database or open an existing one. In this tutorial, you'll close that dialog box without choosing either option since they are discussed in later sections.

☐ **1-1 DRILL.** To do any useful work on a computer you must first start an application program. In this drill you practice that procedure with Access.

1-2 OPENING AND CLOSING DATABASES

To use Access you must know how to open and close databases. You open a database just as you open documents in all Windows programs. You can open an existing database when you first start Access or at any later time. Unlike many other applications with which you are likely familiar, you can have only one database open at a time.

Opening an Existing Database When Starting Access

When you first start Access, the Microsoft Access dialog box opens so you can open an existing database or create a new one. (Creating new databases is covered in PicTorial 2.)

Q U I C K S T E P S

Opening an Existing Database When Starting Access

1. With Access not yet open, click the **Start** button on the Windows taskbar to display the Start menu.

2. Point to the **Programs** folder on the Start menu to cascade the menu.

3. Click the **Microsoft Access** program name or icon to start it and display the Microsoft Access dialog box. The **Open an Existing Database** option button should be on (◉) and a list of the most recently opened databases appears below.

4. How you proceed depends on whether you are opening a listed or unlisted database:

   ▶ If the database you want to open is listed, click it to select it, then click the **OK** button (or double-click its name) to open it.

   ▶ If the database isn't listed, click the *More Files* choice on the list to select it, then click the **OK** button to display the Open dialog box. This dialog box is discussed in the next section, "Opening an Existing Database Using the Open Dialog Box."

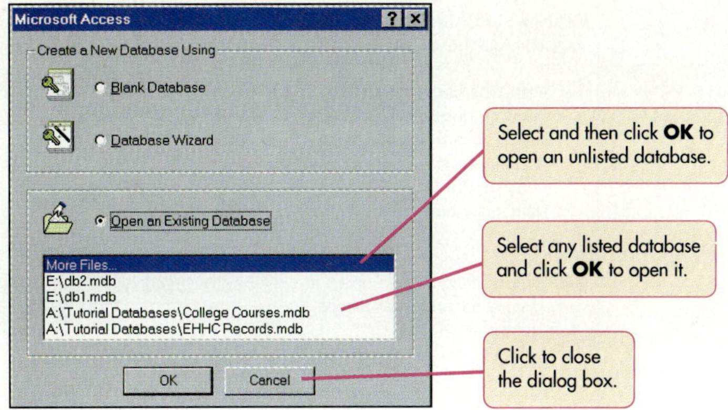

Opening an Existing Database Using the Open Dialog Box

Unlike many application programs, Access is designed so you can have only one database open at a time. If you open a new database when one is already open, the one that is opened will automatically close. Usually you open a database when you start Access. However, you can open an existing database after you have started Access or worked on another database. To do so, you have to specify the disk it's on, the folder it's in, and its filename. If you want to work with a database you've recently closed, this is easy. The last four databases worked on are listed at the bottom of the **File** menu. (Four is the default number but you can change it.) If the database you want is listed there, all you have to do to open it again is click its name.

QUICKSTEPS

Opening an Existing Database Using the Open Dialog Box

1. With Access started, click the **Open Database** button on the toolbar, or pull down the **File** menu and click the **Open Database** command to display the Open dialog box.

2. To specify the drive the database is on, click the **Look in** drop-down arrow (▼) and select the drive from the list that appears. A list of folders or databases on that drive appears in one of the dialog box's windows—how it looks and what is shown depends not only on its contents but also on whether the **List**, **Details**, or **Properties** button on the toolbar is on.

3. The name of the open drive or folder is displayed in the **Look in** box and a list of the databases or folders it contains appears in the box below. To open the folder the database is stored in:

   ▶ Move down the tree by double-clicking a folder you want to open.

   ▶ Move up the tree by clicking the **Up One Level** button on the toolbar.

4. To open a database once you locate it, click its name or icon to select it and then click the **Open** button. You can also double-click the database's name to open it without clicking the **Open** button.

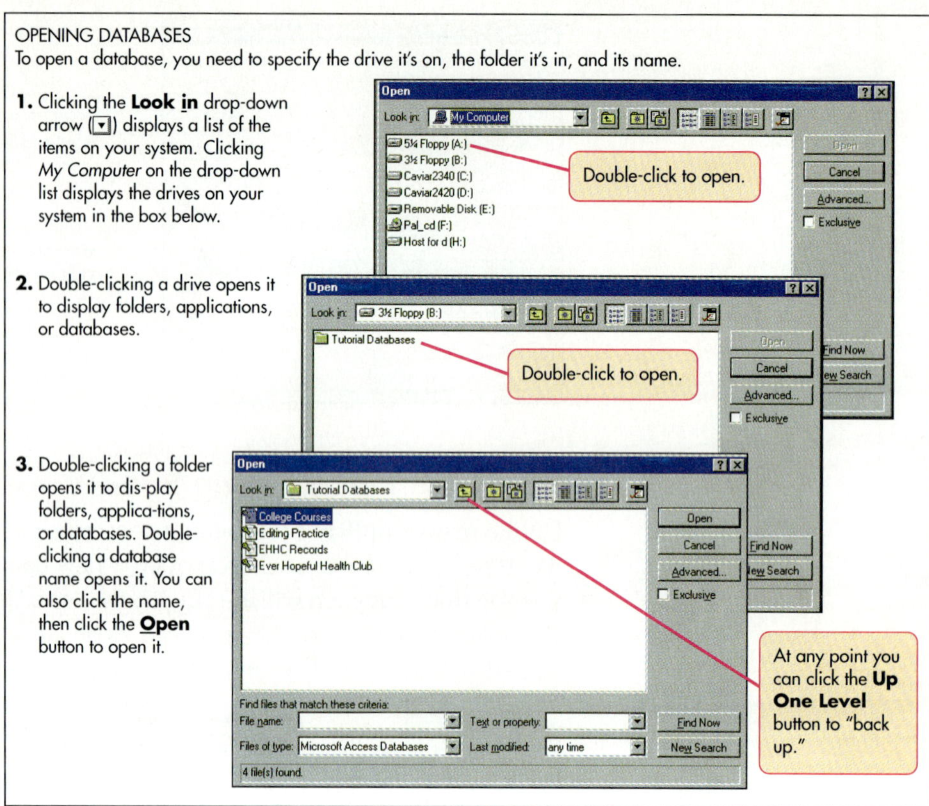

When the Open dialog box is displayed, you can also enter the name of a database you want to find in the **File name** text box and click the **Find Now** button to search for it. It will search the drive or folder listed in the **Look in** text box at the top of the dialog box.

UNDERSTANDING
The Toolbar

When the Open (or Save As) dialog box is displayed, you can click buttons on its *toolbar* to change the way database names are displayed.

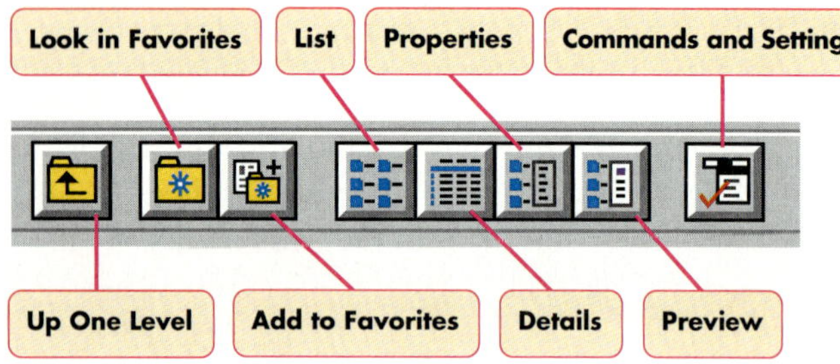

▶ **Up One Level** moves you up the tree.

▶ **Look in Favorites** displays a list of databases that you have designated as favorites with the **Add to Favorites** button (see below).

▶ **Add to Favorites** adds any selected folder or database to your list of favorite databases so you can access them

quickly in the future. When you click this icon, menu choices allow you to add whatever folder is displayed in the **Look in** text box, or any folder or database selected on the list.

▶ **List** displays just icons and the names of folders or databases.

▶ **Details** displays information about databases including their size, type, and date last modified.

▶ **Properties** displays information about any highlighted database including the name of its creator, the date and time of its last revision, and its size in bytes.

▶ **Preview** does not work with databases but it is a standard Windows feature that works with most other types of documents.

▶ **Commands and Settings** displays a menu you can use to print selected databases, sort the list of databases, or perform other procedures.

Opening a Recently Open Database

After you've opened and then closed a database, there may be a shortcut to opening it again. The four most recently opened databases are listed at the bottom of Access's **File** menu. (Four is the default number but you can change it.) The fifteen most recently opened documents of any type are listed on Windows' Start menu in the **Documents** folder.

QUICKSTEPS
Opening a Recently Open Database

▶ If Access is already running, pull down Access's **File** menu and click one of the most recently opened databases listed at the bottom of the menu.

▶ With Access running close any open database, then click the **Start** button on the Windows taskbar to display the Start menu. Point to the **Documents** folder to cascade the menu and display the fifteen most recently opened documents of all kinds. Click the name of the database you want to open. If Access isn't already running, Windows will start it for you. (If an Access database is already open when you do this, a second copy of Access will be opened.)

COMMON WRONG TURNS
Removing a Floppy Disk Too Soon

When you work on Access databases, Windows creates temporary files on the disk. When working on a database, do not remove the disk from the drive until you have quit Access. If you do, you may see a message telling you that there is a disk error. If this message appears, reinsert the disk and follow the instructions on the screen.

Closing Databases

When you are finished with a database, you close it. This removes it from the computer's memory and removes its window from the Access window.

QUICKSTEPS
Closing a Database

To close a database, do any of the following:

▶ Click the database's **Close** button. It's at the far right of the title bar when the database is displayed restored and at the far right of the menu bar when it's displayed maximized. (When a database is open, there are two **Close** buttons. Clicking the upper one closes Access; clicking the lower one closes the open database.)

▶ Pull down the Access **File** menu and click the **Close** command.

▶ Locate the Access database icon at the far left of the database's title bar when the database is displayed restored and at the far left of the menu bar when it's displayed maximized. Double-click the icon to close the database, or click it to display a shortcut menu, and click the **Close** command.

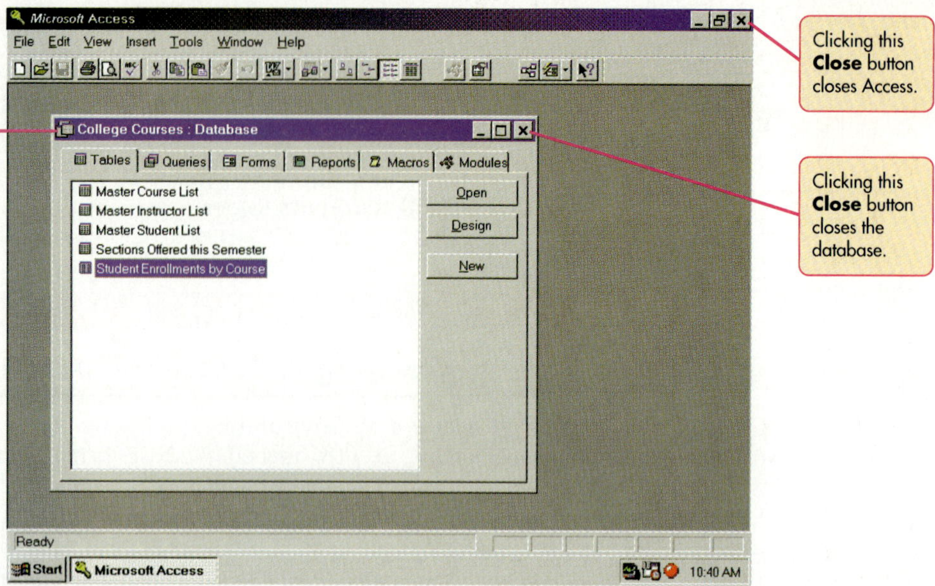

Double-clicking this icon closes the database; clicking it displays a shortcut menu with the **Close** command.

Clicking this **Close** button closes Access.

Clicking this **Close** button closes the database.

TIP
Minimizing Databases

When you click a database's **Minimize** button, the database is displayed at the bottom of the screen above the status bar as an icon that looks like a small title bar. Click the **Restore** or **Maximize** button to open it.

PAL ON-LINE ACTIVITIES CHECKLIST

☐ **1-2 CONCEPTS**. Opening and closing databases is one of the most basic of all skills. In this concepts section you are introduced to these procedures.

☐ **1-2 TUTORIAL**. In this tutorial you open an existing database supplied to you on the *Access Student Resource Disks* designed to be used with this text. These disks contains all of the databases on which you work while completing the lab activities in this PAL. If you do not have a copy of these disks, you will need to make one using the *MakeSRD* program on your PAL CD. The database you will open contains a number of tables similar to those a college might use to keep track of students, instructors, and courses to be sure everyone is in the right classes at the right time.

☐ **1-2 DRILL**. One of the most basic skills you need to master is opening and closing databases in directories on your *Access Student Resource Disks*. In this drill you practice the procedures you use to do so. You will have to switch disks as you do the drill.

Databases to Open and Close		
Done	**Folder**	**Filename**
☐	*Tutorial Databases*	*College Courses*
☐	*Tutorial Databases*	*Editing Practice*
☐	*Drill Databases*	*Publisher Records*
☐	*Exercise Databases*	*Store Records*
☐	*Exercise Databases*	*General Store*
☐	*Project Databases*	*College Records*

When you first open Access and a database, the database is displayed within the Access window. Either window can be independently maximized or restored by clicking the **Maximize** button, minimized by clicking the **Minimize** button, or restored by clicking the **Restore** button. **Close** buttons close the application or the database. These buttons for the application are on Access's title bar. The database's buttons are on the database's title bar when the Database window is restored, and on the menu bar when it is maximized.

The Access Window

The Access startup window appears on the screen whenever you start the application. The startup window displays a number of elements that you should become familiar with.

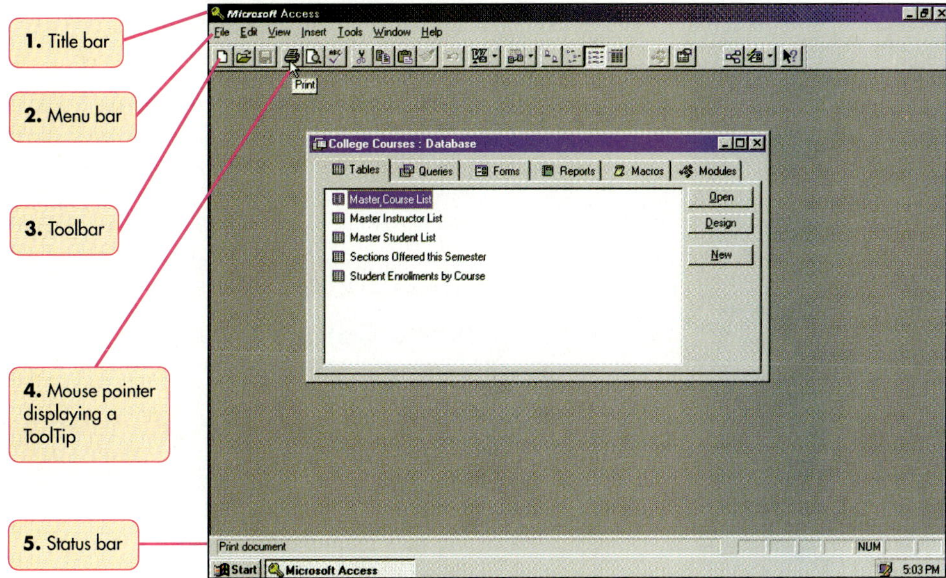

The Microsoft Access startup window with a ToolTip displayed

1. The *title bar* lists the name of the application. It also displays an icon at the left end that you can click to display a shortcut menu, or double-click to close the application. At the right end are the **Minimize**, **Maximize** or **Restore**, and **Close** buttons that affect the application's window.

2. The *menu bar* lists the names of menus you pull down by clicking. Each pulled-down menu contains a list of commands from which you can choose. The menu names listed on this menu bar change as you work with databases. A dimmed menu name means you cannot use it at that point in the program.

3. The *toolbar* contains buttons you can click to execute the most frequently used commands. Buttons and toolbars automatically change as you work with the program depending on what you are doing. Initially, the toolbar named *Database* is displayed. Until a database is opened, most of the buttons are dimmed because they are not available. (They will not remain dimmed once you open a database.) If you point to any button with the mouse pointer, its name will be displayed in a little box called a ToolTip. A

description of its function will be displayed on the status bar at the bottom of the window.

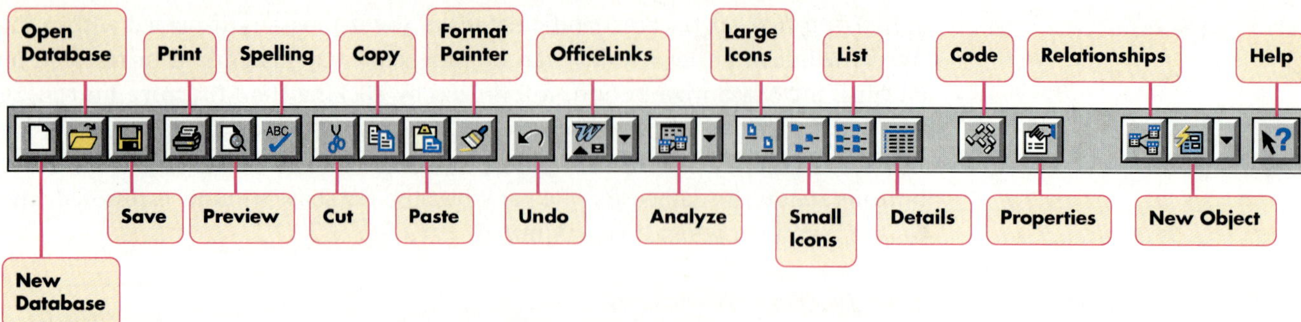

The Database toolbar

4. The *mouse pointer* moves when you move the mouse so you can point to things on the screen and click to select them. Until you begin working on databases, it is shaped like an arrow (▷) so you can click on menu commands and toolbar buttons. Later, when you are working on databases, it sometimes takes the shape of an I-beam (I) so you can position it correctly between letters or words.

5. The *status bar* describes highlighted commands or buttons you point to, prompts you for the information the program needs you to enter to complete a command, and informs you of the progress of some commands.

QUICKSTEPS

Executing Menu Commands

Executing Menu Commands

1. To pull down a menu, point to its name with the mouse and click once, or hold down [Alt] while you press the underlined letter or number in the menu name. (The underlined letter or number is called a *mnemonic*.)

2. To choose a command from a pulled-down menu, point to the command and click once, or press the letter on the alphabetic keyboard that is underlined in the command name.

Canceling Menu Commands

▶ To close a pulled-down menu without selecting a command, point anywhere outside of the menu or menu bar and click the mouse button or press [Esc].

▶ To cancel a command when a dialog box is displayed, press [Esc] or click the box's **Close** or **Cancel** button.

TIP
ToolTips or Toolbars Are Not Displayed

If ToolTips or toolbars are not displayed correctly but a database is open, pull down the **View** menu, and click the **Toolbars** command to display the Toolbars dialog box. If a database isn't open, the **View** command is on the **File** menu. (You can also right-click a clear area of the toolbar.)

▶ To display ToolTips, click the **Sho̱w ToolTips** check box (☑) to turn it on.

▶ To display the Database toolbar, click its check box on the **Toolbars** list to turn it on (☑). Click any other check boxes that are on to turn them off.

When finished, click the **Close** button.

The Database Window

When you work with Access, you create tables to hold your data, queries to find data, forms to make data entry easier, and reports to share your data with others. Each of these (table, form, and report) is called an *object*. An object is simply something you can select and manipulate as a unit. The Database window has a series of tabs across the top that you can click to see the various types of objects that are related to the database.

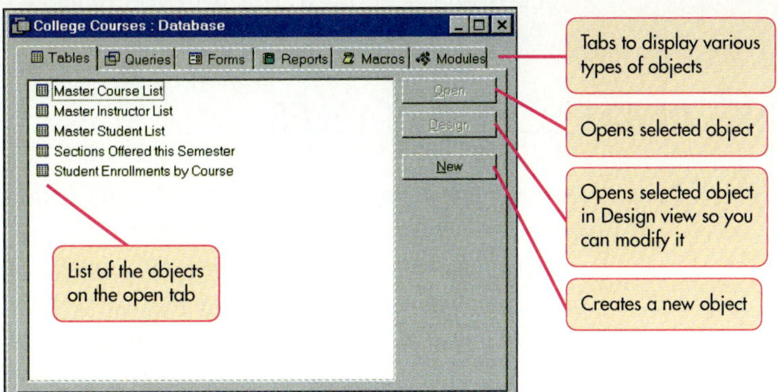

The Database window

▶ *Tables* are where you store the actual data. A database can contain several tables, and they can be related to one another.

▶ *Queries* are used to get specific data out of the database. For example, you can use a query to locate just the students enrolled in the Algebra I course offered by the college. When you create and then use a query, the result is very similar to a table. However, the query may contain only selected fields and records and it may draw fields from more than one table.

▶ *Forms* are used to display, enter, and edit data in a more attractive and user-friendly format than a table presents.

▶ *Reports* are formats used to print the data in the database in a useful and attractive way.

▶ *Macros and Modules* are used to automate Access and build custom applications. Macros and modules are beyond the scope of this text.

The way objects are displayed in the Database window depends on the view that has been chosen by clicking a button on the toolbar. There are four possible displays:

▶ **Large Icons** displays objects as large labeled icons.

▶ **Small Icons** displays objects as small labeled icons.

▶ **List** displays small icons and names for each object.

▶ **Details** displays not only icons and names of objects but also their description, date and time created and last modified, and object type.

PAL ON-LINE ACTIVITIES CHECKLIST

☐ **1-3 CONCEPTS.** When you start Access, its startup window is displayed. In this concepts section you are introduced to the parts of this screen.

☐ **1-3 TUTORIAL.** The Access startup window supplies you with information about the program and makes it easy to execute commands. Almost all commands can be executed by clicking buttons on the toolbar or selecting commands from menus. In this tutorial you explore elements of the Access startup window. If you make any mistakes during this tutorial, just press Esc twice and repeat the step.

☐ **1-3 DRILL.** All application windows have buttons you can click to change the size of the window. In this drill you practice using these buttons.

1-4 OPENING AND CLOSING TABLES

As you have seen, the Database window contains all of the objects related to the database. The most important of these objects are the tables that contain the actual data. To work on a table you must first open it. You can then close it or minimize it to an icon when you are finished with it. Although you can have only one database open at a time, that database can contain many different tables, and more than one table can be open at the same time.

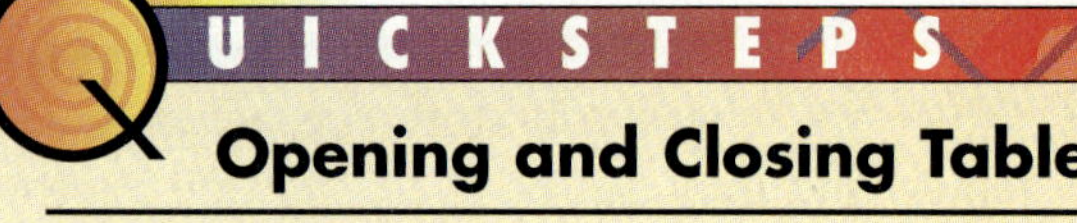

Opening and Closing Tables

Opening Tables

1. Click the **Tables** tab on the Database window to display the names of any tables in the database.

2. Either double-click the table's name, or click the table's name to select it and then click the **Open** button on the Database window.

Closing Tables

▶ Click the table's **Close** button (⊠).

▶ With the table the active window, pull down the **File** menu and click the **Close** command.

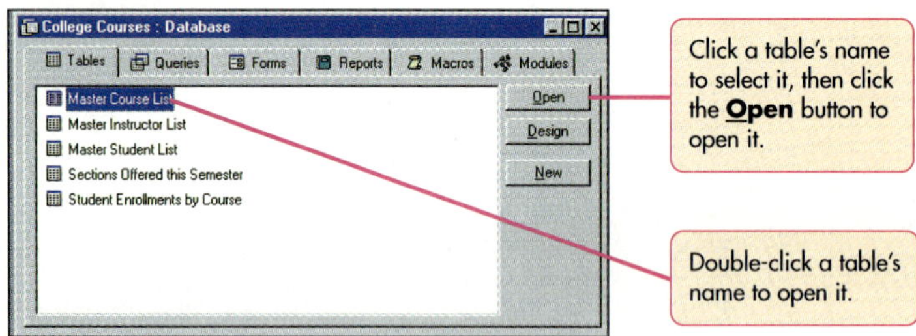

Opening a table

☐ **1-4 CONCEPTS.** The tables in a database are where your data is stored. In this concepts section you are introduced to opening and closing existing tables.

☐ **1-4 TUTORIAL.** When you open a database, its tables and all other related objects such as forms or reports are listed in the Database window under the appropriate tab. In this tutorial you open database tables listed when the **Tables** tab is clicked. The procedures you learn here apply to all objects listed in the Database window.

☐ **1-4 DRILL.** In this drill, you open and close a number of tables in the *College Courses* database.

1-5 VIEWING DATABASE TABLES

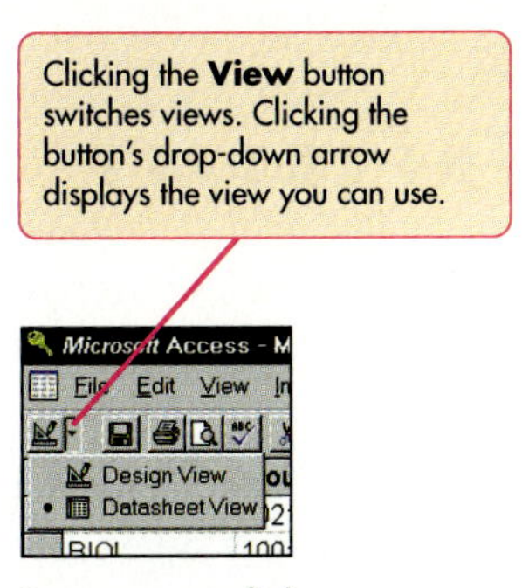

Buttons you click to change views

There are two basic ways to view a table in a database: you can view either its contents or its design. (This is also true of many other objects that you will encounter when working with Access and some of them have more than two views.) To switch between the two views of a table, you click the **View** button on the toolbar. This button displays different icons depending on what view is currently displayed. It always displays the one that will change you to the other view. To see a list of possible views, you can also click the **View** button's drop-down arrow. The current view is marked with a round bullet. You can click any other view to change to it. (See the Note box "Nonspecific ToolTip.")

Datasheet view displays the contents of a table as tabular columns. In this view, each row is a record and each column is a field. The window in which the table is displayed has scroll bars so you can scroll vertically through records or horizontally through fields.

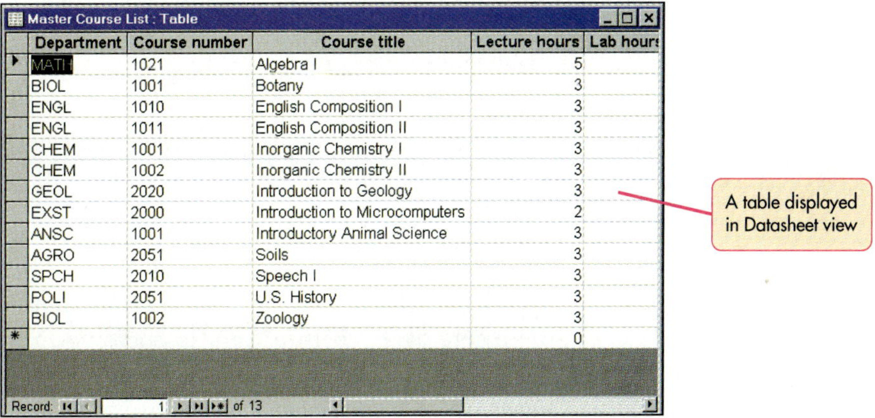

A table displayed in Datasheet view

Design view shows the names and properties of the fields in the database so you can see how they should work. These entries are displayed in cells called *boxes*. Later you will see how you edit the contents of these boxes to modify the fields.

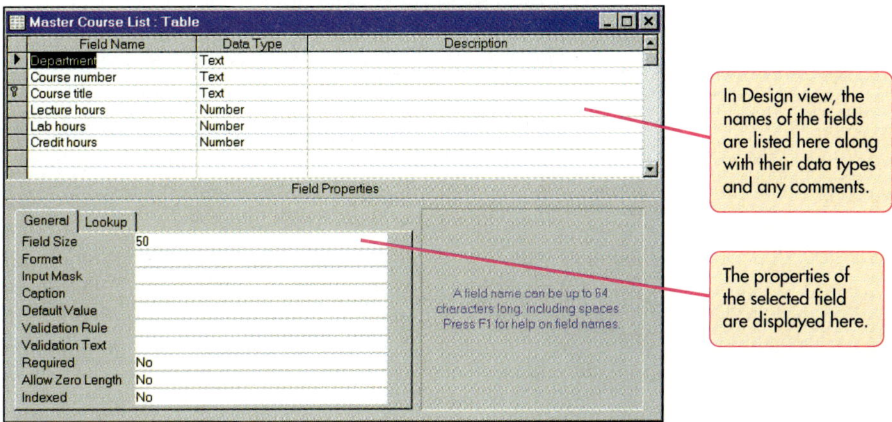

In Design view, the names of the fields are listed here along with their data types and any comments.

The properties of the selected field are displayed here.

NOTE
Nonspecific ToolTip

The ToolTip for the **View** button gives you the general name for the button's function—for instance, "Table View" when you are viewing a table—rather than the name of the specific button that is shown—such as **Datasheet View** or **Design View**. If you don't remember what view the specific button represents, you can always click the drop-down arrow next to the button to see a list of the possible views, then click the one you want to change to it.

PAL ON-LINE ACTIVITIES CHECKLIST

- ☐ **1-5 CONCEPTS.** Tables can be displayed in Datasheet or Design View. In this concepts section you are introduced to these two views and the procedures you use to switch between them.

- ☐ **1-5 TUTORIAL.** In this tutorial you change back and forth between viewing a table's contents and its design. As you do so, you will see how it is organized into fields and records.

- ☐ **1-5 DRILL.** You can view a table's contents or its design. (This is also true of many other objects that you will encounter when working with Access.) In this drill you practice switching between these two views of a table.

1-6 USING A FORM TO VIEW AND ENTER DATA

You've seen how you can use the Datasheet view to see a table's contents organized as a table. However, you can create a form (or have Access do it for you) so you can display data the way you want. You can then use these custom forms to view, enter, or change data. When a form is open, you can switch between Form view and Design view by clicking the **View** button on the toolbar. Remember, only the button that will change to the other view is displayed. To see all views available, including Datasheet view, click the **View** button's drop-down arrow. The current view is marked with a round bullet. You can change to any other listed view by clicking it.

☐ **1-6 CONCEPTS.** Forms can make it easier and faster to enter new data into a database or view the records that it contains. In this concepts section, you are briefly introduced to forms.

☐ **1-6 TUTORIAL.** In this tutorial you view the data in a database using forms that have already been created. Later on you will learn how easy it is to create your own.

☐ **1-6 DRILL.** Forms are used to view, enter, or change data. In this drill, you practice displaying forms and switching between Form view and Datasheet view.

1-7 SORTING TABLES

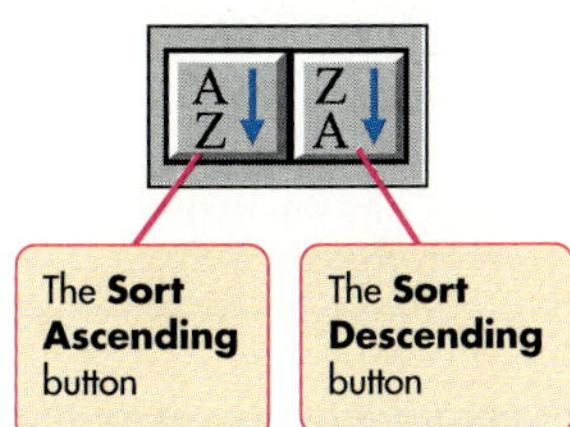

The **Sort Ascending** button

The **Sort Descending** button

When you need to sort a table based on the contents of a single column or field, you can do so with just a couple of mouse clicks. For example, to sort a table so it's arranged by people's last names, click anywhere in the column where last names are listed and then click one of the **Sort** buttons on the toolbar.

QUICKSTEPS

Sorting Records

1. Display the table in Datasheet or Form view.
2. Click in the field you want to sort by.
3. Click the **Sort Ascending** or **Sort Descending** button on the toolbar, or pull down the **Records** menu, point to the **Sort** command to cascade the menu, and click **Ascending** or **Descending**.

☐ **1-7 CONCEPTS.** The data in a table can be sorted into ascending or descending order. In this concepts section you explore how this is done.

☐ **1-7 TUTORIAL.** In this tutorial you use simple sorting to arrange a table into ascending or descending order based on the contents of a single field.

☐ **1-7 DRILL.** Sorting arranges a table based on the contents of a single field. In this drill you practice sorting tables using the **Sort** buttons on the toolbar.

1-8 PREVIEWING AND PRINTING TABLES

When you want to share a table with others or file a copy for future reference, you usually make a printout. Before you do so, you can also preview how the table will look when printed. This way, if you find that you need to make adjustments, you can do so without wasting a sheet of paper. Before you begin printing, be sure there is a printer connected to your system and that it is on and has paper in it.

Previewing a Table

You can preview what a table will look like when printed so you can catch layout mistakes before wasting time and paper printing the database.

The **Print Preview** button

Previewing Printouts

1. Open the table or click its name in the Database window to select it.
2. Click the **Print Preview** button on the toolbar, or pull down the **File** menu and click the **Print Preview** command. The first page of the table is displayed in the Print Preview window.
3. Click any of the buttons described in the box "Understanding the Print Preview Toolbar." Use the navigation buttons in the lower-left corner of the window to page through a table that has more pages than are currently displayed.
4. Click the **Close** button on the toolbar to close the Print Preview window.

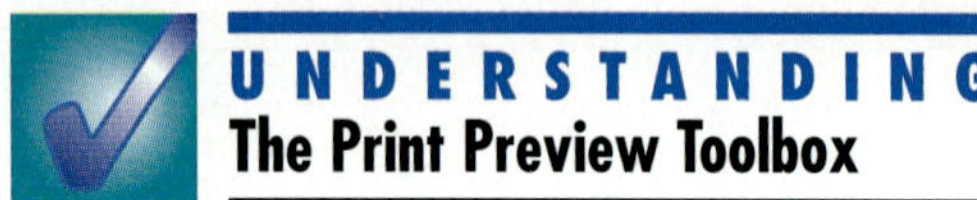

UNDERSTANDING
The Print Preview Toolbox

When you pull down the **File** menu and click the **Print Preview** command, the Print Preview window and toolbar are displayed.

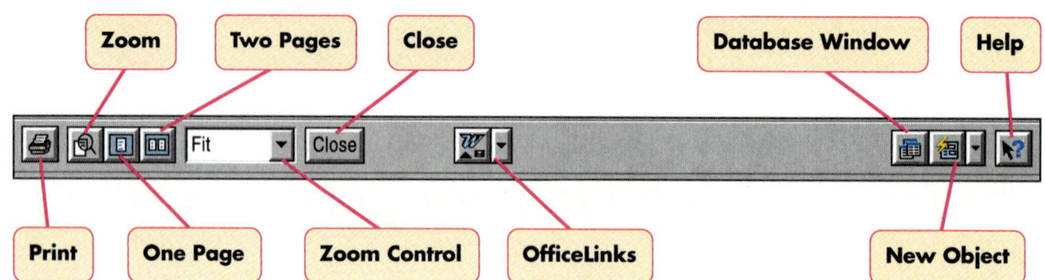

Print prints the database.

Zoom zooms in or zooms out on the database when you click it. You can also click in the database with the magnifier to do the same thing. When the database is zoomed in, a scroll bar appears so you can scroll to see more of the database.

One Page displays one page of the table.

Two Pages displays two pages of the table.

Zoom Control allows you to specify the size of the table on the screen.

Close closes the Print Preview window.

OfficeLinks' drop-down arrow displays the following options:

▶ **Merge It** allows you to merge the data into a Word document.

▶ **Publish It with MS Word** transfers a copy of the database table to Word and opens Word so you can edit the table (see Section 4-8).

▶ **Analyze It with MS Excel** transfers a copy of the database table to Excel and opens Excel so you can add formulas or create charts of the data (see Section 4-8).

Database Window returns you to the Database window.

New Object displays a drop-down list so you can create new forms, tables, queries, and such.

Printing Tables

When you print the table displayed on the screen, you can print the entire table, specific pages, or a selected section.

Printing Tables

The **Print** button

1. Open the table in Datasheet view or click its name in the Database window to select it.
2. Do one of the following:
   - To print the entire table using the current print settings, click the **Print** button on the toolbar or on the Print Preview toolbar.
   - To print specific pages or choose other options, pull down the **File** menu and click the **Print** command to display the Print dialog box that allows you to specify options. Change any of the settings described in the box "Understanding the Print Dialog Box" and then click the **OK** button.

UNDERSTANDING
The Print Dialog Box

When you pull down the **File** menu and click the **Print** command, the Print dialog box appears. This box allows you to control all aspects of the printout.

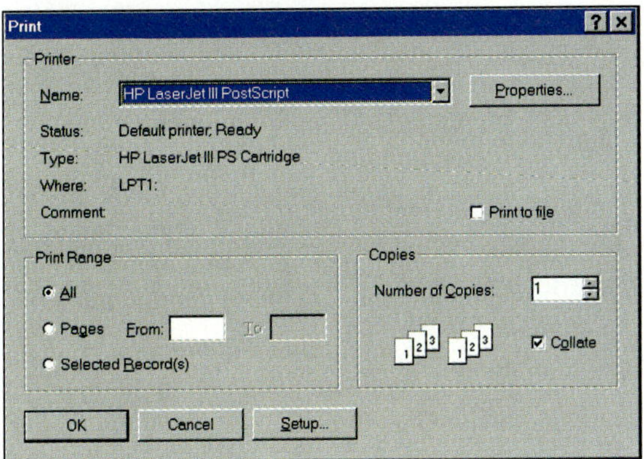

Printer Section

Name lists the currently selected printer. To select another printer, click the drop-down arrow (▾) and select one from the list.

Properties button displays a tabbed dialog box you use to change paper sizes, page orientation (portrait or landscape), and the number of copies. It also has advanced settings for graphics, device options, and PostScript. After making changes, you can always click the **Restore Defaults** button to cancel them. Click the **OK** button to return to the Print dialog box.

Print to File check box, when on (☑), prints the item to a file on the disk.

Page Range Section

Print Range section allows you to specify pages to be printed:

- **All** (the default setting) prints the entire object (table, report, form, and so on).
- **Pages** prints ranges of pages you enter in the **From** and **To** text boxes.
- **Selected Records** prints the selected (highlighted) records in the table.

Setup button displays the Print Setup dialog box where you can specify other printers, change page orientation between portrait and landscape, and set margins.

Copies Section

Number of Copies specifies the number of copies to be printed.

Collate check box, when on (☑), collates copies when you print more than one copy of a multipage table. Each collated copy has all of its pages following one another in sequence. When uncollated, all copies of the first page are together, then all of the next page, and so on.

☐ **1-8 CONCEPTS**. When working on a database, you may want to check data or share it with others. In this concepts section you explore one way to do this—by printing out part or all of a table.

☐ **1-8 TUTORIAL**. Printing is as easy as clicking a button. However, as you'll see in this tutorial, you can catch mistakes and save paper by previewing databases before you print them. You can save additional paper by printing only the pages you are interested in.

☐ **1-8 DRILL**. Printing a database table is as simple as opening it and clicking a button on the toolbar. In this drill, you preview and then print a small database table to see what fields and records it contains.

1-9 USING REPORTS

Most people do not actually use the database file itself. Generally, they use reports created from part of the information stored in the file. *Reports* are simply selected parts of the database displayed on the screen or printed out in a specified way. Each report provides only the specific information needed.

PAL ON-LINE ACTIVITIES CHECKLIST

☐ **1-9 CONCEPTS**. When it comes time to seriously analyze the data in a database or present it to others, you use reports. In this concepts section, you are briefly introduced to reports.

☐ **1-9 TUTORIAL**. In this tutorial you present the data in a database using reports that have already been created. Later in this text you will learn how easy it is to create your own.

☐ **1-9 DRILL**. Reports are printed documents that include all or just part of the data in a table. In this drill you practice opening a report to preview it on the screen.

1-10 QUERYING THE DATABASE

Databases are not just created and stored; they are used over and over again. One thing they are used for most frequently is to provide information. For example, you can look up which students are enrolled in which courses. The way you do so is to query the database. A query is simply a question you ask the database in a specific way. The set of records that is displayed as a result of your query is called a *dynaset* or *record set*—a dynamic set of records that changes when the query changes.

PAL ON-LINE ACTIVITIES CHECKLIST

☐ **1-10 CONCEPTS**. Databases are not static collections of data. They are used to make decisions. To help you do so, you need to find patterns or relationships in the data. You do this using questions, called queries. The answer you get is a set of records that match the criteria you specified. This set of records is called a dynaset. In this concepts section you are introduced to queries.

- ☐ **1-10 TUTORIAL.** In this tutorial you query the database using a query that has already been created. Later in this text you will learn how easy it is to create your own queries.

- ☐ **1-10 DRILL.** In this drill, you practice viewing a query and a dynaset.

1-11 USING ON-LINE HELP

When you are using Access, you can have tips automatically displayed as you go about your usual tasks, or you can ask for detailed help whenever you want information on a specific procedure.

ScreenTips

If you click the **Help** button on the Standard toolbar, it adds a question mark to the mouse pointer. You can then click buttons or areas of the screen to display a pop-up description called a ScreenTip. To close the ScreenTip, click it. Also, many Help windows and dialog boxes have a question mark button on their title bar. If there is no question mark button, look for a **Help** button or try pressing F1.

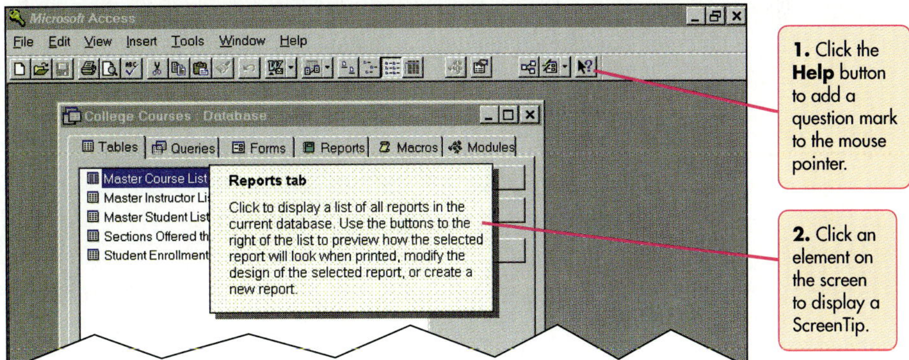

The Help System

Access has extensive *on-line help* available from almost anywhere in the program. When you call up Help, you'll find that it is organized into topics, much like sections in a book. To find help on a specific topic, you double-click the **Help** button on the Standard toolbar, then click one of the four tabs in the Help Topics window: *Contents*, *Index*, *Find*, and *Answer Wizard*. Each tab uses a different method of locating help.

The Contents Tab

The *Contents* tab lists topics grouped by subject much as the table of contents in a book. Double-clicking a book opens it to display a list of topics or closes it to hide the list. Double-clicking a topic opens it to display Help.

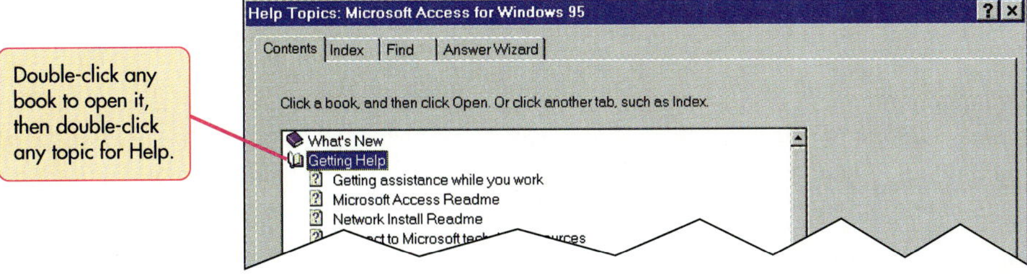

The Index Tab

The *Index* tab lets you look up topics much as you would in the index of a book.

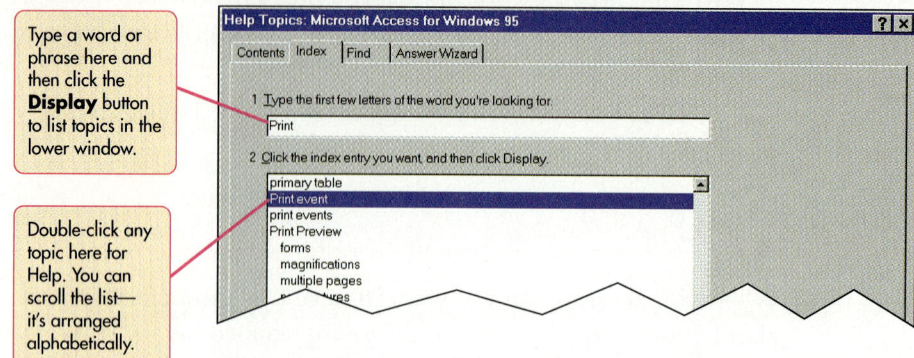

The Find Tab

The *Find* tab lets you search for words or phrases that might appear in a Help topic's title.

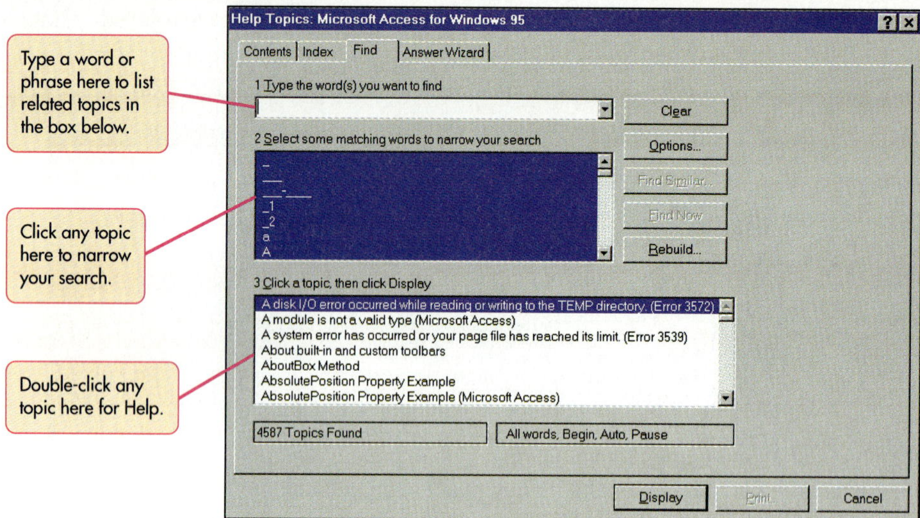

The Answer Wizard Tab

The *Answer Wizard* tab gives you help and guides you through many procedures step by step. It also has a *Tell Me About* section that explains the principles behind many parts of the program.

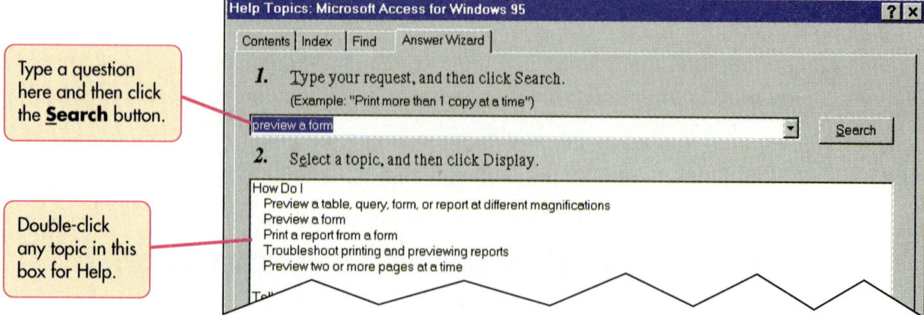

Displaying Help

1. Double-click the **Help** button on the Standard toolbar, or pull down the **Help** menu and click the **Microsoft Access Help Topics** command to display the Help Topics dialog box.

2. Locate Help using the tabs *Contents*, *Index*, *Find*, or *Answer Wizard* as shown in the illustrations in the section "The Help System." You may see *hypertext links* within the Help windows that take you directly to other places. Hypertext links are simply "hot spots" you click to jump to another location. (You know you are pointing to a hypertext link when the mouse pointer turns into a pointing finger.)

▸ *Shortcut buttons* take you directly to the dialog box where you make the changes related to the Help topic.

▸ *Pop-ups* are displayed when you click words with green underlines. Click in a pop-up or any area but a button or menu command to close it.

3. After locating and reading Help, do one of the following:

▸ Pull down the **Options** menu and click the **Print Topic** command.

▸ Click the **Help Topics** button to return to the Help Topics dialog box.

▸ Click the Help window's **Minimize** button to display it as a button on the taskbar.

▸ Click the Help window's **Close** button to close it.

▸ Click the shortcut button to perform the procedure.

PAL ON-LINE ACTIVITIES CHECKLIST

☐ **1-11 CONCEPTS.** Help is always just a few keystrokes away. In this concepts section you explore the ways it's organized.

☐ **1-11 TUTORIAL.** In this tutorial you practice using Access's on-line Help to locate information on some of the topics you have explored in this PicTorial.

☐ **1-11 DRILL.** Access's on-line Help is always available, even long after you've lost the manual. In this drill you use Help's Answer Wizard to learn more about databases.

1-12 MANAGING DATABASES

What if you want to copy, move, delete, rename, or explore databases or folders? You can do so from within Access without opening Windows' My Computer or Windows Explorer. To do so, you right-click on a database or folder displayed in the Open or Save As dialog boxes, and a shortcut menu appears. Which menu appears depends on whether you right-click on a database, a folder, or anywhere in the box except on a folder or database. The commands listed on the menus are described below although not all of these commands appear on the same menu.

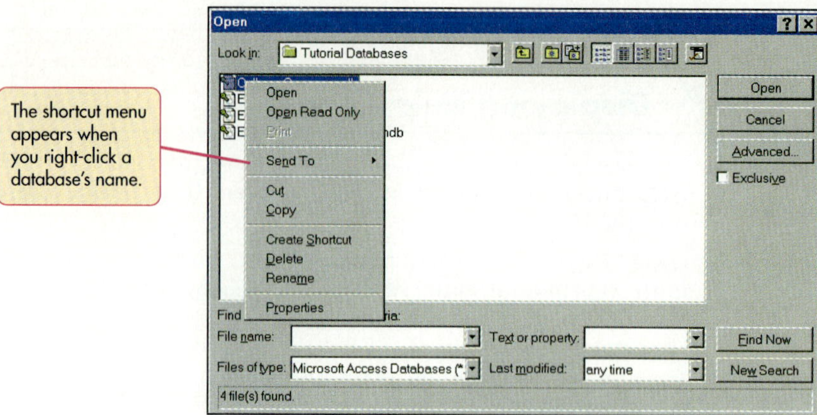

▶ **Open** opens the selected folder in the dialog box.

▶ **Open Read Only** opens the database so you can read it but not change it.

▶ **Print** prints the selected database.

▶ **Explore** opens the selected folder and displays it in Windows Explorer.

▶ **Send To** sends the selected database or folder to a floppy disk, or to a fax or e-mail recipient.

▶ **Cut** moves the selected folder or database to the clipboard.

▶ **Copy** copies the selected folder or database to the clipboard.

▶ **Paste** pastes the cut or copied database or folder into the current folder. You must have cut or copied something for the **Paste** command to appear.

▶ **Create Shortcut** creates a shortcut to the selected folder or database in the same location. You can then drag or move this shortcut to another folder or to the desktop.

▶ **Delete** deletes the selected folder or database to the Recycle Bin.

▶ **Rename** highlights the name of the selected folder or database so you can type a new one. (If the filename includes a period followed by a three-character extension such as *.mdb*, be sure not to change or delete that extension. If you do, Access will not be able to recognize the database.)

▶ **Properties** displays the properties of the selected folder or database.

Managing Databases

1. To manage your databases, do one of the following:
   - ▶ Click the **Open Database** button on the toolbar, or pull down the **File** menu and click the **Open Database** command to display the Open dialog box.
   - ▶ Click the **Save** button on the toolbar, or pull down the **File** menu and click the **Save** or **Save As/Export** command to display the Save As dialog box.
2. Locate the folder or database you want to manage, and right-click it to display a shortcut menu. If you right-click in the box, but not on a specific folder or database, the shortcut menu choices apply to the folder up one level, not to those in the window.
3. Click any of the menu commands described in the text.

PAL ON-LINE ACTIVITIES CHECKLIST

☐ **1-12 CONCEPTS.** You don't have to leave Access to copy, move, or delete documents. You can do so when opening or saving documents. In this concepts section you are introduced to these procedures.

☐ **1-12 TUTORIAL.** In this tutorial you use the Open dialog box to manage a few databases.

☐ **1-12 DRILL.** In this drill you practice managing documents when the Open dialog box is displayed.

PicTorial 1

LAB ACTIVITIES

EXERCISES

1-1 Loading Access on Your Own System

For future reference, list the steps here that you use to load Access.

1. ____

2. ____

3. ____

4. ____

5. ____

The figure "The Access screen display" shows the Access display that appears when you open a database. In the spaces provided, write down the name of each of the lettered elements.

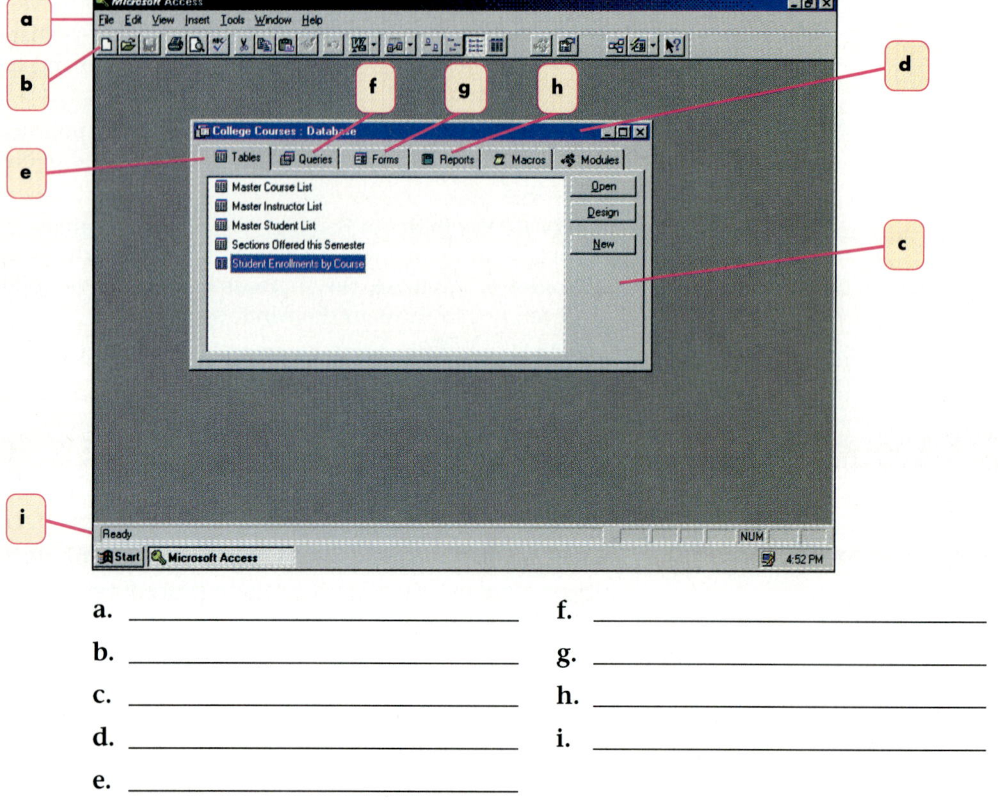

a. _______________________________   f. _______________________________

b. _______________________________   g. _______________________________

c. _______________________________   h. _______________________________

d. _______________________________   i. _______________________________

e. _______________________________

PROJECT

1-1 Using Help to Learn About Databases

In this project you use Help to learn more about Access and about databases in general.

1. Start Access and open the *College Courses* database stored in the *Tutorial Databases* folder on the *Access Student Resource Disk*.

2. Double-click the **Help** button on the toolbar to display the Help dialog box.

3. Use the **Contents** tab to open the book *Visual Introduction to Microsoft Access* and then open the topic *Visual Introduction to Microsoft Access*. This displays a Help page with a number of topics on it that you can explore by clicking their button. This page is the starting point.

4. Click the *What is a database* button and then use the **Next** button to read through the pages of the description. Eventually you'll return to the starting point.

5. Click the *Tables: What they are and how they work* button and then use the **Next** button to read through the pages of the description. Eventually you'll return to the starting point.

6. Continue exploring topics until you have learned everything you can understand at this point.

7. Click the **Close** buttons on any open Help window(s).

CREATING DATABASES

After completing this PicTorial, you will be able to:

▸ **Explain how to plan a database**
▸ **Create a new database**
▸ **Design and modify a database table**
▸ **Define fields in a table**
▸ **Describe and select a primary key**
▸ **Change the properties of fields**
▸ **Enter and edit data in a table**
▸ **Preview and print a table**
▸ **Analyze and document a database**

T HE first step in using a database management application is to create a database and then design the tables you want to store data in. A table is a set of data that describes or refers to a specific category of things and is arranged into records (rows) and fields (columns) like a grid. For example, one table could contain the names and addresses of your customers and another table a complete description of your products. Each column in the table is a field and each row is a record.

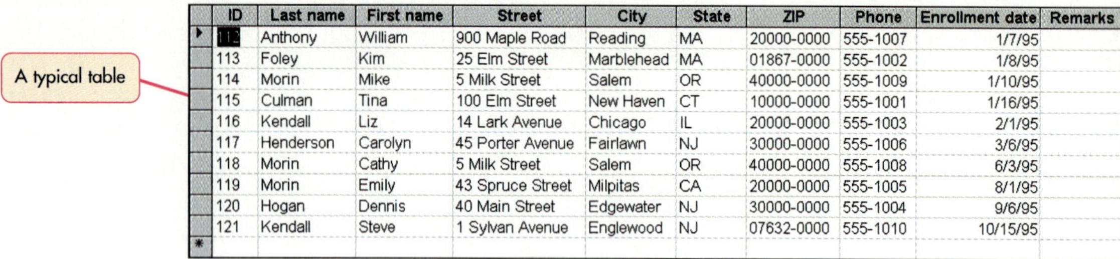

	ID	Last name	First name	Street	City	State	ZIP	Phone	Enrollment date	Remarks
▶	112	Anthony	William	900 Maple Road	Reading	MA	20000-0000	555-1007	1/7/95	
	113	Foley	Kim	25 Elm Street	Marblehead	MA	01867-0000	555-1002	1/8/95	
	114	Morin	Mike	5 Milk Street	Salem	OR	40000-0000	555-1009	1/10/95	
	115	Culman	Tina	100 Elm Street	New Haven	CT	10000-0000	555-1001	1/16/95	
	116	Kendall	Liz	14 Lark Avenue	Chicago	IL	20000-0000	555-1003	2/1/95	
	117	Henderson	Carolyn	45 Porter Avenue	Fairlawn	NJ	30000-0000	555-1006	3/6/95	
	118	Morin	Cathy	5 Milk Street	Salem	OR	40000-0000	555-1008	6/3/95	
	119	Morin	Emily	43 Spruce Street	Milpitas	CA	20000-0000	555-1005	8/1/95	
	120	Hogan	Dennis	40 Main Street	Edgewater	NJ	30000-0000	555-1004	9/6/95	
	121	Kendall	Steve	1 Sylvan Avenue	Englewood	NJ	07632-0000	555-1010	10/15/95	
*										

When you create a table, you define each field. To do so, you specify its name and data type, and, if you like, add a description.

Designing a Database

Planning what information to store in a database table is vital to the usefulness of the database. This is not as straightforward as you might think. When asked what information they need, many managers will say, "Everything." But it is usually impossible to include *everything* because of the limited availability of information, the cost of collecting available information, and the cost of recording and holding the information collected. Therefore, when deciding what information to keep, you should spend some time thinking about what type of questions you wish to have answered by the data. A good way to do this is to first design the reports that you will want to generate from the data in the database. You can also decide what questions (queries) you want to be able to ask it. For example, you might want a report like the one shown in the figure "Student class assignments" that shows what courses each student is enrolled in. From it, you could immediately tell that you needed to store information about each student, such as name, address, ID, college, major, and year. You would also have to store information about each course, such as its name, section, type, day and time, building and room, instructor, and credit hours.

Central University
Spring Schedule

Cleary, Michael   129338673   College: AGRI   Major: ANSC   Year: 1
4152 Main
Hacberry, LA 70645

Course	Section	Type	Days	Time	Bldg/Room	Instructor	Credits
ANSC 1001	1	LEC	M W F	7:30 - 8:30	ANSC 58	Roberts, Paul	3
BIOL 1002	1	LEC	T TH	7:30 - 9:00	LIFE 135	Long, Charles	4
		LAB	TH	2:30 - 4:30	LIFE B26	Long, Charles	
CHEM 1002	1	LEC	M W F	8:30 - 9:30	CHEM 145	Zolki, Matt	4
		LAB	W	2:30 - 5:30	CHEM 105	Zolki, Matt	
EXST 2000	1	LEC	M W F	9:30 - 10:30	COATES 155	Morris, Stanley	3
		LAB	M	10:30 -12:30	ACGAD 48	Cammack, Evelyn	
SPCH 2010	1	LEC	T TH	1:30 - 3:00	LOCKETT 20	Miller, Michael	3

Total credit hrs: 17

Student class assignments

As you compile a list of the data you want to store, you can sketch it out, assigning field names and specifying the type and length of the data to be entered into each field.

You may need to divide certain basic information into more than one field so that you can manipulate it more easily. For example, if you used only one field for both first and last names and then entered names like John Smith, Betty Lewis, and Roger Wentworth, you could not sort the data by last name. To enable you to sort by last name, set up two fields, one for the first name and one for the last name. Similarly, with addresses, if you enter ZIP codes into the same field as another part of the address, you will not be able to sort the records by ZIP codes (which can save you money when printing envelopes or mailing labels because the U.S. Postal Service gives discounts for mail sorted by ZIP code). When entering addresses, you should enter the street address in one field, the city or town in one field, the state in one field, and the ZIP code in one field.

You may also decide that not all information should be stored in a single table. For example, to print the report shown in the figure "Student class assignments," the information on students should be stored in one table, information on courses in another, and information on instructors in a third. Storing related information together in separate tables increases a database's flexibility and reduces duplication.

Revising a Database's Design

Occasionally, a database's design has to be changed after it has been created. You may need to add or delete fields or modify the properties or formats of existing fields. For example, a few years ago, many databases had to be restructured when the ZIP code was changed from five to nine characters long. If a change like this is necessary, or if fields must be added or deleted, the design can be modified.

2-1 CREATING DATABASES

An Access database is a collection of objects, all stored together so they are easy to find and work with. When you first create a new database, you have to decide three things: the drive to save it on, the folder to save it in, and its name. When you create a new database, the File New Database dialog box appears so you can specify this information. The Database window is then displayed so you can create objects such as tables, forms, queries, and reports for the new database.

When you create a database, you need to specify the drive to save it on, the folder to save it in, and the name to save it under.

1. Clicking the **Save in** drop-down arrow (▾) displays a list of the drives on your system. Selecting *My Computer* from the list displays the drives on your system in the box below.

2. Double-clicking a drive opens it to display folders, applications, or databases.

3. Double-clicking a folder opens it to display folders, applications, or databases. Type the name of the database in the **File name** text box and then click the **Create** button to save it and display the Database window.

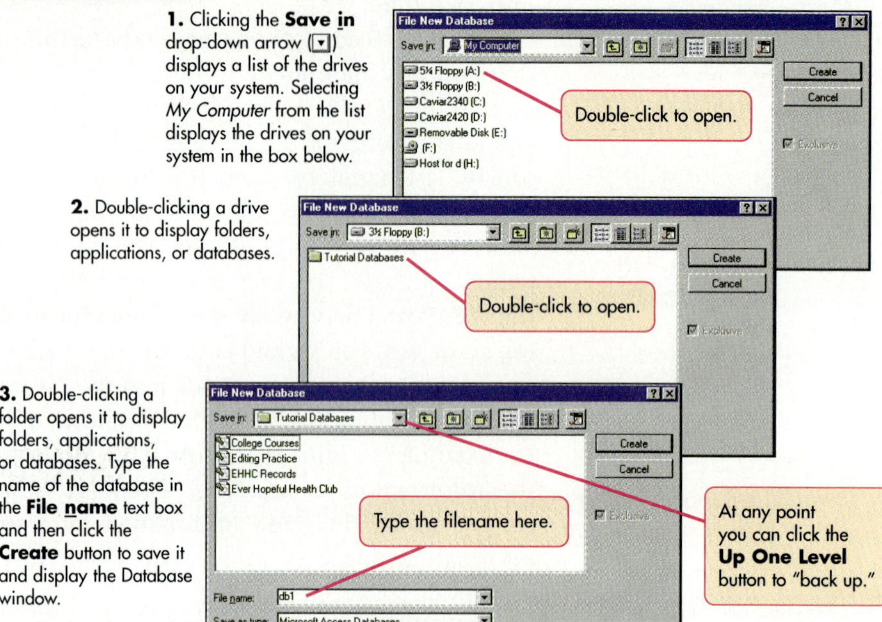

Keep in mind these rules when naming databases:

▸ Filenames can be up to 255 characters long.

▸ Filenames can include spaces and as many periods as you want.

▸ Filenames cannot include the characters \ / : * ? " < > or |. If you use any of these characters, a message box appears and lists them so you can correct the name.

▸ Each filename should be unique. If you assign a database the same name as a file that is already on the disk in the same folder, a message box appears and asks if you want the new file to overwrite the previous file and erase it.

▸ Filenames retain the capitalization you use to enter them. For example, you could type a filename as *filename*, *Filename*, *FileName*, or *FILENAME*.

When you create a new database, a tabbed dialog box lists available *templates*. A template is a stored database with an accompanying Wizard that guides you through the creation of a database for a specific task. There are templates for such tasks as managing addresses, assets, book collections, contracts, donations, events, expenses, and so on. Both templates and Wizards are topics beyond the scope of this text although you can use Access's Help to locate information on them.

Opening a New Database

The **New Database** button

1. To open a new database, do one of the following:

   ▶ When starting Access, click the <u>B</u>lank Database option button on the Microsoft Access dialog box, then click the **OK** button to display the File New Database dialog box.

   ▶ With Access already started, click the **New Database** button on the toolbar, or pull down the <u>F</u>ile menu and click the <u>N</u>ew Database command to display the New dialog box. On the *General* tab click the *Blank Database* icon to select it, then click the **OK** button to display the File New Database dialog box.

2. To specify the drive to save the database on, click the **Save <u>i</u>n** drop-down arrow and select the drive from the list that appears. (You can click buttons on the toolbar to change the way databases are displayed. These buttons are described in the box "Understanding the Toolbar" in Section 1-2.

3. To open the folder the database is to be saved in:

   ▶ To move down the tree, double-click the folder in the box.

   ▶ To move up the tree, click the **Up One Level** button on the toolbar.

4. Type the name you want to use in the **File <u>n</u>ame** text box (up to 255 characters) and then click the **Create** button.

☐ **2-1 CONCEPTS.** The first step in using a database is to create it. Once created it becomes a container for any tables, queries, forms, or reports that you create. In this concepts sections you are introduced to creating and saving a database.

☐ **2-1 TUTORIAL.** Two recent college graduates who were interested in physical conditioning started the *Ever Hopeful Health Club*. One of the first management steps was to create a database in which they could store information about their members. Their plan was to use this database to determine when dues were paid, keep track of customer charges, and prepare mailings on special events. In this tutorial, you create the *Club Records* database in which this information will be stored.

Field Name	Data Type	Description
ID	Text	ID number
Last name	Text	Last name
First name	Text	First name
Street	Text	Street address
City	Text	City of residence
State	Text	State
ZIP	Text	ZIP code
Phone	Text	Home phone number
Enrollment date	Date/Time	Date first enrolled
Remarks	Memo	Comments on health and physical condition

The Club Member Table

☐ **2-1 DRILL.** In this drill you create a new database in which to store tables related to the publishing business.

2-2 CREATING DATABASE TABLES

After creating a database, you design one or more tables in which to store your data. Once you have created tables, you can add other objects such as forms, reports, and queries. When you create a table, you specify each field's name, data type, and description. You then specify a primary key for the table—a field or fields that will uniquely identify each record. You do all of this in the Table window.

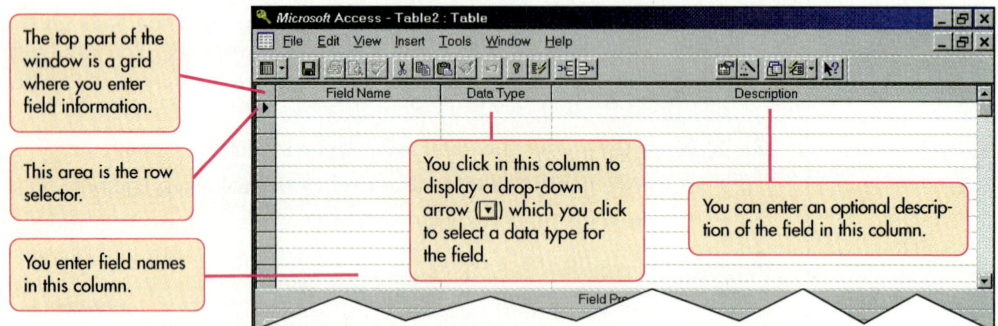

The Table window

Field Names

A field name describes or identifies the contents of the field. For example, if the field is to store phone numbers, its name might be *Phone*, *Phone Number*, or *Phone #*. When naming fields in a database file, observe the following rules:

▸ Field names must be unique in the table; the same field name cannot be used twice in the same table. (Access ignores the case of letters so the field names *Phone* and *PHONE* are the same and couldn't be used in the same table.)

▸ Field names can be up to 64 characters including spaces.

▸ Field names cannot include periods, exclamation points, backquote characters (`), or brackets ([ ]).

T I P
Changing Field Names

Once you have created a database table and entered data into it, be careful when changing field names. If you change a field name that other objects, such as forms or reports, refer to, all of those objects will have to be revised.

T I P
To Space or Not to Space

Field names with spaces between words, such as *Enrollment Date* or *Last Name*, are much easier to read than names without them such as *EnrollDate* or *LastName*. Although we use spaces in field names in this text, you might not always want to do so. Tables with spaces in field names may not be easily exportable to other database management programs because most older programs don't allow spaces in field names.

Data Types

For each field, you must specify a data type. Access uses this information to determine what data you can enter into the field and how it is displayed and used. For example, if you specify a field's data type as Currency, you can enter numbers such as *100.25* in the field but not text such as *two hundred*. Access provides the following eight data types from which to choose:

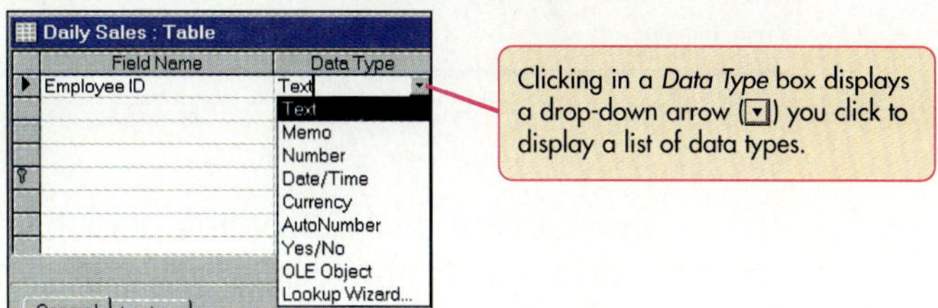

Clicking in a *Data Type* box displays a drop-down arrow (▾) you click to display a list of data types.

▶ **Text fields** store names and names and numbers, such as addresses, phone numbers, Social Security numbers, and ZIP codes. Numbers entered into a text field are treated as text, not as values. Therefore they cannot be used in calculations but will retain leading zeros, such as the zero that begins a 01945 ZIP code. A text field can hold up to 255 characters of data. The default setting is 50 characters.

▶ **Memo fields** store general descriptive text and do not have a fixed length. They expand as you enter up to 64,000 characters of data.

▶ **Number fields** store numbers that can be used in calculations. Entries in these fields can have only numbers, a decimal point, and a plus or minus sign. (To store dollars or other monetary data, use a Currency field.)

▶ **Date/Time fields** store dates and times, which can then be used in calculations. For example, you can add or subtract dates, or add or subtract numbers to or from them. This allows you to get answers to questions like "What is the average number of days between orders?" or "How old is someone?" or "Is the invoice over 30 days past due?"

▶ **Currency fields** are used for currency such as dollars, pounds, or francs. You should use this data type instead of a Number data type to store any kind of monetary values.

▶ **AutoNumber fields** automatically number fields in the order in which they are entered. These numbers uniquely identify each record.

▶ **Yes/No fields** store only Yes or No (which you can enter as Yes/No, True/False, or On/Off).

▶ **OLE Object fields** store objects created by other applications that support object linking and embedding (OLE). These objects can be graphics, sound, animations, or videos.

▶ **Lookup Wizard** creates a lookup column that you can use to choose values from a list. The values on the list are taken from the column you specify in another table in the same database.

You can quickly enter a data type by typing its mnemonic, its first character, in a *Data Type* box. For example, you can type **t** (for Text), **m** (for Memo), **n** (for Number), **d** (for Date/Time), **c** for Currency, **a** for AutoNumber, **y** (for Yes/No), and **o** (for OLE Object). You can also double-click in a *Data Type* box to scroll through the data types one by one.

Description

You can enter an optional description of each field to provide more information about the field than is provided by its name. A field's description is displayed on the status bar when you select the field in Datasheet view or move the insertion point into its entry space in a form. This is especially helpful when the person entering and maintaining the database is not the person who created it or when more than one person will be entering data.

Primary Keys

Ideally, each table should have a field that uniquely identifies each record. Such a field can be specified as the table's *primary key*. Tables with primary keys operate faster and can be related to other tables in the database that use the same key (related tables are discussed in PicTorial 5). For a field to be designated a primary key, each record in the field must contain unique data. Access will not allow you to store duplicate data in the primary key field. For example, fields containing data such as last names will not suffice as the primary key, because there will almost certainly be duplication in names. If the last name field contains two or more *Jones*, that data no longer uniquely identifies the field. Many kinds of data can uniquely identify records, including:

- ▶ Social Security numbers
- ▶ Serial numbers
- ▶ Driver's license numbers
- ▶ Dates and times
- ▶ Employee ID numbers
- ▶ Telephone numbers
- ▶ Policy numbers

- ▶ Part numbers
- ▶ Vehicle license numbers
- ▶ Bank account numbers
- ▶ Customer account numbers
- ▶ Purchase order numbers
- ▶ Credit card numbers

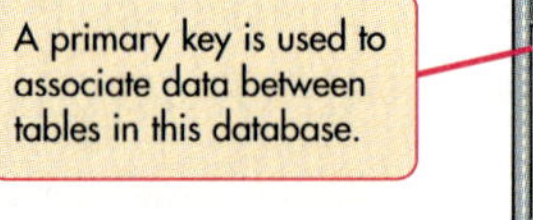

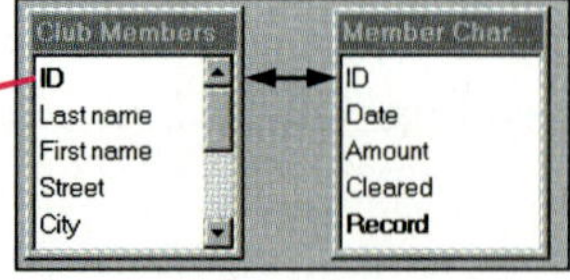

Primary keys relate tables

When possible, the primary key is a single field, such as an employee ID field. At other times it is a combination of fields that together contain unique data.

If you do not have a field that contains unique data, you can create a separate AutoNumber field where Access assigns a unique number to each record. If you don't specify a primary key, Access will ask if you want to specify one when you save the table. If you click the **Yes** button, it adds an AutoNumber field to the database.

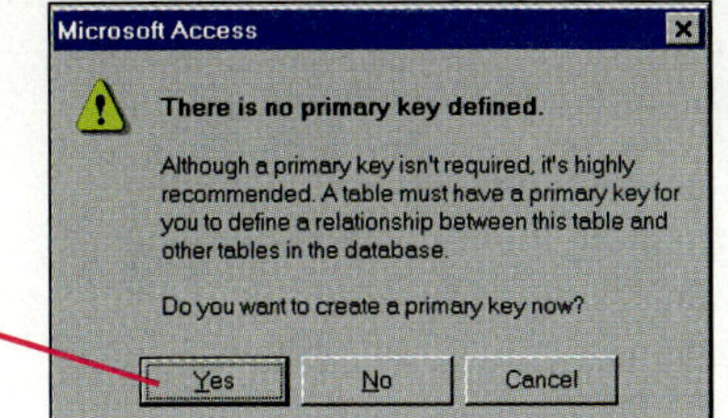

The message that appears when you close a table without specifying a primary key

Designing a New Table

Keep in mind as you design a table that you can quickly switch back and forth between Design and Datasheet views by clicking the **View** button on the toolbar or its drop-down arrow. However, to switch from Design view to Datasheet view you must first save the table if you made any changes. (If you forget to save the design, when you try to switch views a dialog box will remind you.)

Table designs are not saved automatically. To save one, click the **Save** button on the toolbar or click the **Yes** button when a message asks if you want to save the table. The name of a table, or any Access object, can contain up to 64 characters including spaces.

Designing a New Table

1. Open the database for which you want to create a new table and click the **Tables** tab in the Database window to make sure it is on top.

2. Click the **New** button on the Database window, or pull down the **Insert** menu, click the **Table** command to display the New Table dialog box.

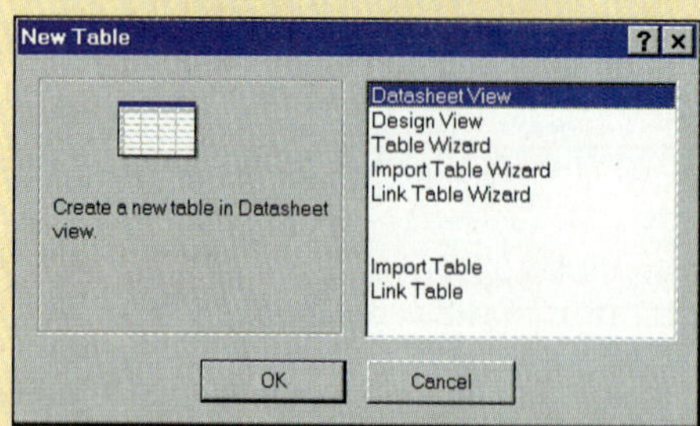

3. Click the **Design View** choice on the list to select it, then click the **OK** button to display the Table window. The Table window has a grid at the top of the screen into which you enter field names, data types, and optional descriptions of the fields. (Pressing Tab⇥ is the fastest way to move from field to field.)

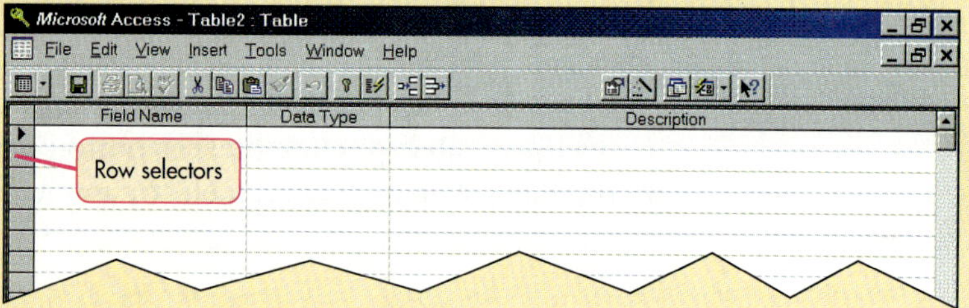

▸ To enter a field name, tab to or click in one of the boxes in the *Field Name* column and type in the name.

▸ To enter a data type (*Text* is the default), tab to or click in a box in the *Data Type* column, click the drop-down arrow (▾) that appears, and click the data type you want to specify.

▸ To enter an optional description, tab to or click in one of the boxes in the *Description* column and type in the information.

4. Click the row selector for the field you want to use as the primary key. (To use more than one field, click the row selector for the first field to be included, then hold down Ctrl while you click others.) Click the **Primary Key** button on the toolbar, or pull down the **Edit** menu and click the **Primary Key** command. The row selector for the field(s) displays a key-shaped icon to indicate that it is a primary key.

5. Click the **Save** button on the toolbar to display the Save As dialog box, type a name of up to 64 characters into the **Table Name** text box, and then click the **OK** button to save the table's design.

6. Click the **View** button on the toolbar to begin entering data, or click the dialog box's **Close** button to close it. (If you close it, it will be listed on the **Tables** tab of the Database window so you can open it again.)

Assistance in Table Design

When you create a new table, Access has built-in guidance—**Build** buttons and Wizards.

When specifying fields in a table, you can use built-in samples of tables with sample fields. You can automatically enter fields by using Access's **Build** command. To do so, click in a *Field Name* box and then click the **Build** button on the toolbar. Selecting a table on the **Sample Tables** list displays a list of **Sample Fields** from which you can choose. Selecting one automatically specifies the field name, data type, and other properties for the field.

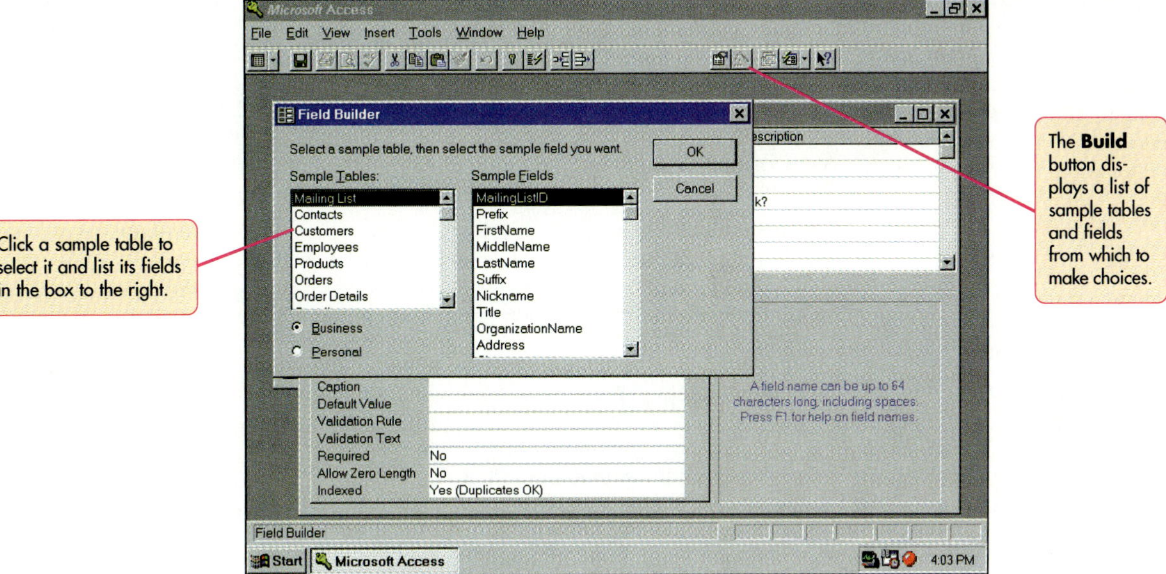

When you create a new table (or a query, form, or report), a dialog box gives you the choice of starting with a blank object and creating the object yourself, or using a Wizard to guide you through the process. An Access Wizard asks you a series of questions step by step and then creates the object based on the answers you provide. When you are familiar with table design, you can click the **Table Wizard** choice on the New Table dialog box to be guided through the creation of a table. In this text we don't use the Wizard because we're focusing on database concepts, not automatic procedures. When you're finished reading this text you should be able to build and use your own database, and understand each step in the process.

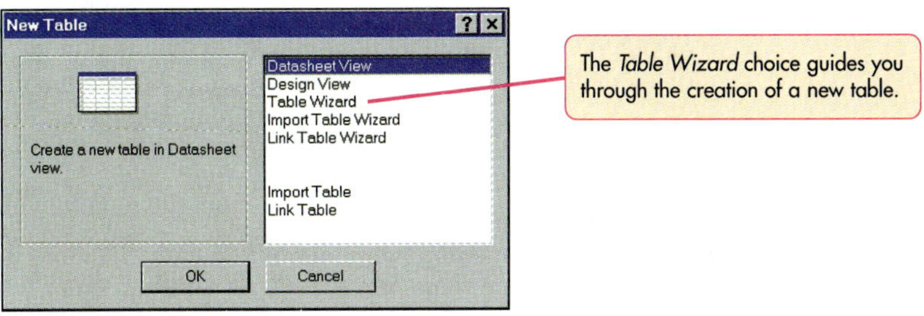

☐ **2-2 CONCEPTS**. Once a database has been created, the next step is to create its tables. When you create them, you specify what fields they are to contain and what the properties of those fields are. In this concepts section you explore these procedures.

☐ **2-2 TUTORIAL**. In this tutorial, you create a table for the *Club Records* database that you created in Section 2-1. The table will be used to store membership information.

☐ **2-2 DRILL**. In this drill you create the first table for the publisher database. It will store the quarterly sales of various titles by department.

Field Name	Data Type	Description
ISBN	Text	International Standard Book Number
Sales Period	Text	Quarter in which books were sold
Trade Sales	Number	Unit sales in Trade Department
Educational Sales	Number	Unit sales in Educational Department
Mail Order Sales	Number	Unit sales in Mail Order Department
International Sales	Number	Unit sales in International Department

2-3 SPECIFYING FIELD PROPERTIES

When you click anywhere on a row to enter or edit a field's name, data type, or description, the properties of that field are displayed in the lower part of the window.

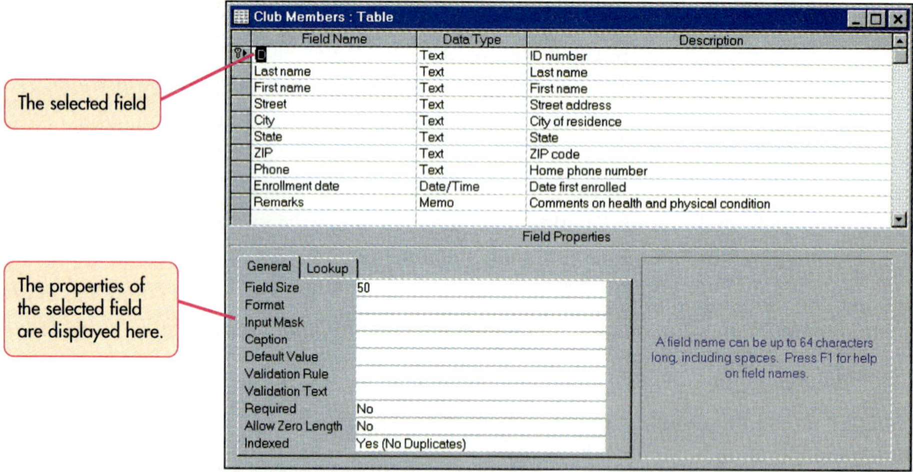

The properties of the selected field

The properties of a field are initially set to the default values for the specified data type, but you can change these properties at any time. Properties are the characteristics of the fields such as their size, format, number of decimal places, and so on, that specify how the field stores, handles, and displays data. For example, if you specify a medium date format for a field, dates will be displayed as 01-Jan-98. If you specify a short format, the same date will be displayed as 1/1/98. Changing a property changes the way data is displayed in a datasheet, form, or report, but it does not necessarily change the underlying data. However, if you change a property to make a field smaller after entering data in the table, you may lose data. Text fields may be shortened to fit, or numbers may be rounded off to the nearest whole number. There are many properties to work with, but which are available depends on the field's data types. The available properties are summarized in the table "Properties of Various Data Types."

Properties of Various Data Types								
Property	**Text**	**Memo**	**Number**	**Date/Time**	**Currency**	**AutoNumber**	**Yes/No**	**OLE**
Field Size	■	□	■	□	□	□	□	□
Format	■	■	■	■	■	■	■	□
Decimal Places	□	□	■	□	■	□	□	□
Input Mask	■	□	■	■	■	□	□	□
Caption	■	■	■	■	■	■	■	■
Default Value	■	□	■	■	■	□	■	□
Validation Rule	■	■	■	■	■	□	■	□
Validation Text	■	■	■	■	■	□	■	□
Required	■	■	■	■	■	□	■	■
Allow Zero Length	■	■	□	□	□	□	□	□
Indexed	■	□	■	■	■	■	■	□

■ = available

□ = not available

Changing Field Sizes

The *Field Size* property specifies the maximum number of characters that you can enter in a field. You should specify the smallest possible Field Size setting because the table will then take less space and can be processed more quickly. The default width of most data types is set automatically, but you can change Text and Number fields. Text fields can be between 0 and 255 characters long (the default is 50). When choosing one of these data types, keep the following points in mind:

▸ To store numbers with decimal places, select Single or Double.

▸ To store monetary values (dollars), select the Currency data type instead of the Number type.

Changing Formats

The *Format* property specifies how the field's contents will be displayed. Number, Date, and Yes/No field formats from which you can choose are shown in the figures at the left.

The Decimal Places Property

The *Decimal Places* property specifies how many decimal places are displayed for Number fields. This command overrides or modifies the Format property. For example, fields formatted as Currency normally display only 2 decimal places. By changing the Decimal Places property, you can change this to between 0 and 15. This property has no effect on fields where the format is set to General Number. The Auto setting (the default) displays numbers as specified by the field's Format property setting.

The Input Mask Property

The *Input Mask* property specifies a pattern for data entry. A *mask* is like a template that only allows you to enter data of a specific type in a specific format. You can type in the mask, or click the **Build** button with the three dots (see the Note

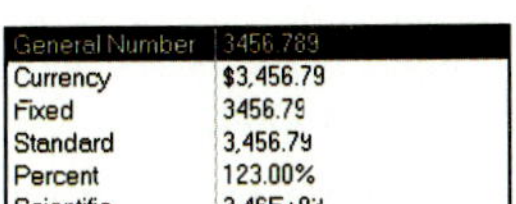

Number field formats

Date field formats

Yes/No field formats

box "Build Not Installed") in Text or Date/Time fields to display a list of pre-designed masks specific to the field. For example, in a Text field there are predefined masks for phone numbers, extensions, Social Security numbers, ZIP codes, passwords, dates, and times. In a Date/Time field the predefined masks include those that display dates in such formats as 16-Mar-97 and 3/16/97.

NOTE
Build Not Installed

If you click the **Build** button and get a message that this feature is not installed, it isn't on your system. To use it, you must install Access's developer tools.

The Caption Property

The *Caption* property creates a label that is used in place of a field name in a form. (Forms are discussed in detail in PicTorial 4.) If you leave this property blank, the field name will be used on the form instead.

The Default Value Property

The *Default Value* property specifies a value that is automatically entered into the field for all new records. For example, if most of your business is within the state of Texas, you could make TX the default for the state field. You can type in the default value or click the **Build** button to display the Expression Builder screen.

The Validation Rule and Validation Text Properties

The *Validation Rule* property sets rules for the data that Access will accept in the field. If you enter data that violates the rule, when you try to move to the next field a message displays whatever error message you set up in the *Validation Text* box. This is an important feature that prevents the wrong data from being entered into the database. Some validation rules are built in. For example, you can't enter text in number fields. However, other validation rules must be set. (The symbols and conventions used in these rules are discussed in sections 3-1 and 3-3.) For example:

▸ **Not > 1000** only allows numbers of 1000 or less in the field.

▸ **Between 10 And 20** allows only numbers of at least 10 and no more than 20 in the field.

▸ **= NY** allows only the abbreviation for New York in the field.

▸ **=NY Or CA** allows only abbreviations for New York or California in the field.

▸ **Between #1/1/96# And #12/30/98#** allows only dates between January 1, 1996, and December 30, 1998, in the field.

▸ **Like "???"** allows only text with three characters in the field.

The Required and Allow Zero Length Properties

The *Required* and *Allow Zero Length* properties specify whether data must be entered in the field. The Allow Zero Length property controls Text and Memo fields. The Required property controls all field types except AutoNumber fields. Using these properties you can ensure, for example, that a last name or price is entered for every field.

The Indexed Property

When you want to find data in a field or sort a table based on a field, these operations work faster if that field is indexed. The index contains only two things: the record numbers that Access assigned when you entered the records and the contents of the indexed field.

When you use an indexed field to find a particular record, you specify the value to be looked for in the indexed field. The program first reads the indexed file and scans the records there. Since the index is generally much smaller than the table, this can be done quickly. When it finds an entry in the index that matches the search criteria you entered, it looks for its record number, or record pointer, and goes directly to where that record is stored on the disk.

Although indexes speed finding and sorting in the indexed field, they can slow down the adding, editing, and deleting of data because the index must also be automatically updated. For this reason, try to avoid indexing too many fields within one table. Also, the field you specify as the primary key is indexed automatically.

Specifying a Field's Properties

1. Display the table in Design view.
2. Click anywhere on the row in the grid at the top of the window to display the field's current properties in the *Field Properties* section at the bottom of the window.
3. In the *Field Properties* section, click in the box next to the field whose properties you want to change, then do one of the following:
   ▶ Type in the property.
   ▶ Click the drop-down arrow (▾) that appears and select the property from the menu.
   ▶ Click the **Build** button (with the three dots that appears to the right of the field's property) and select choices from the options offered.

PAL ON-LINE ACTIVITIES CHECKLIST

☐ **2-3 CONCEPTS.** The properties of a field determine both the type of data it can contain and how that data is displayed. In this concepts section you explore how you specify these properties and others.

☐ **2-3 TUTORIAL.** In this tutorial you change some field properties so data in those fields is displayed in the chosen format or must be entered only in a specific way.

☐ **2-3 DRILL.** In this drill you change the properties of some of the fields you created for the *Quarterly Sales* table from their default values.

Quarterly Sales Field Properties		
Field Name	**Property**	**Setting**
ISBN	*Field Size*	**13**
Sales Period	*Validation Rule*	**Spring Or Summer Or Fall Or Winter**
	Validation Text	**Must enter Spring, Summer, Fall, or Winter**
Trade Sales	*Format*	**Standard**
	Decimal Places	**0**
Educational Sales	*Format*	**Standard**
	Decimal Places	**0**
Mail Order Sales	*Format*	**Standard**
	Decimal Places	**0**
International Sales	*Format*	**Standard**
	Decimal Places	**0**

2-4 ENTERING AND EDITING DATA

Unlike a card index file, where you insert the card in the proper order as you fill it out, the database management program will add a new record (the equivalent of an index card) to the end of the file. You can enter new records one after another without worrying about their order. As you saw in PicTorial 1, a file can be sorted after you enter the records.

It is often necessary to edit or update records in a database file; for example, when club members change addresses, their records must be updated. To do this, you first find the specific record to be updated and display it on the screen. You then revise the contents of the appropriate fields, or if the record is no longer needed, delete it.

You can enter or edit data into a table in either Datasheet or Form view (Form view is discussed in detail in PicTorial 4). In Datasheet view your table looks like a grid of rows (records) and columns (fields). The elements are illustrated in the figure "Datasheet view screen elements."

You don't have to save your data when you enter or edit records. That is done automatically when you move to another record or close the table.

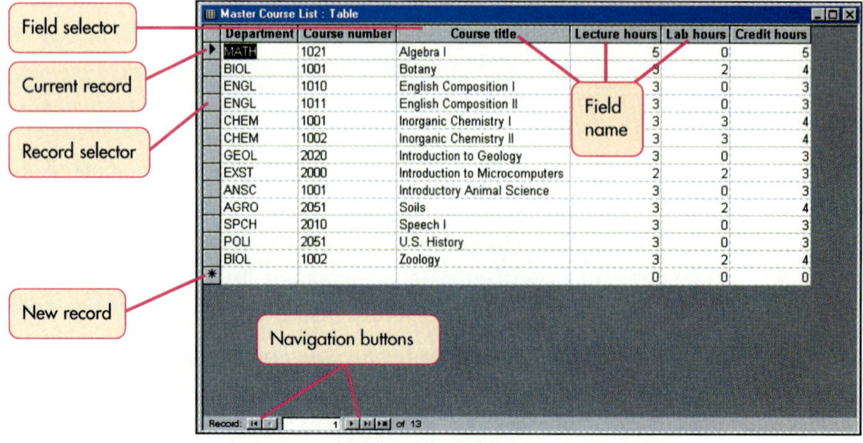

Datasheet view screen elements

Entering and Editing Data in Datasheet View

1. Display the table in Datasheet view.

2. Enter and edit records as follows:

   ▶ To enter data in a field, click in the field and type in the data. You can use the scroll bar to scroll the table and any of the keys described in the table "Keyboard Commands in Datasheet View" to enter and edit data.

   ▶ To delete a record, click its row selector to highlight it and then press Del or click the **Delete Record** button on the toolbar.

   ▶ To add a new record, enter it on the last row of the table or click the **New Record** button on the toolbar.

3. Click the table's **Close** button (⊠) to close the table when finished entering or editing data. The data you have entered is saved automatically.

Keyboard Commands in Datasheet View

Task	Press
Finding Records	
Go to a specific record in a datasheet	F5
Editing Records	
Select or unselect all data in the current field	F2
Undo changes to the current field	Esc
Insert the same value as the same field in the previous record	Ctrl+'
Enter the default value assigned to a field (see Section 2-3)	Ctrl+Alt+Spacebar
Moving Within a Table	
Move to the next field	Tab, →, or Enter
Move to the previous field	Shift+Tab, or ←
Move to the first or last field in the current record	Home or End
Move to the current field in the next or previous record	↓ or ↑
Move to the current field in the first or last record	Ctrl+↑ or Ctrl+↓
Move to the first field in the first record	Ctrl+Home
Move to the last field in the last record	Ctrl+End
Scrolling the Screen	
Move up or down one screen	PgUp or PgDn
Move left or right one screen	Ctrl+PgUp or Ctrl+PgDn

RECORD SELECTOR SYMBOLS

Record selector symbols indicate the current record—the only record you can work on.

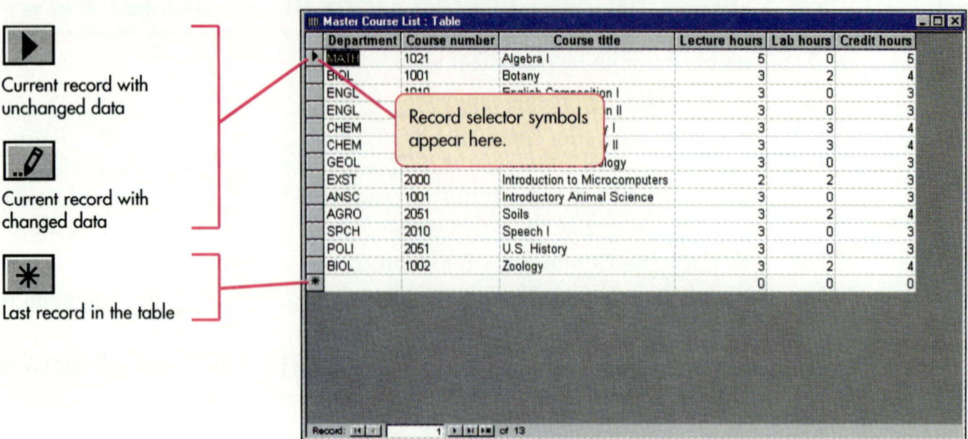

Current record with
unchanged data

Current record with
changed data

Last record in the table

> A pencil symbol () indicates the record's contents have been changed but not saved.

> A triangle symbol (▶) means the record is current, but its contents haven't been changed.

> An asterisk symbol (✳) marks the empty record at the end of the table. (This blank record isn't counted as one of the records.) As soon as you begin to enter data into this record, a new record is created, the asterisk moves down, and is replaced with a pencil symbol.

Editing Data: Navigation vs. Editing Mode

When you press `Tab` to move to a field containing data, or click in it with the mouse pointer shaped like a right-pointing diagonal arrow, the field's entire contents is highlighted. This is called navigation mode. If you type any data, the new data immediately replaces the highlighted data. To edit, not replace, the existing data, click in the field when the mouse pointer is shaped like an I-beam (I), or press `F2` to change from navigation to editing mode. Then use the arrow keys to move the insertion point to insert or delete characters.

COMMON WRONG TURNS
Can't Enter Data

If you can't enter data in a field, you may be having one of the following problems:

> You are trying to enter the wrong data type. For example, you can't enter text in a Number field.

> The data violates a validation rule. For example, you can't enter 12 or 1234 in a field with a validation rule *Like "???"* since that rule specifies that three characters must be entered.

> The entry is too long. For example, you can enter only 255 characters in a Text field.

> The **Allow Editing** command is turned off. (Pull down the **Tools** menu, click **Options**, and on the dialog box's **Advanced** tab, make sure the **No Locks** option button is on.)

Undoing Mistakes

If you make a mistake, press [Esc] or pull down the **Edit** menu and use one of the **Undo** commands to undo it. The commands on the menu change depending on what you have been doing. For example, **Undo Typing** undoes the last typing you did, and **Undo Current Field** (same as pressing [Esc]) and **Undo Current Record** undo changes to the current field or record respectively.

PAL ON-LINE ACTIVITIES CHECKLIST

☐ **2-4 CONCEPTS.** Once the database's tables have been created, you can begin entering data. To do so you just move the insertion point into a field and type in the data. In this concepts section you are introduced to entering the data and then editing it.

☐ **2-4 TUTORIAL.** In this tutorial you enter data into the *Club Members* table that you created earlier in this PicTorial.

	ID	Last name	First name	Street	City	State	ZIP	Phone	Enrollment date	Remarks
▶	112	Anthony	William	900 Maple Road	Reading	MA	20000-0000	555-1007	1/7/95	
	113	Foley	Kim	25 Elm Street	Marblehead	MA	01867-0000	555-1002	1/8/95	
	114	Morin	Mike	5 Milk Street	Salem	OR	40000-0000	555-1009	1/10/95	
	115	Culman	Tina	100 Elm Street	New Haven	CT	10000-0000	555-1001	1/16/95	
	116	Kendall	Liz	14 Lark Avenue	Chicago	IL	20000-0000	555-1003	2/1/95	
	117	Henderson	Carolyn	45 Porter Avenue	Fairlawn	NJ	30000-0000	555-1006	3/6/95	
	118	Morin	Cathy	5 Milk Street	Salem	OR	40000-0000	555-1008	6/3/95	
	119	Morin	Emily	43 Spruce Street	Milpitas	CA	20000-0000	555-1005	8/1/95	
	120	Hogan	Dennis	40 Main Street	Edgewater	NJ	30000-0000	555-1004	9/6/95	
	121	Kendall	Steve	1 Sylvan Avenue	Englewood	NJ	07632-0000	555-1010	10/15/95	
✳										

Records to add to the *Club Members* table

☐ 2-4 **DRILL.** In this drill you enter data into the *Quarterly Sales* table.

ISBN	Sales Period	Trade Sales	Educational Sales	Mail Order Sales	International Sales
96102	spring	1,500	300	25	1,300
96103	spring	600	200	100	50
96104	spring	4,000	1,000	3,000	500
96105	spring	6,000	3,000	8,000	1,200
96106	spring	3,000	750	925	225
96107	spring	75	25	10	0
96108	spring	100	2,000	156	2,000
96100	fall	300	1,100	150	75
96101	fall	200	800	500	125
96102	fall	1,300	200	75	600
96103	fall	800	100	75	25
96104	fall	4,000	900	2,500	250
96105	fall	5,000	2,000	6,000	0
96106	fall	2,500	500	625	160
96107	fall	0	10	5	0
96108	fall	375	1,100	100	50

The quarterly sales records

After creating a database table, you can import it from one database into another. This is especially useful when you are creating a new database and want to use other Access tables that have already been created. It's also useful when changing from one database application to another. For example, millions of databases have been created in a program called dBASE over the years. To use these tables with Microsoft Access, you don't have to redo them: they can be imported directly into Access with little effort. You can also import data from spreadsheets and word processing programs. This eliminates retyping data and can greatly speed up the development of a database.

QUICKSTEPS

Importing an Access Table from Another Database

1. Open the database into which you want to import a table.
2. Do one of the following to display the Import dialog box:
   - Click the **New** button on the Database window, click **Import Table** to select it, then click the **OK** button.
   - Pull down the **File** menu, point to the **Get External Data** command to cascade the menu, then click the **Import** command.
3. Click the **Files of type** drop-down arrow and click the type of file you want to import. (Microsoft Access databases is the default.)
4. Specify the drive, folder, and filename of the database containing the table you want to import and click the **Import** button. Depending on the type of file you are importing, a dialog box or a Wizard that guides you through the process may appear.
5. Select the table you want to import and click the **OK** button. In a few moments the table is listed in the Database window.

PAL ON-LINE ACTIVITIES CHECKLIST

- ☐ **2-5 CONCEPTS.** If you are working on a database and want to include in it a table from another database, you can import it. In this concepts section you are introduced to this procedure.

- ☐ **2-5 TUTORIAL.** Earlier in this PicTorial you created the *Club Members* table in the *Club Records* database. We would like to have another table in the database to store customer charges. To speed things along, in the tutorial we import the table instead of creating it.

- ☐ **2-5 DRILL.** The *Publisher sales* database should contain two tables, the one you've created and a second listing details about each title sold. In this drill you import that *Titles and Publishers* table from another Access database.

There are times when a table has to be changed after it has been created. Changes might include adding new fields, deleting existing fields, or changing the properties of existing ones. To modify a table's design, you use Datasheet or Design view. Any changes you make in one view also appear in the other view.

N O T E
Two-Digit Years—Yikes!

For the past forty or so years, databases have been designed to hold only the last two digits of the year's date. For example, 1996 is stored as 96. With the millennium just around the corner, a disaster looms because computers using dates in this way cannot tell the difference between 1996 and 2096. There is a lot of scrambling going on at the moment as this problem looms larger and larger. Vast sums will be spent to modify databases and avert complete chaos.

Datasheet View

In Datasheet view, you can change column (field) widths or positions and row (record) heights. In Access, the basic rule is to select something and then choose the operation you want to perform on it. To select elements in Datasheet view, you use the procedures described in the table "Selecting in Datasheet View."

Selecting in Datasheet View	
To Select	**Do This**
A record	Click the record selector, or click anywhere in a record then pull down the **Edit** menu and click the **Select Record** command.
Multiple consecutive records	Point to the first record selector and holding down the left mouse button, drag down the others.
All records	Pull down the **Edit** menu and click the **Select All Records** command, or click the topmost record selector (the one on the same row as the column headings), or press Ctrl + A.
A field	Click the field selector (the column heading).
Multiple consecutive fields	Point to the first selector and drag across the others.
Single cell	Click just inside the left edge when the mouse pointer is displayed as a plus pointer.
Multiple adjacent cells	Click just inside the left edge when the mouse pointer is displayed as a plus pointer and drag across the cells.

Resizing Columns and Rows and Moving Columns

▶ To change the order of columns, click the field selector (the column heading) when the mouse pointer is displayed as a downward-pointing arrow to select the column. Then point to the selected column heading again, hold down the left mouse button, and drag the column to a new position.

▶ To resize a column or field, point to the field selector's right border so the mouse pointer changes to a split arrow and drag the column wider. You can also double-click the field selector's right border to automatically size the column to the longest entry. You can also select a group of columns and click the right edge of any selected column's header to size them all. Sizing the fields does not affect the data stored within them, just the way they are displayed.

▶ To resize rows or records, point to one row border so the mouse pointer changes to a split arrow and drag it taller or narrower. When you change one row, they all change.

Design View

In Design view, you can move, delete, or insert fields. To select a row (field) in Design view, click the row selector illustrated in the figure "Design view screen elements."

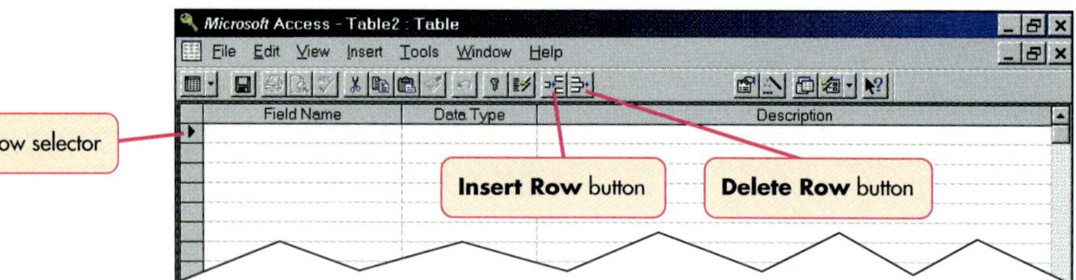

Design view screen elements

Moving, Deleting, and Inserting Fields

▶ To move a field, click the row selector to select the field. Then point to the selected row selector again, hold down the left mouse button, and drag the row to a new position. When the pointer is where you want the field moved, release the mouse button.

▶ To delete a field, click the row selector to select the field, then click the **Delete Row** button on the toolbar, or pull down the **Edit** menu and click the **Delete Row** command. (Respond to the warning box that you do want to permanently delete the selected field.)

▶ To insert a field, click the row selector of the row below where you want the new field inserted. Then click the **Insert Row** button on the toolbar, or pull down the **Insert** menu and click the **Field** command.

Saving Changes

Changes to a table's design are not saved automatically.

> **QUICKSTEPS**
>
> **Saving Changes**
>
> ▶ Click the **Save** button on the toolbar, or pull down the **File** menu and click the **Save** command.

PAL ON-LINE ACTIVITIES CHECKLIST

☐ **2-6 CONCEPTS.** Once a table has been created, some needed improvements might become apparent. In this concepts section you are introduced to the procedures you use to modify a design.

☐ **2-6 TUTORIAL.** When you defined the *Club Members* table, you may have made some mistakes. In this tutorial, you open a similar database and correct the table's design. Using what you have learned, you should then be able to modify your own file so that it is correct.

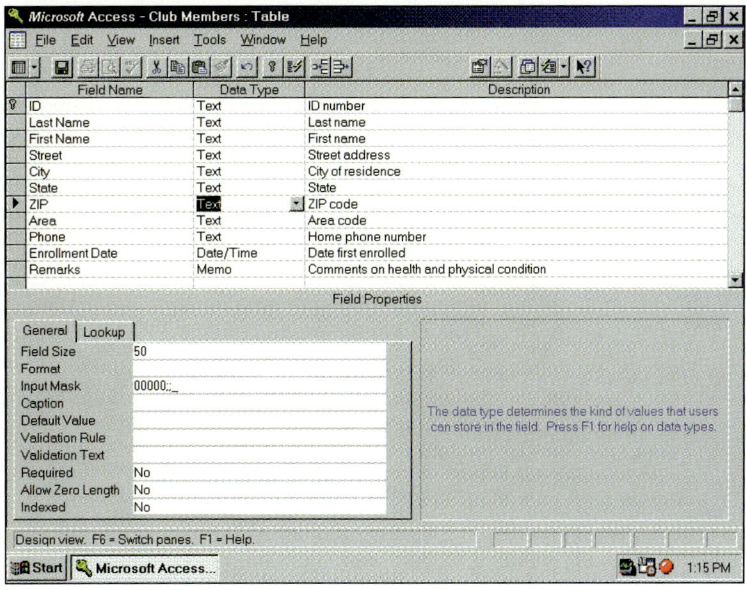

The modified *Club Members* table

☐ **2-6 DRILL.** In this drill you modify the design of the *Titles and Publishers* table that you imported into the new database.

2-7 ANALYZING A DATABASE

There might be times when you would like to document a database's design or you'd like some suggestions on how to improve it. You can do so by analyzing a table's performance and by printing a description of its objects.

Analyzing Tables

The worst thing you can do in a database is store duplicate information. It makes the database hard to update and it will lose accuracy over time as changes are made to some data and not to other. Access provides you with a tool that will analyze your database tables for duplicate information. If Access finds duplication it will recommend how to split one table into two to correct the problem, or will even split the table for you.

Analyzing Tables

1. Open the database that you want to analyze.
2. Do one of the following to analyze a specific table in the database:
   - Click the **Analyze** button on the toolbar.
   - Click the **Analyze** button's drop-down arrow on the toolbar, and click the **Analyze Table** command.
   - Pull down the **Tools** menu, point to the **Analyze** command to cascade the menu, then click the **Table** command.
3. Follow the instructions as the Wizard guides you through the process.

Analyzing Performance

The performance of a large database is very important. Imagine trying to make an airline reservation when the system is slow. The agent would have lines a mile long forming at the counter or people fretting on the phone. Maximizing performance is an advanced skill, but Access gives you a tool you can use to improve your own designs.

Analyzing Performance

1. Open the database that you want to analyze.
2. Do one of the following to analyze performance:
   - Click the **Analyze** button's drop-down arrow on the toolbar, and click the **Analyze Performance** command.
   - Pull down the **Tools** menu, point to the **Analyze** command to cascade the menu, then click the **Performance** command.
3. Click the **Object Type** drop-down arrow and select the type of object you want to analyze.
4. Click the check box in front of each object you want analyzed.
5. Click the OK button and in a moment a list of suggestions appears.
6. Select any suggestion you want to accept and then click the **Optimize** button to have the change made for you.

Documenting a Database

Documenting the design of a database is important for two reasons. First, it gives you a record to keep on file in case you need it to reconstruct the database or create a similar database. Second, it gives you information you need to trace errors, make changes, or plan improvements and additions.

Documenting a Database

1. Open the database that you want to document.

2. Do one of the following to document the database:
   - Click the **Analyze** button's drop-down arrow on the toolbar, and click the **Documentor** command.
   - Pull down the **Tools** menu, point to the **Analyze** command to cascade the menu, then click the **Documentor** command.

3. Click the **Object Type** drop-down arrow and select the type of object you want to document.

4. Click the check box in front of each object you want documented.

5. Click the **OK** button and in a moment a document appears in Print Preview listing the object's characteristics.

6. Click the **Print** button on the toolbar to print the documentation or click the **Close** button to close the Print Preview window.

PAL ON-LINE ACTIVITIES CHECKLIST

☐ **2-7 CONCEPTS**. Designing large databases is a specialty requiring a lot of experience. However, access has some tools that make it easier by analyzing the database's performance. In this concepts section you are introduced to the database Documentor.

☐ **2-7 TUTORIAL**. In this tutorial you document the *Club Records* database so you have a complete record to work from when troubleshooting, improving, or recreating the database.

☐ **2-7 DRILL**. In this drill you document the design of the *Quarterly Sales* table that you created in preceding drills.

LAB ACTIVITIES

EXERCISE

2-1 The General Store Database

In this exercise you create a database for a small general store. The database already contains one table (*Employees*) but you design a second (*Daily Sales*) and import a third (*Inventory*). In the process of designing the database you set field properties, add and delete fields, and enter records.

Opening the Database

1. Open the database named *General Store* stored in the *Exercise Databases* folder of the *Access Student Resource Disk*. The database contains a single table, *Employees*.

Designing the Database

2. Click the **New** button on the Database window and using *Design View*, design a table with the following fields.

Field Name	Data Type	Description
Employee ID	Text	Employee ID number
Item Number	Text	Item's stock number
Selling Price	Number	List price of item
Date Sold	Date/Time	Date item was sold
Record	AutoNumber	Record number

Changing Field Properties

3. With the table still displayed in Design view, specify the *Record* field as the primary key.

4. With the table still displayed in Design view, change the properties of the fields as follows:

Field Name	Property	Setting
Employee ID	*Input Mask*	**A000** (note that the 0s are zeros)
Item Number	*Input Mask*	**A000** (note that the 0s are zeros)
Selling Price	*Field Size*	**Double**
	Format	**Currency**
Date Sold	*Format*	**Short Date**

5. Save the design under the name *Daily Sales*.

Entering Data

6. Click the **View** button on the toolbar and enter the records shown in the figure "The daily sales table."

Employee ID	Item Number	Selling Price	Date Sold	Record
S001	A111	$11.85	3/22/97	1
S001	A112	$15.55	3/22/97	2
S001	E111	$399.00	3/22/97	3
S001	G110	$4.65	3/22/97	4
S001	G112	$0.58	3/22/97	5

The daily sales table

7. Print out the records in the table and then close the table so just the Database window is displayed.

Importing a Table

8. Use the **New** button on the Database window and the *Import Table* choice to import the Microsoft Access table *Inventory* stored in the *Store Records* database in the *Exercise Databases* folder of the *Access Student Resource Disk*.

Changing Field Properties

9. Display the *Inventory* table in Design view, examine it, then change the properties of the fields as follows:

Field Name	Property	Setting
Item Number	Input Mask	**A000** (note that the 0s are zeros)
Selling Price	Format	**Currency**
	Decimal Places	**2**
Cost	Format	**Currency**
	Decimal Places	**2**

Modifying the Table's Design

10. With the *Inventory* table displayed in Design view, delete the *Comments* field, and then save the revised design.

11. With the *Inventory* table displayed in Datasheet view, adjust all column widths to the longest entry.

12. Save the modified design.

Displaying the Table's Definition

13. Close the table.

14. Use the **Analyze** button's drop-down arrow to document the *Daily Sales*. After scrolling though it, close the Object Definition window.

Finishing Up

15. Close all open windows including the Database window.

PROJECT

2-1 The College Database

In this project you create a database used to match students, courses, and instructors in a college.

1. Create a new database named *College Courses* based on the blank template and save it in the *Project Databases* folder on the *Access Student Resource Disk*.

2. Design a table that allows you to enter the records shown in the figure "The *Master Course List* table." As you do so, keep the following points in mind:

   ▸ The fields listing Lecture hours, Lab hours, and Credit hours should be Number data types and the rest Text data types.

   ▸ The *Course title* field should be the primary key.

   ▸ Save the table as **Master Course List**.

3. After designing the table, enter the records shown in the figure "The *Master Course List* table." Adjust all column widths to the width of the longest entry then save the table and close it.

Department	Course number	Course title	Lecture hours	Lab hours	Credit hours
MATH	1021	Algebra 1	5	0	5
BIOL	1001	Botany	3	2	4
ENGL	1010	English Composition I	3	0	3
ENGL	1011	English Composition II	3	0	3
CHEM	1001	Inorganic Chemistry I	3	3	4
CHEM	1002	Inorganic Chemistry II	3	3	4
GEOL	2020	Introduction to Geology	3	0	3
EXST	2000	Introduction to Computers	2	2	3
ANSC	1001	Introductory Animal Science	3	0	3
AGRO	2051	Soils	3	2	4
SPCH	2010	Speech I	3	0	3
POLI	2051	U.S. History	3	0	3
BIOL	1002	Zoology	3	2	4

The *Master Course List* table

4. Import the following Microsoft Access tables stored in the *College Records* database in the *Project Databases* folder of the *Access Student Resource Disk*:

   ▸ *Master Instructor List*

   ▸ *Master Student List*

   ▸ *Sections Offered This Semester*

   ▸ *Student Enrollments by Course*

5. Close any open windows including the Database window.

USING DATABASES

After completing this PicTorial, you will be able to:

▸ **Find and replace data in a database table**
▸ **Filter records**
▸ **Use criteria expressions to filter records**
▸ **Create queries and describe dynasets**
▸ **Change the properties in a query's dynaset**
▸ **Calculate with queries**

THE tables in a database store raw data, things like names, addresses, and numbers. Having this data stored in a structured way is not useful in and of itself. To make this raw data useful, it must be analyzed to turn it into information. The real power of a database comes from using it to supply you with information. You do this by using the **Find** command, filters, and queries to specify what information is displayed and in what order. You can also calculate the values in one or more fields and even use calculations such as sums, averages, standard deviations, and variances. In this PicTorial you explore these powerful aspects of Access.

3-1 FINDING DATA IN A TABLE

Besides death and taxes there is at least one other certainty in life: The sooner you collect all the information you need, the sooner it will become outdated and require modifications to bring it up to date. With small tables you can easily scan your data. But once tables begin to hold hundreds or thousands of records, you need tools to expedite your search. The simplest tool to which you will be introduced is the **Find** command, which locates the record you want to view, update, or delete. (This command works for tables, queries, and forms.)

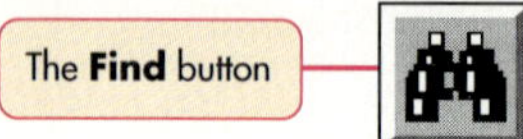

QUICKSTEPS

Finding Data

1. With the table open in Datasheet view, move the insertion point into the field you want to find data in. (If you want to find it everywhere, leave the insertion point anywhere.)

2. Click the **Find** button on the toolbar, or pull down the **Edit** menu and click the **Find** command to display the Find dialog box. (The dialog box title is *Find in field* when the **Search Only Current Field** check box is on (☑), and *Find* when it isn't.)

3. Enter the data you want to find in the **Find What** text box and make any of the other settings described in the box "Understanding the Find in Field Dialog Box."

4. Click the **Find First** button to locate and highlight the first occurrence of the data you are searching for.

5. Click the **Find Next** button to find additional occurrences, or click the **Close** command to close the dialog box and then press ⇧Shift+F4 to find additional occurrences.

UNDERSTANDING
The Find in Field Dialog Box

When you use the **Find** command, the Find dialog box appears with the following options.

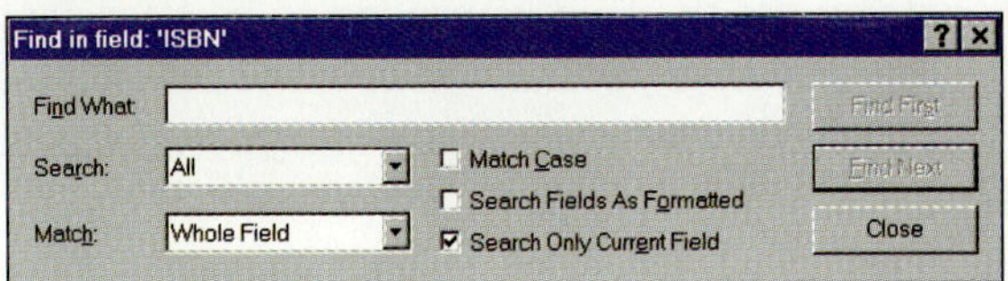

Fi<u>n</u>d What text box is where you enter the data (or string) you want to find. You can use wildcard characters in the text you enter to find patterns. For details, see the TIP box "Using Wildcard Characters."

Drop-Down Arrows

Sea<u>r</u>ch drop-down arrow lets you specify whether Access looks at **All** of the table or just **Up** or **Down**.

Matc<u>h</u> drop-down arrow lets you specify what part of the field's contents is checked.

▶ **Any Part of Field** searches for any occurrence of the string even if it is part of another word. For example, searching for *York* will find *York, Yorkville,* and *New York*.

▶ **Whole Field** searches only for occurrences where the string matches the exact contents of the field. For example, searching for *York* will find *York* but not *Yorkville* or *New York*.

▶ **Start of Field** command searches for occurrences that fall at the beginning of the field. For example, searching for *York* will find *York* or *Yorkville* but not *New York*.

Check Boxes

Match <u>C</u>ase check box, when on (☑), searches only for occurrences that exactly match the case you enter. For example, searching for *Adams* will find *Adams* but not *adams* or *ADAMS*.

Search Fields As F<u>o</u>rmatted check box, when on (☑), searches fields for data as it is displayed rather than the way it is stored. For example, dates are stored as numbers such as *1/1/98* but can be formatted to be displayed in a variety of ways such as *01-Jan-98* or *Monday 01-Jan-98*.

Search Only Curr<u>e</u>nt Field check box, when on (☑), searches only in the current field in all records. This is always faster than searching all fields, and is much faster when the field is indexed (see Section 2-3).

Buttons

Find Fir<u>s</u>t button finds the first occurrence in the table of the data in the **Fi<u>n</u>d What** text box.

Fi<u>n</u>d Next button finds the second and subsequent occurrences of the data. (You can also close the Find dialog box and press ⇧ Shift + F4 to find additional occurrences.)

Close button closes the Find dialog box.

TIP
Using Wildcard Characters

When you use the **Find** command, you can enter wildcard characters in the **Fi<u>n</u>d What** text box.

▶ **?** stands for a single character. For example, **h?t** will find *hat* and *hot*.

▶ ***** stands for any sequence of characters. For example, **h*t** will find *hat, host,* and *habitat.*

▶ **[ ]** will match any single character of those listed within the brackets. For example, **h[ai]t** will find *hat* and *hit* but not *hot*.

▶ **[!]** will not match any single character listed within the brackets. For example, **h[!ai]t** will find *hot* but not *hat* and *hit*.

▶ **-** will match any one of a range of characters. For example, **h[a-m]t** will find *hat* and *hit* but not *hot*.

▶ **#** stands for any digit. For example, **Runway #L** will find *Runway 1L* and *Runway 2L*.

☐ **3-1 CONCEPTS.** As database tables increase in size, it becomes harder to find specific records. One tool that makes it easier is the Find command to which you are introduced in this concepts section.

☐ **3-1 TUTORIAL.** In this tutorial you use the Find command to look for data in the *Member Charges* table in the *Ever Hopeful Health Club* database. (The *Ever Hopeful Health Club* database is an enlarged version of the *Club Records* database that you created in PicTorial 2.)

☐ **3-1 DRILL.** In this drill you use the Find command to locate information in the *Titles and Publishers* table in the *Publisher Sales* database.

3-2 REPLACING DATA IN A TABLE

You can replace data in a table using the **Replace** command. This works much like the **Replace** command in a word processing program.

QUICKSTEPS

Using Replace

1. With the table open in Datasheet view, move the insertion point into the field you want to replace data in. (If you want to replace it everywhere, leave the insertion point anywhere.)

2. Pull down the **Edit** menu and click the **Replace** command to display the Replace dialog box. (The box title is *Replace in field* when the **Search Only Current Field** check box is on, and *Replace* when it isn't.)

3. Enter the data you want replaced in the **Find What** text box and the data you want to replace it with in the **Replace With** text box.

4. Use any of the options and click any of the buttons described in the box "Understanding the Replace Dialog Box."

When you use the **Replace** command, the Replace dialog box offers you the following options.

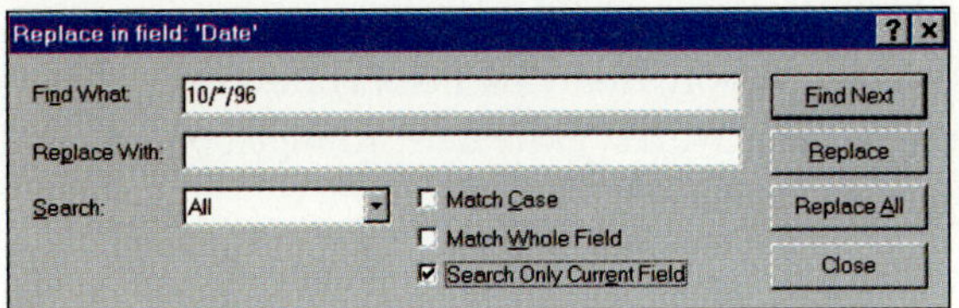

Text Boxes

Find What text box is where you enter the data you want replaced. You can also enter the wildcard characters described in the tip box "Using Wildcard Characters" in Section 3-1.

Replace With text box is where you enter the data you want to use to replace the other data.

Search drop-down arrow lets you specify whether Access looks at **All** of the table or just **Up** or **Down**.

Check Boxes

Match Case check box, when on (☑), locates only data with the same case. For example, searching for *New* will find *New* but not *new* or *NEW*.

Match Whole Field check box, when on (☑), locates only data that matches the **Find What** data and that fills the field. For example, when on, searching for *New* will find *New* but not *New York*.

Search Only Current Field check box, when on (☑), limits the search to the field in which the insertion point is located.

Command Buttons

Find Next button locates the next occurrence of the data currently in the **Find What** text box.

Replace button replaces the highlighted data with the data currently in the **Replace With** text box.

Replace All button replaces all occurrences of the data in the **Find What** text box that match the criteria of the check boxes with the data in the **Replace With** text box.

Close button ends the replace operation and closes the dialog box.

PAL ON-LINE ACTIVITIES CHECKLIST

☐ **3-2 CONCEPTS.** There are times when you need to replace data in a table. In this concepts section you are introduced to the Replace command that you would use to do that.

☐ **3-2 TUTORIAL.** In this tutorial you use the Replace command to replace data in one of the *Ever Hopeful Health Club* database tables.

☐ **3-2 DRILL.** In this drill you use the Replace command to replace information in the *Titles and Publishers* table in the *Publisher Sales* database.

3-3 FILTERING RECORDS IN A TABLE

You have used commands that display records so that you can read or edit them. Those commands were useful in a small database, but when the number of records increases, it becomes harder to find the record you want. There are times when only part of a table is of interest. For example, you may have a national membership list but want to work with only records for those members living in California. In cases such as these, you can hide the records of all other people by filtering the table. To filter a table you enter a *criteria expression* such as **CA** (for California) into one of the fields. Access compares the same field in each record to the criteria and displays only those that match—in this case, records with CA in the field. The filter temporarily hides all records that do not match the criteria and displays those that do. Filtering records is useful when you want to:

▸ See only those records that are of interest at the moment. For example, you may only want to see records from California.

▸ Find records that meet multiple criteria. For example, you may only want to see records from California where payments are past due.

▸ Sort records based on the contents of more than one field. For example, you may want to sort by state and have records within each state arranged by city.

It's easy to work with filters because you can use toolbar buttons, commands on the **Records** menu, or right-click an open table to display a shortcut menu to create or edit a filter, apply it, and then redisplay all hidden records.

Filtering by Selection

The fastest way to filter a table is to select all or part of the data in a field. When you then apply the filter, only records with matching data in the same field are displayed. For example, if you select the date *1/1/98* in the *Date* field, when you apply the filter, only records with that date are displayed.

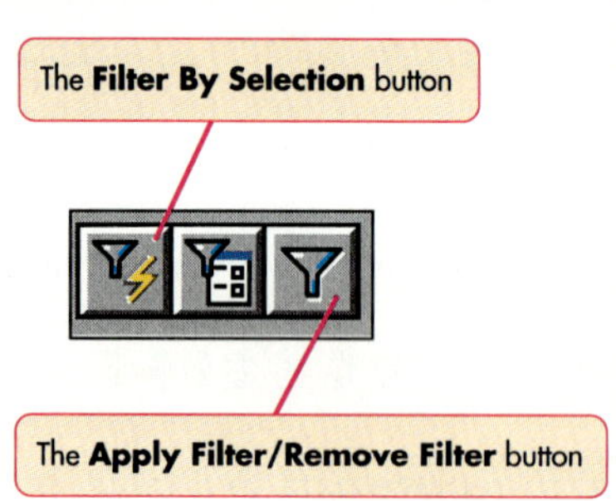

QUICKSTEPS

Filtering by Selection

1. Select any part of, or all of, a field's entry.
2. Click the **Filter By Selection** button on the toolbar or right-click in the selection and then click the shortcut menu's **Filter By Selection** command. Only records that contain the same data in the same field as that which you have selected are displayed.
3. Click the **Remove Filter** button on the toolbar to see all of the records again. (When no filter has been applied, this is the **Apply Filter** button.)

TIP
Filtering Out the Selection

Normally, the data you select determines which records are displayed. However you can turn this around and hide all of the records containing the selected data. To do so, select the data, right-click it, then click the shortcut menu's **Filter Excluding Selection** command. Only those records that don't contain the selected data are listed. Click the **Remove Filter** button on the toolbar to display all of the records again.

Filtering by Form

When you want to filter using data in two or more fields, you can use the **Filter by Form** command. This command displays a Filter by Form window, which contains a blank version of the active table or form.

If you enter data to filter by in more than one field, you are telling the filter command that the record must contain both to be listed. For example, if you enter *Jones* in one field and *1/1/98* in another, only records with both Jones and 1/1/98 will be listed. This is called an AND criteria since the first criteria AND the second criteria must both be met.

The Filter by Form window has both a **Look for** and an **Or** tab. If you enter data to filter by on the **Look for** tab and other data on the **Or** tab, the filtered table will contain records with one OR the other. For example, if you enter *Jones* on the **Look for** tab and *1/1/98* the **Or** tab, all records with Jones or 1/1/98 will be listed. This is called an OR criteria since either the first criteria OR the second criteria must be met.

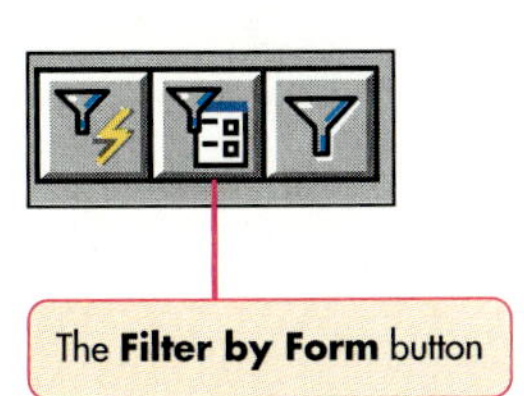

QUICKSTEPS

Filtering by Form

1. With the table displayed in Datasheet view, click the **Filter By Form** button on the toolbar to display the Filter by Form window. Click the **Clear Grid** button on the toolbar to remove any previous filters.

2. Click in the field you want to filter by to display a drop-down arrow. Click this drop-down arrow and select the value you want to filter by from the list that appears.

3. Click the **Apply Filter** button on the toolbar to filter the table.

4. Click the **Remove Filter** button on the toolbar, or pull down the **Records** menu and click the **Remove Filter/Sort** to redisplay all of the records in the table.

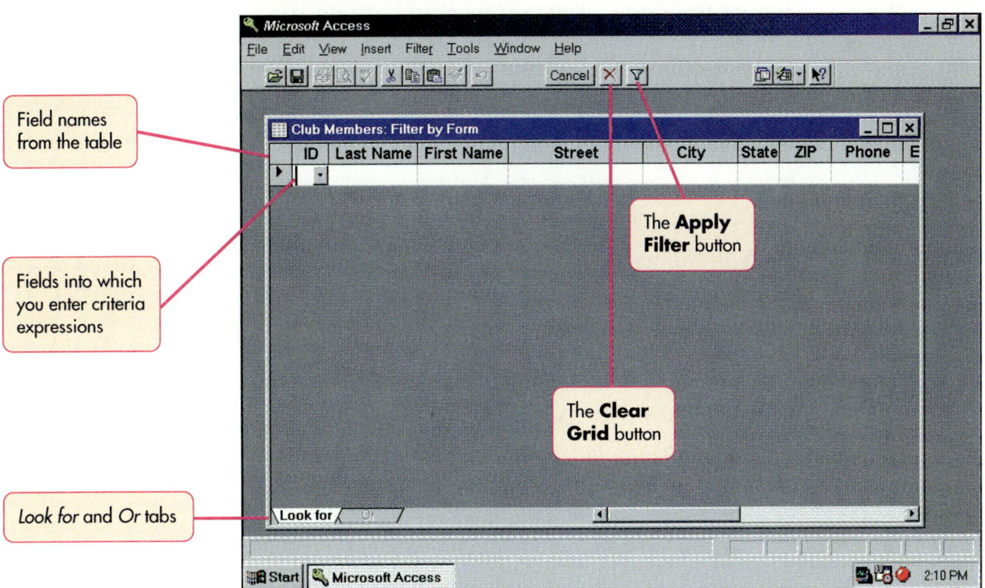

The Filter by Form window

Advanced Filtering

Sometimes you want to more than just match data when you filter a database. For example, instead of finding records with the date of 1/1/98, you may want to find all records later than 1/1/98 or earlier than 12/31/97. To do so, you use an advanced filter. Pull down the **Records** menu, point to the **Filter** command to cascade the menu, then click the **Advanced Filter/Sort** command to display the Filter window. This window has two sections. In the upper half is a list of the fields in your table. In the lower half is a grid with a number of columns and rows that divide the grid into areas called boxes, cells, or input areas.

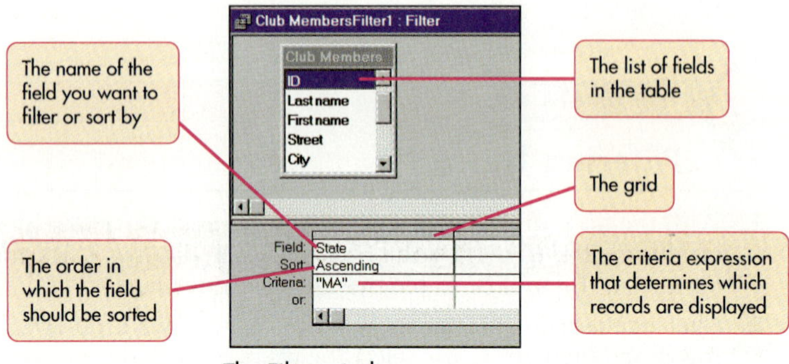

The Filter window

Specifying Fields to Use for a Filter or Sort

Using the grid's cell, you specify the fields to use for the filter or sort, the order in which the records are to be sorted, and the criteria by which they will be filtered.

To specify a field to filter or sort, you need to enter a field's name on the *Field* row of the grid. There are four ways to do so:

▸ Drag the field's name from the field list at the top of the window into one of the cells on the *Field* row of the grid.

▸ Double-click the field's name on the field list at the top of the window.

▸ Click in any cell on the Field row of the grid to display a drop-down arrow that lists fields you can choose from.

▸ Type the name in a cell.

Specifying a Sort Order

You can use the Filter window to filter and sort, or just to sort the table. In either case, you can sort using more than one field. To do so, drag down the names of the fields you want to sort by, keeping in mind that Access will sort them from left to right. (You can't sort Memo or OLE fields.) The most important field should be to the left and the least important to the right. For example, if you want to sort by state and then have cities arranged alphabetically within each state, you would list the state field first and then the city field. To then specify a sort order for a field, click on its *Sort* row and click the drop-down arrow (▾) that appears to list the choices. *Ascending* sorts the field from 0–9 or A–Z; *Descending* sorts it 9–0 or Z–A. If you select the *not sorted* choice, the table is arranged in the same order as the original table on the disk.

Specifying Criteria

A criteria expression determines what records are included in the table after it has been filtered. The simplest criteria expression tells Access to display only records that contain the specified data in the field. (You'll explore more powerful criteria expressions in the next section.) To enter a criteria expression, you just type it into the *Criteria* row on the grid. For example:

▶ **"Jones"** displays only those records with *Jones* in the field.

▶ **10.00** displays only those records where the value in the field is 10.00.

▶ **#1/10/99#** displays only those records with January 10, 1999 dates in the field.

The data type in the field determines how you enter a criteria expression in a cell on the *Criteria* row and how it's displayed.

▶ Enter numbers using digits and a decimal point if it's required. Don't enter currency symbols ($) or commas to separate thousands.

▶ Enter text with or without quotation marks. If you don't enter quotation marks, Access will do so when you press [Enter◄┘] or click elsewhere. You can enter text in upper- or lowercase or any combination. Entering **MA** is the same as entering **ma** or **Ma**.

▶ Enter dates with or without beginning and ending pound signs (#). If you don't enter pound signs, Access will do so when you press [Enter◄┘] or click elsewhere. You can enter dates in a variety of formats. For example, you can enter January 12, 1998 as **12 January 1998**, **1/12/98**, **12-Jan-98**, or **Jan 12 98**.

Displaying text in quotation marks and dates in pound signs is called the *standard format* and acts as a visual cue. If you enter a number into a Text field, it will be enclosed in quotation marks, telling you it is being treated as text, not as a value.

T I P
The Zoom Box

To get extra space to enter and edit a criteria expression, put the insertion point in any cell in the Filter window's grid and press [⇧ Shift]+[F2], or right-click the cell and then click the shortcut menu's **Zoom** command. This opens a Zoom box or window. When finished, click the **OK** button to close the box.

Editing a Filter

At any time you are using a filter, you can display the Filter window and edit the filter. You can add and delete fields in the grid, change sort orders in any field, rearrange the order of the columns, type in new criteria, and change column widths in the grid.

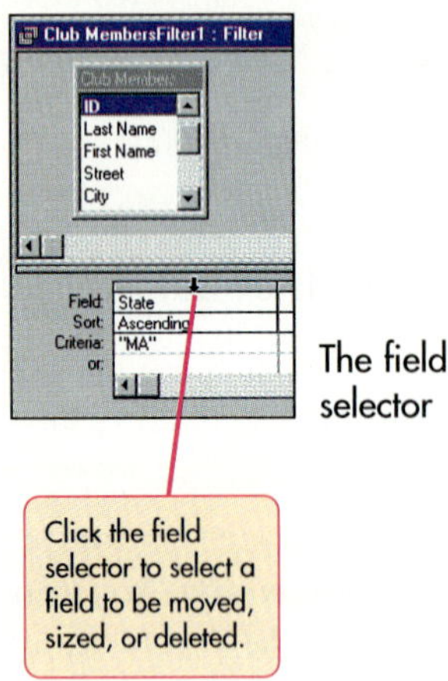

The field
selector

Click the field
selector to select a
field to be moved,
sized, or deleted.

PAL ON-LINE ACTIVITIES CHECKLIST

☐ **3-3 CONCEPTS.** There are many times when you want to work just with the records from a specific state, company, or ZIP code. In these kinds of situations you can filter the table. In this concepts section you are introduced to this procedure.

☐ **3-3 TUTORIAL.** In this tutorial you sort and filter records in the *Club Members* table in the *Ever Hopeful Health Club* database.

☐ **3-3 DRILL.** In this drill you filter the *Titles and Publishers* table in the *Publisher Sales* database so only selected groups of records are displayed.

3-4 USING CRITERIA EXPRESSIONS IN FILTERS

What if a customer calls about his or her credit card account and wants to know what date a specific purchase was made? Using the customer ID number and the amount of the purchase, you can immediately locate the date of the purchase by filtering the table to display any charges to the customer's account for the specified amount. When using filters, and later in Section 3-5 when you use queries, you often specify *criteria* that narrow your search. Criteria specify a field to look in and a value to look for. To do so, you use the **Advanced Filter/Sort** command and enter a criteria expression in the *Criteria* row of the Filter grid in the field you want to filter by. Only those records that match the criteria expression are then displayed. The criteria can be a text string, a date, a number, or any other data type.

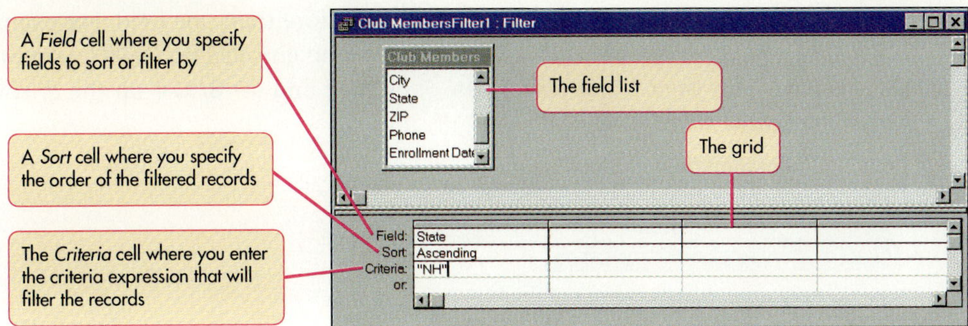

A *Field* cell where you specify fields to sort or filter by

A *Sort* cell where you specify the order of the filtered records

The *Criteria* cell where you enter the criteria expression that will filter the records

The filter grid elements

Finding Records That Match a Single Criteria Expression

As you have already seen in Section 3-3, to display only exact matches you enter a specific text or value as the criteria expression. When you do this, Access assumes the expression includes the comparison operator "is equal to" (=). And in fact you can enter that operator yourself if you want to. Let's look at some examples:

- ▶ "Jones" or ="Jones" finds all records with *Jones* in the field.
- ▶ 10.00 or =10.00 finds all records equal to 10.00.
- ▶ #1/10/98# or =#1/10/98# finds all records dated January 10, 1998.

Finding Records Using Multiple Criteria

Many times, a single criteria does not filter a table enough to make it easy to find records. In these cases you enter multiple criteria expressions using logical operators such as *and* and *or* and others shown in the table "Logical and Other Operators Used in Criteria." In the following sections, we'll look at examples of these operators at work.

Logical and Other Operators Used in Criteria	
Operator	**Description**
And	Result is true only when both expressions are true.
Or	Result is true when either expression is true.
Not	Result is true when the expression is not true.
In	Determines if the value of an expression is equal to any of several values in a list.
Is Null	Determines if a field is empty or null.

Finding Records with Or Criteria Expressions

What if you want to find all of the records from *New Hampshire* OR *Massachusetts*? There are two ways to do this. You can search for one value or another in the same field with a statement such as **"NH" Or "MA"** which will display records with *NH* or *MA* in the field. You can also enter the criteria beneath one another on the grid. For example, enter **"NH"** on the *Criteria* row and **"MA"** on the *or* row. (The quotes enclosing characters indicate that it's text. If you don't enter them, Access will do it for you.)

A criteria expression that will display records with *NH* or *MA* in the *State* field

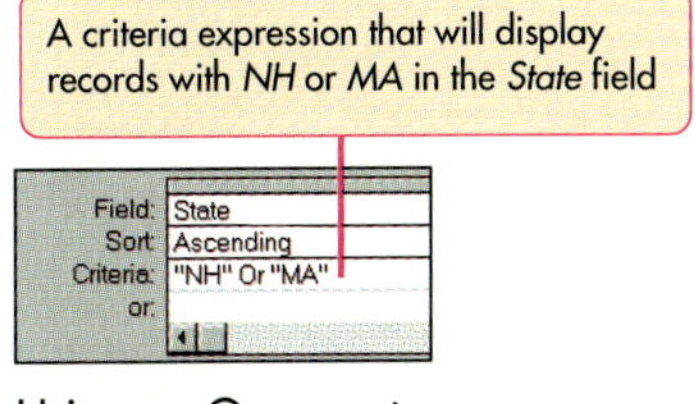

Using an Or operator in a single field

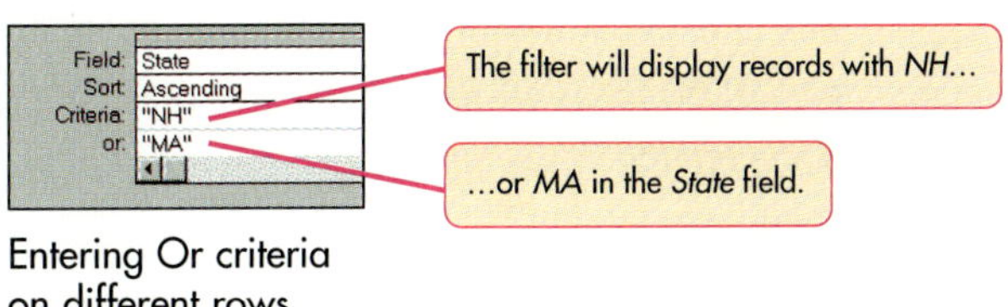

Entering Or criteria on different rows

You can also use Or-type criteria expressions in more than one field. For example, to find all people who live in *MA* or all people who enrolled on *9/8/97*, you would enter "**MA**" on the *Criteria* row in the *State* field and **#9/8/97#** on the *or* row in the *Enrollment Date* field.

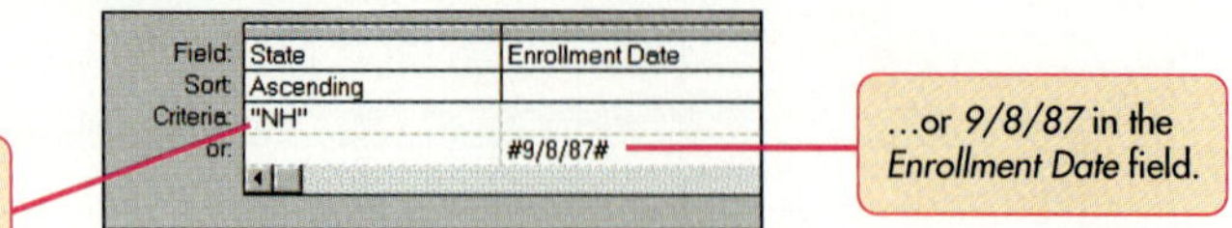

Using Or criteria in multiple fields

Finding Records with And Criteria

You can also display records that meet all criteria. For example, what if you wanted to find all people in *NH* who enrolled on *10/20/97*. To do this you could enter "**NH**" on the *Criteria* row of the *State* field and **#10/20/97#** on the same row in the *Enrollment Date* field.

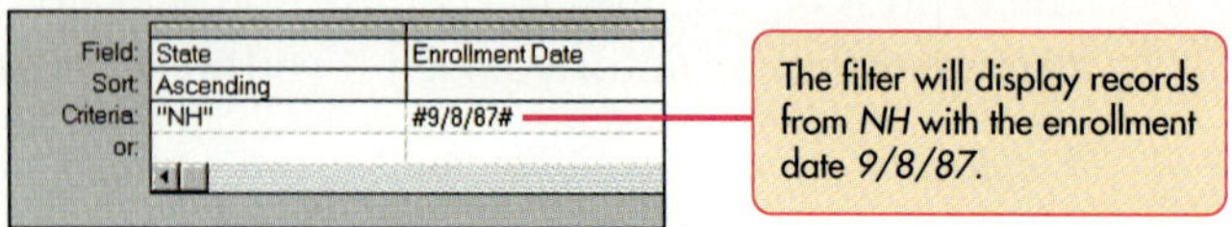

Using And criteria in multiple fields

TIP
Rule to Remember

When you specify criteria in multiple fields, those entered on the same row (And criteria) mean both criteria must be met for a record to be displayed. Those entered on different rows (Or criteria) mean either criterion must be met.

Finding Records Within a Range

Many times you are not looking for exact matches, but rather records that fall within a range. To display records that fall within a range, you frequently use the operators shown in the table "Comparison Operators Used in Criteria." Let's look at some examples:

Comparison Operators Used in Criteria	
Operator	**Name**
=	Equal to
>	Greater than
<	Less than
>=	Greater than or equal to
<=	Less than or equal to
<>	Not equal to

▶ The greater-than operator (>) finds all records greater than the criteria you specify; for example:

   ▶ >"**Jones**" displays all records alphabetically after *Jones*.

   ▶ >**10.00** finds all records greater than 10.00.

   ▶ >**1/10/98** finds all records dated later than January 10, 1998.

- The less-than operator (<) finds all records less than the criteria you specify; for example:
  - <"**Jones**" displays all records alphabetically before *Jones*.
  - <**10.00** finds all records less than 10.00.
  - <**1/10/98** finds all records dated earlier than January 10, 1998.
- The greater-than-or-equal-to operator (>=) finds all records greater than or equal to the criteria you specify; for example:
  - >="**Jones**" finds all records with *Jones* in the field and all entries in that field that follow Jones alphabetically.
  - >=**10.00** finds all records where the number is 10.00 or more.
  - >= **1/10/98** finds all records dated January 10, 1998 or later.
- The less-than-or-equal-to operator (<=) finds all records less than or equal to the criteria you specify; for example:
  - <="**Jones**" finds all records with *Jones* in the field and all entries in that field that precede Jones alphabetically.
  - <=**10.00** finds all records where the number is 10.00 or less.
  - <=**1/10/98** finds all records dated January 10, 1998 or earlier.
- The not-equal-to operator (<>) or the logical operator **Not** finds all records not exactly equal to the criteria you specify; for example:
  - <>"**Jones**" displays all records except those with *Jones* in the field.
  - <>**10.00** finds all records where the number is not 10.00.
  - <>**1/10/98** finds all records not dated January 10, 1998.
  - **Not "CA"** will display all records that don't have CA in the field.
  - **Not 1/10/98** will display all records that don't have a January 10, 1998 date.

Special Operators

In addition to the more common operators, Access has a number of operators and other features that perform useful functions.

Using Wildcards

You can enter asterisk or question mark wildcards to search for patterns in any field that has a Text or Date/Time data type.

- The asterisk stands for any sequence of characters in the same position as the asterisk. For example, to see all records for people whose last name begins with the letter *C*, enter **C*** in the *Criteria* cell of the field. To find all dates in January 1998, enter *1/*/98*.
- The question mark stands for any single character in the same position. For example, to find all records with *hat*, *hot*, or *hit* in the field, enter a question mark, as in *h?t*.

When you enter a criteria expression with a wildcard and then move the insertion point out of the cell, Access converts it to a Like expression. For example, it changes **C*** to *Like "C*"* and **h?t** to *Like "h?t"*.

There are many uses of wildcard characters. For example, what if you want to find all of the records that begin with National AND end with Inc. To do this you would enter the criteria expression **Like "National*" And Like "*Inc."**.

Finding Records Between Two Values

The Between operator finds all records that fall between two dates or two values. For example, you can find all records between two dates in January, all values between 100 and 200, or all names that start with letters between C and F.

- **Between #5-Jan-96# And #5-Jan-98#** will display records with dates between January 5, 1996 and January 5, 1998 inclusive.
- **Between 100 And 200** will display records with numbers between 100 and 200.
- **Between "C*" and "F*"** will display records with names that begin with any letter between *C* and *F*.

Finding Records Like a Pattern

The Like operator displays all records matching a pattern that you specify. You can use the complete value or you can use wildcards for the pattern.

- **Like "A*"** will display all records that begin with the letter *A*.
- **Like "*A"** will display all records that end in the letter *A*.
- **Like "[CA-MA]"** will display all records with states alphabetically between *CA* and *MA* inclusive.
- **Like "10/*/96"** will display all records from October 1996.

Finding Records That Match Any Value on a List

The In operator displays all records matching any one of a list of values.

- **In ("MA","CA","NJ")** displays all records for MA, CA, and NJ. (Note that you place the commas outside the quotation marks, not inside them as you would write them in a document.) You could also enter this as **"MA" Or "CA" Or "NJ"**.

Finding Records That Contain Values

To display all records with values of any kind in a field, enter the criteria as **Not Null** or **Is Not Null**. To find records that are blank in the field, enter the criteria as **Null** or **Is Null**. Finding records with blank fields is important because in many cases these records won't be found with normal filters or queries.

PAL ON-LINE ACTIVITIES CHECKLIST

- ☐ **3-4 CONCEPTS.** Criteria allow you to narrow your search to specific records. For example, you can enter a criteria expression that displays just those records with *Bobby Jones*, or *NY*, or *more than $100*. In this concepts section you are introduced to this procedure.

- ☐ **3-4 TUTORIAL.** In this tutorial you use criteria expressions to filter records in the *Club Members* table. This is a long tutorial because this it covers the most important aspect of using databases—finding the data you want. The procedures and principles you learn here apply to queries, which you'll learn about in Section 3-5, and to almost all other database programs.

- ☐ **3-4 DRILL.** In this drill you will use operators to enhance the power of your criteria expressions. Criteria expressions allow you to see ranges of records and those that fall above, below, or between certain values.

You've seen how useful filtering a table can be. However, a much more powerful tool is available to you—queries. Everything you've learned about filters can be used with queries—you only need to know a few more things to be a master.

A query is a question you ask your database to answer for you. For example, you may ask a subscription database what subscriptions will expire next month. When you use a query, it creates a *dynaset* that looks just like a table. The data in a dynaset is always current. If you change any data in a dynaset, Access updates the data in the underlying (source) tables. If you change any data in the underlying tables, the data in the dynaset changes. In a multiuser system, you can see changes that others make to dynasets right away. Data is stored only in the underlying tables, not in the dynaset. The dynaset is only a *virtual table*.

You can use this dynaset just as you use tables—in fact, it looks just like a table. The difference is that it is dynamic: it can have just some of the fields and records from the underlying table (or tables); and both the fields and records can be arranged in a different order. You can sort the dynaset, create forms for it, or use it as the basis for reports.

Having been introduced to filters, you may wonder how a query differs. Queries differ from filters in the following ways:

▶ You can save a query. (You can also save a filter, but when you do so, it is saved as a query.)

▶ If you like, you can display just selected fields, not all of them.

▶ You can display fields in any order.

▶ You can draw fields from more than one table.

▶ You can use the query as the basis for a form or report.

▶ You can calculate.

The most common type of query is called a *select query* because you use it to select data from the database. Although you can create other types of queries using the Query Wizard, you can't create select queries with the Wizard.

Queries can be displayed in Design view and Datasheet view. You switch back and forth between these two views by clicking the **View** button on the toolbar and its drop-down arrow when the query is open. (A third view, *SQL View*, is beyond the scope of this text.)

The Datasheet view will show you the query's dynaset, not the underlying table. In a multiuser environment, you would see changes to the dynaset as soon as someone else made them. And if you change any data in the dynaset, the change is carried to the underlying table. For example, if you create a query that displays phone numbers and change any phone numbers in the query's dynaset, the phone numbers are also changed in the underlying table that you queried.

Queries and Filters—Similarities

To create a query, you specify the fields and records you want to see in the Select Query window. This window is a graphical query-by-example (QBE) tool. QBE interfaces are now the most common way of creating queries in all leading database management programs. The Select Query window is almost identical to the Filter window described in Section 3-3 (with a few exceptions, which we'll discuss in a moment). And creating a query is almost exactly like creating a filter. The things that are the same (see Sections 3-3 and 3-4 for details on these procedures) include the following:

▶ Moving field names from a field list in the top part of the window to the grid in the bottom part.

▶ Editing the query by adding, deleting, and moving columns and changing their widths.

▶ Specifying a sort order.

▶ Entering criteria expressions.

Creating a Query

A query is much more powerful and flexible than a filter, so you would expect there to be some differences. The things that are different include the following:

▶ The grid is called the QBE (Query-By-Example) grid.

▶ You can click the check box on the *Show* row to show (☑) or hide (☐) the field in the dynaset. You do this when you want to use the field as a criteria to sort the dynaset but don't want to actually see its contents.

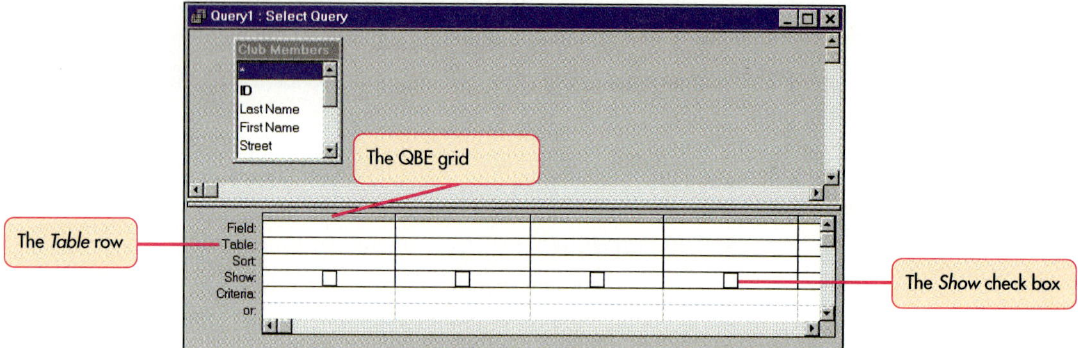

The Select Query window's parts

When you create a query, keep the following points in mind:

▶ The table need not be open to create a query as it does to create a filter.

▶ A query dynaset displays only those fields you list in the QBE grid. Fields are listed in the dynaset in the order in which they appear on the grid. (In a filter, all fields appear, and field names on the grid only specify criteria and sort orders.)

▶ You can save a query so you can use it again. When you save it, it's listed as a Query object in the Database window.

▶ The part of the grid that you click to select a column is called a *field selector* in the Filter window and a *column selector* in the Select Query window.

▶ To edit the design of a query displayed in Datasheet view, click the **View** button on the toolbar, or pull down the **View** menu and click the **Query Design** command.

▶ To execute a query displayed in Design view, click the **View** button on the toolbar, or pull down the **View** menu and click the **Table View** command. (Alternatively, you can click the **Run** button on the toolbar, or pull down the **Query** menu and click the **Run** command.)

Being Prompted to Enter the Criteria Expression

If you enter a prompt in the *Criteria* cell of the QBE grid, it will be displayed when you run the query. You can then enter the criteria in a dialog box that appears when you run the query. For example, if you enter **[Enter the last name you want to find]** in a *Criteria* cell, that will appear as the prompt in a dialog box. This is called a *parameter query*.

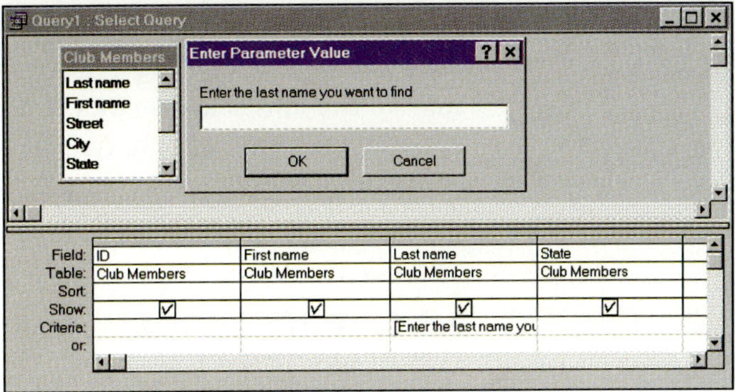

Creating a Query

1. Click the **Queries** tab in the Database window.
2. Click the **New** button on the Database window, or pull down the **Insert** menu, and click the **Query** command to display the New Query dialog box.
3. Click the **Design View** choice to select it, then click the **OK** button to display the Show Table dialog box.
4. Click the name of the table that you want to query and then click the **Add** button to list its fields in the top part of the Select Query window. (To select more than one table, hold down Ctrl as you click the table names.)
5. Click the **Close** button to close the Show Table dialog box.
6. Add fields to the QBE grid (see the Looking Back box *Specifying Fields for a Query*) and specify criteria in the QBE grid just as you did for creating filters. Click the **Run** or **View** buttons on the toolbar to see the query's dynaset.
7. Click the **Save** button on the toolbar or pull down the **File** menu and click the **Save** command to display the Save As dialog box. Enter the name of the query in the **Query Name** text box and click the **OK** button. The query is then added to the list of Query objects in the Database window.

Specifying Fields for a Query

To specify what fields are included in a query, you include the field's name in the QBE grid. There are four ways to do this.

▶ Drag the field's name from the field list at the top of the window into one of the cells on the *Field* row of the QBE grid. When the pointer is shaped like a field, release the mouse button to drop it.

▶ Double-click the field's name on the field list at the top of the window.

▶ Click in the cell on the *Field* row of the QBE grid to display a drop-down arrow (▾), and click that arrow to display a list of the fields you can choose from.

▶ Type the name in a cell.

After clicking in a field's *Criteria* row in the QBE grid, you can click the **Build** button on the toolbar to display the Expression Builder.

Editing a Query

At any time you are using a query, you can display it in Design view and edit it. You can add and delete fields, change sort orders in any field, rearrange the order of the columns in the grid, type in new criteria, and change column widths. The procedures for doing so are discussed in the QuickSteps box "Editing a Filter" in Section 3-3.

PAL ON-LINE ACTIVITIES CHECKLIST

☐ **3-5 CONCEPTS.** Queries are among the most powerful and useful database management skills. In this concepts section you are introduced to these almost universal tools. What you learn here applies not only to Access but to finding information in library databases, corporate databases, and even on the Internet.

☐ **3-5 TUTORIAL.** In this tutorial you create and save a query for the *Club Members* table in the *Ever Hopeful Health Club* database.

☐ **3-5 DRILL.** In this drill you query the *Titles and Publishers* table in the *Publisher Sales* database so only selected groups of records are displayed.

3-6 CALCULATING WITH QUERIES

Queries can do more than just display records; they can also perform calculations. You can add a field that calculates the contents of other fields in the table or calculate totals for all records or groups of records.

Adding a Calculated Field

To calculate other fields in a table, first create a new field and then enter an expression into its *Field* cell. The expression can include the names of other fields (enclosed in square brackets), values, or operators. For example, the expression **[Price] *.20** display 20% of whatever value is in the *Price* field. The expression **[Price]*[Quantity]** multiples the value in the *Price* field times the value in the *Quantity* field. After running the query, any changes you make in the fields referred to by the calculated field are automatically reflected in the calculation.

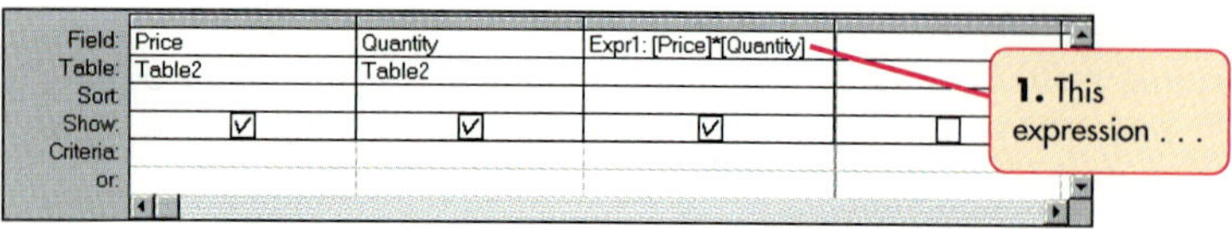

You can also join data from two or more fields with an expression. For example, to join first and last names when they are stored in separate fields, enter an expression such as **[First Name]&" "&[Last Name]**. The ampersands join the fields and the " " includes a space between the names.

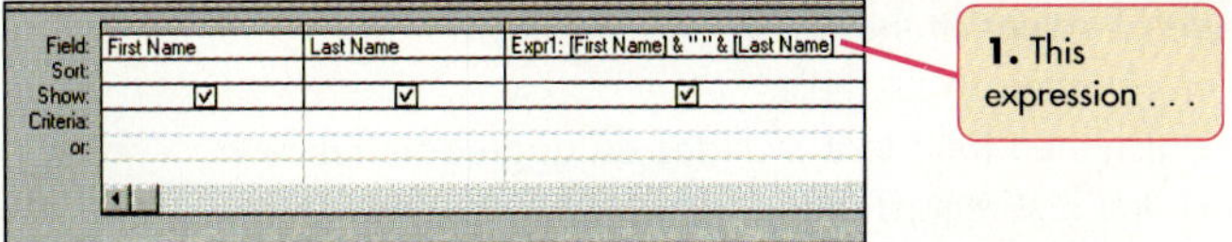

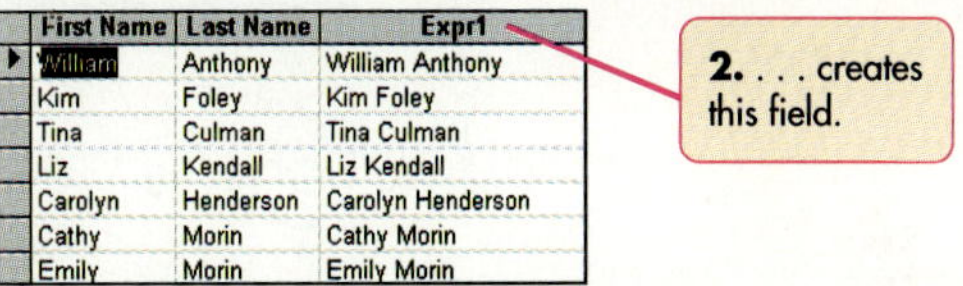

1. This expression . . .

2. . . . creates this field.

When you enter an expression in a calculated field, it is assigned a default name such as *Expr 1:*. You can rename the field to a name that means more to you but the name must end in a colon. To format the display of the calculated field, you will have to change its properties since it doesn't inherit them from any underlying table. (You'll see how to do so in the next section.)

Calculating Totals

What if you want to know the total number of widgits in inventory, or the average score on a test? You can make such calculations using an aggregate query—one that uses a function that will calculate averages or sums. Keep in mind that you can also enter criteria expression just as you do in other queries so you only total those items that meet the criteria.

QUICKSTEPS

Calculating Totals for All Records in the Table

1. Create a query with the fields you want to total and display it in Design view. The simplest way to do this is to add only two fields, the one you want to group by and the one you want to total. For example, to find all *Sales by State*, add just the *Sales* and *State* fields so you can group by *State* and Sum the *Sales* field.

2. Click the **Totals** button on the toolbar, or pull down the **View** menu and click the **Totals** command. A *Total* row is added to the QBE grid and *Group By* is the default setting on this row for each field.

3. Click in the *Total* cell under each field to display a drop-down arrow ([▼]) and click it to select a type of aggregate total. (See the box "Understanding Totals.")

4. Click the **View** button on the toolbar to see the results.

UNDERSTANDING
Totals

When you click in the *Total* cell under a field on the grid, it displays a drop-down arrow ([▼]), which you click to select a type of aggregate total.

▶ The various functions from which you can choose are listed in the table "Aggregate Functions You Can Use."

▶ Each field must have some setting on the *Total* row.

▶ To calculate a total for any column, select one of the aggregate functions.

▶ To remove the *Total* row and any calculations, click the **Totals** button on the toolbar.

▶ The field with the aggregate function is named with a combination of the function name and the field name, for example, *CountOfNames*.

<table>
<tr><td colspan="2">Aggregate Functions You Can Use</td></tr>
<tr><td>Function</td><td>Description</td></tr>
<tr><td>Avg</td><td>The average of values in the field</td></tr>
<tr><td>Count</td><td>The number of values in the field</td></tr>
<tr><td>Expression</td><td>Creates a calculated field that includes an aggregate function.</td></tr>
<tr><td>First</td><td>The value of the first record in the field</td></tr>
<tr><td>Group By</td><td>Defines the groups you want calculated. For example to total sales by state, group by the State field.</td></tr>
<tr><td>Last</td><td>The value of the last record in the field</td></tr>
<tr><td>Max</td><td>The largest value in the field</td></tr>
<tr><td>Min</td><td>The smallest value in the field</td></tr>
<tr><td>StDev</td><td>The standard deviation of values in the field</td></tr>
<tr><td>Sum</td><td>The total of values in the field</td></tr>
<tr><td>Var</td><td>The variance of values in the field</td></tr>
<tr><td>Where</td><td>Specifies criteria for a field you aren't using to define groupings.</td></tr>
</table>

PAL ON-LINE ACTIVITIES CHECKLIST

☐ **3-6 CONCEPTS.** Queries can be used to calculate values in a database by multiplying, dividing, adding, or subtracting the values stored in the tables. There are also functions you can use to calculate averages, count records, calculate standard deviations, and so on. In this concepts section you are introduced to the procedures you use to calculate.

☐ **3-6 TUTORIAL.** In this tutorial you calculate fields and totals in the *Member Charges* table from the *Ever Hopeful Health Club* database.

☐ **3-6 DRILL.** In this drill you use a query to calculate a discounted price for the books in the *Titles and Publishers* table when a 20% discount is offered.

3-7 CHANGING PROPERTIES IN A QUERY'S DYNASET

When you create a query, the fields in the dynaset inherit the properties of the fields in the underlying table. If you want to, you can change these so data in the dynaset is displayed differently from the table.

QUICKSTEPS

Changing a Field's Properties

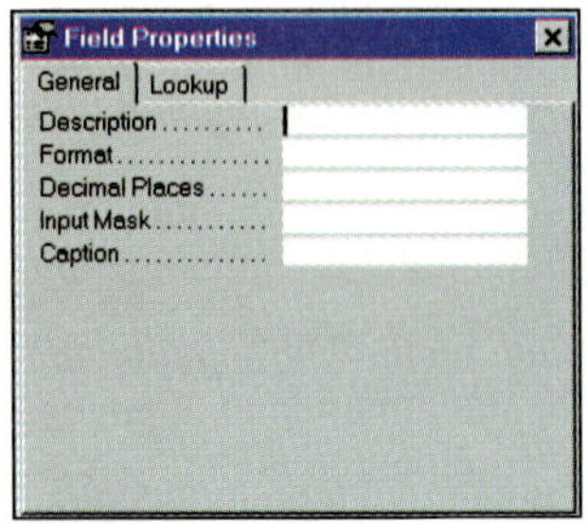

A property sheet

1. Display the query in Design view.

2. Click the cell in the *Field* row for the field whose properties you want to set or change.

3. Click the **Properties** button on the toolbar, or pull down the **View** menu and click the **Properties** command to display the property sheet for the field.

4. The properties vary depending on the data type stored in the field. However, Number, Date, and Text field data properties can be set as follows:

   ▶ Click in the *Description* text box and type a description that will appear on the status bar when the insertion point is in the field.

   ▶ Click in the *Format* or *Decimal Place* text box, click the drop-down arrow (▼) that appears, then select a property for the field.

   ▶ Click in the *Input Mask* text box and type an input mask or click the **Build** button to select one from the menu. The input mask specifies a pattern for data entry.

   ▶ Click in the *Caption* text box and type a caption that will be used for the field's label when you create a form.

☐ **3-7 CONCEPTS.** Dynasets are much like tables. You can change the properties of any of their fields. In this concepts section you are introduced to this procedure.

☐ **3-7 TUTORIAL.** In this tutorial you change the properties of the calculated field you added to the *Service Charges* query.

☐ **3-7 DRILL.** In this drill you edit a query's properties to display the discount price as currency.

PicTorial 3

LAB ACTIVITIES

EXERCISE

3-1 The General Store Database

In this exercise you locate data in the *General Store* database using the **Find** command, filters, and queries. You also replace data and calculate totals.

Opening the Database

1. Open the database named *General Store* stored in the *Exercise Databases* folder of the *Access Student Resource Disk*.

Finding Data

2. With the *Employees* table open in Datasheet view, use the **Find** button on the toolbar to find records with each of the following data in the specified fields:

Field	Data
Employee	**H999**
Last Name	**Lettuce**
First Name	**Barney**
Department	**Payroll**
Hire Date	**6/1/87**

Replacing Data

3. Use the **Replace** command on the **Edit** menu to make the following replacements (be sure to watch what check boxes are on in the dialog box):

Field	Replace	With
Last Name	**Varroom**	**Varoom**
Supervisor	**Varroom**	**Varoom**
First Name	**Cassandria**	**Cassandra**
Department	**Sales**	**Marketing**
Hire Date	**6/1/88**	**6/1/89**

Filtering Records

4. Use the **Filter By Selection** button on the toolbar to filter using the following selections:

   ▶ *Department* of **Automobile**

   ▶ *Department* of **Hardware**

5. Use the **Filter By Form** button on the toolbar to filter using the following selections (after filtering, remove the filter each time):

   ▶ Anyone in the *Automobile* department with the supervisor *Varoom, George*

   ▶ Anyone in the *Marketing* department with the supervisor *Brown, Jim*

6. Use the **Records** menu's **Filter** and **Advanced Filter/Sort** commands to display the Filter grid. Clear any previous entries, then move the following fields to the grid.

   ▶ *Last Name*

   ▶ *Department*

   ▶ *Hire Date*

   ▶ *Supervisor*

7. Filter for records that match each of the following criteria:

   ▶ Any *Hire Date* in **88** (use the **Like */*/88** command)

   ▶ Any *Hire Date* later than **88** (use **>=1/1/89**)

   ▶ Any *Hire Date* in **88** or later

   ▶ Any *Hire Date* in **88** or earlier

   ▶ Any *Hire Date* between **88** and **91**

   ▶ Any *Supervisor* without an entry (**Is Null**)

Querying the Table

8. Use the **New** button on the **Queries** tab to query the *Employees* table. Add first and last names and departments to the grid and query for employees in the *Automobile* department. Save the query as **Automobile Department Employees.**

9. Use the **New** button on the **Queries** tab to query the *Employees* table. Add first and last names and departments to the grid and query for employees in the *Marketing* department. Save the query as **Marketing Department Employees.**

10. Use the **New** button on the **Queries** tab to display last names and hiring dates for employees hired in 88 and save the query as **Employees Hired in 1988.**

Calculating Totals

11. Use the **New** button on the **Queries** tab to create a new query for the *Employees* table and add the *Department* field to the QBE grid twice.

12. Click the **Totals** button on the toolbar to add a *Total* row to the QBE grid and group by one field and count the other. This gives you a list of departments with a count of how many employees are in each.

13. Save the query as **Employee Count by Department** and print its dynaset.

14. Close all windows including the Database window.

3-1 The College Database

In this project you locate data in the *College Records* database using the **Find** command, filters, and queries. You also replace data and calculate totals.

1. Open the database named *College Records* stored in the *Project Databases* folder of the *Access Student Resource Disk*.

2. Find the following records in the *Sections Offered this Semester* table:

Field	Data
Department	**BIOL**
Times	**7:30 - 9:00**
Building/Room	**COATES** (any room)
Instructor ID	**442019756**

3. Make the following replacements:

Field	Replace	With
Department	**EXST**	**ADULT ED**
Time	**2:30 - 4:30**	**2:30 - 4:00**

4. Using the quickest method, filter for records that match each of the following criteria:

   ‣ *Department* of **CHEM**
   ‣ *Department* of **ADULT ED**
   ‣ *Department* of **CHEM** or **ADULT ED**
   ‣ Any *Building/Room* in **COATES** (use a wildcard)
   ‣ Any *Building/Room* in **COATES** or **LOCKETT**
   ‣ Any *Days* of **M W F**
   ‣ Any *Type* of **LAB**
   ‣ Any **LAB** *on* **F**
   ‣ Any **CHEM** department **LAB**
   ‣ Any **CHEM** department **LEC**

5. Query the *Sections Offered this Semester* table to display records of all courses offered by the Chemistry (CHEM) department and save the query as **Chemistry Department Courses**.

6. Query the *Sections Offered this Semester* table to display records of all courses offered by the Adult Education (ADULT ED) department and save the query as **Adult Education Courses**.

7. Query the *Sections Offered this Semester* table to calculate the total number of courses offered by each department and save the query as **Course Count by Department**.

8. Close all windows including the Database window.

PRESENTING DATA

After completing this PicTorial, you will be able to:

- ▶ **Create forms**
- ▶ **Use forms to enter and edit records**
- ▶ **Modify form designs**
- ▶ **Create and print reports and mailing labels**
- ▶ **Modify report designs**
- ▶ **Create a link to other Microsoft Office applications**

USING tables as the way to enter, view, and print your data is fairly primitive and not very user friendly. To present your data so it's more attractive and easier to enter, edit, and interpret, you use forms and reports. Forms are generally used to view data on the screen, and reports are used to print it out.

When you work with a database on the screen, you needn't always display it as a table that looks like a spreadsheet. Instead, you can easily create a form on the screen that looks much like a printed form. You can then use the form to display, enter, revise, and even print records. Forms have many advantages over the now-familiar Datasheet view:

▸ Forms often show all of the fields in a single record one record at a time. This sometimes makes it easier to work with records than the Datasheet view, which shows lots of records.

▸ Forms can be designed to resemble paper forms with which users are already familiar. This makes people more comfortable using the database to enter, edit, and view data.

▸ Forms can include productivity-enhancing features such as list boxes, option buttons, and check boxes. Fields can be arranged in the order in which they are normally filled in, and instructions about what to enter can be displayed. These elements, and others, make data entry faster, easier, and more accurate.

▸ Forms can calculate and display values and graphs.

The **View** button and its drop-down arrow

TIP
Form Views

Once a form has been opened, you can switch between three separate views—Form view, Datasheet view, and Design view—by clicking the **View** button on the toolbar or its drop-down arrow. Which view you use depends on what you are doing.

A form is always based on a table or a query, and any changes you make in the data stored in fields using the form are also made in the underlying table.

Fields in the form are linked to fields in the table.

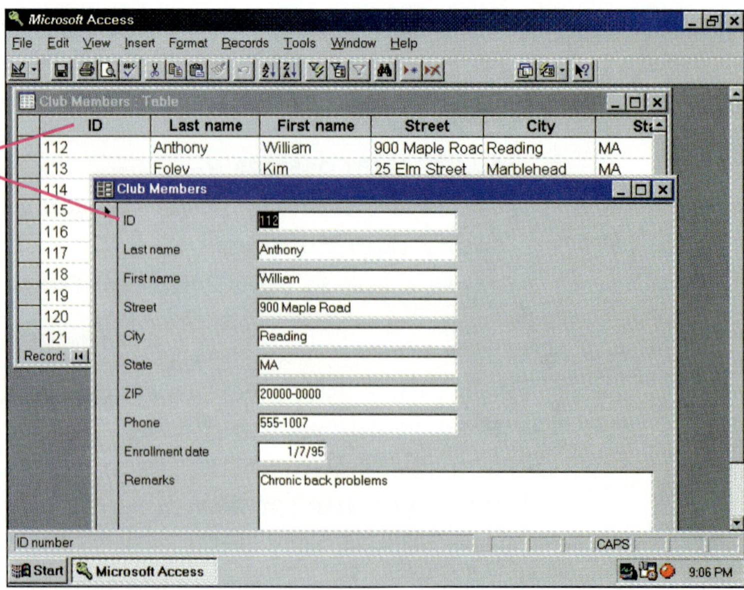

A form based on a table

AutoForms

The easiest way to create a form is to select one of the three predesigned AutoForms. These forms are created without your being asked any questions. They include all of the fields and records in the table unless you base them on a query instead of a table. The three available AutoForms include columnar, tabular, and datasheet. You can modify each type of AutoForm so it better meets your needs.

▶ *Columnar forms* list one record on the screen at a time. Each field is displayed on its own line with a label to its left.

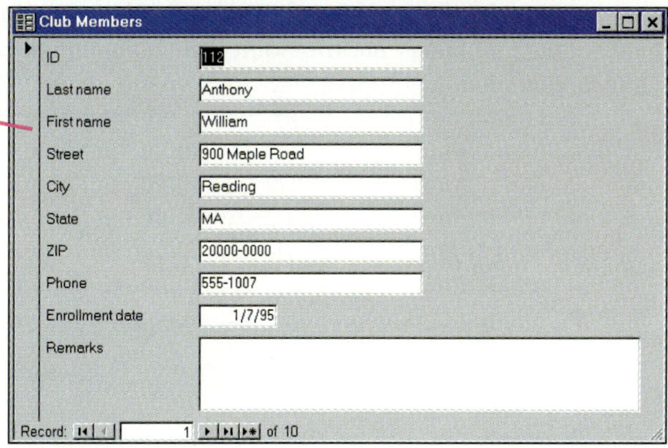

A columnar form

▶ *Tabular forms* are similar to the Datasheet view of a table but are more attractive. They display many records at a time—each on its own row. Fields are arranged in columns with labels at the top of each column—much like a more polished version of the table on which it is based.

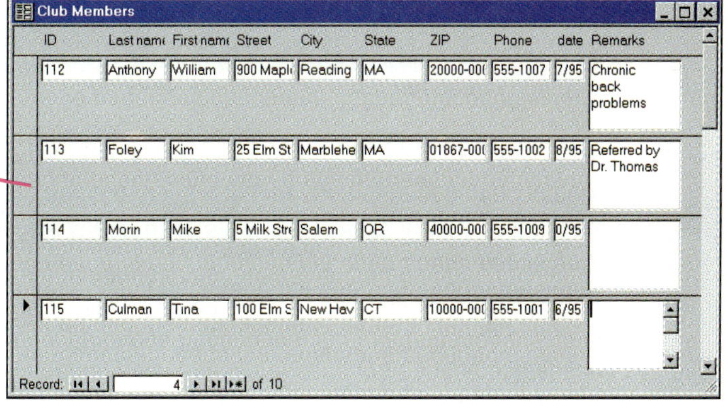

A tabular form

▶ *Datasheet forms* are almost exactly like the Datasheet view of a table.

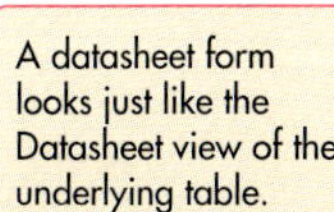
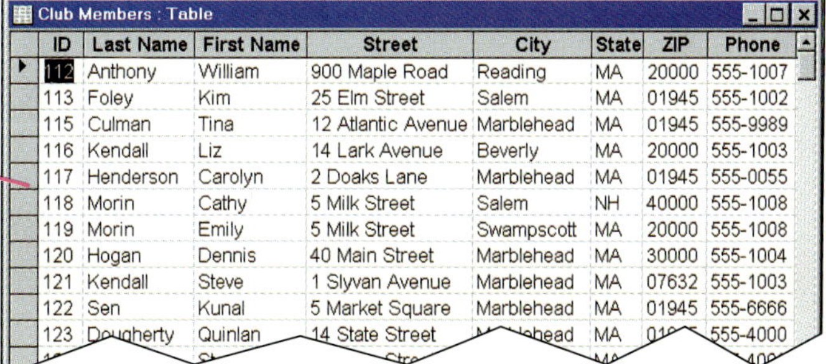

A datasheet form

After creating or modifying a form, you have to save it to save your changes. Saved forms are listed as Form objects in the Database window. When using the form, you don't have to save it since the records are saved automatically, but you can minimize it or close it when you are not using it.

Slightly Different Forms

Access remembers choices made for certain settings when forms are custom designed or created by Form Wizard. These choices will then be used when you create an AutoForm. For this reason, some things, such as background objects, are somewhat unpredictable.

Creating AutoForms

1. Click the **Forms** tab in the Database window.

2. Click the **New** button on the Database window, or pull down the **Insert** menu and click the **Form** command to display the New Form dialog box.

3. Click one of the three **AutoForm** choices to select it and click the drop-down arrow (▼) to select the table or query you want to base the form on.

4. Click the **OK** button and in a few moments the finished form appears on your screen.

5. Click the **Save** button on the toolbar, or pull down the **File** menu and click the **Save** command, enter a name for the form in the **Form Name** text box, and then click the **OK** button.

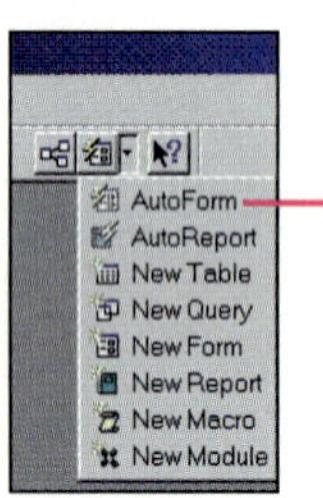

The **New Object** button's drop-down list

AutoForms

When a table is displayed in Datasheet view, you can quickly create an AutoForm by clicking the **New Object** button's drop-down arrow on the toolbar and clicking the **AutoForm** command.

Form Wizard

Using the Form Wizard gives you more control over what is in your form and how it looks. Like AutoForms, the Form Wizard can create columnar, tabular, and datasheet style forms and apply a "look" for the report by choosing from a variety of colorful designs.

QUICKSTEPS

Creating a Form with the Form Wizard

1. Click the **Forms** tab in the Database window.

2. Click the **New** button on the Database window, or pull down the **Insert** menu and click the **Form** command to display the New Form dialog box.

3. Click the *Form Wizard* choice to select it and click the drop-down arrow (▼) to select the table or query you want to base the form on.

4. Click the **OK** button and answer each of the questions displayed by the Form Wizard. Use the **Next** button to advance through the steps and the **Finish** button to finish your design.

   ▶ The first screen lists all of the fields in the underlying table. Click the buttons with the > *or* >> symbols to move one or all fields listed in the **Available Fields** list to the **Selected Fields** list. (How to specify fields is described in the Tip box "Specifying Fields.")

   ▶ The second screen allows you to select a layout from the choices *Columnar*, *Tabular*, and *Datasheet*.

   ▶ The third screen allows you to select a style for the form.

   ▶ The last screen is where you specify the form's name.

TIP
Specifying Fields

When creating forms, you sometimes don't want to include all of the fields in the underlying table. At other times, you have to specify which field should be used for a particular operation such as sorting. In either case, the Form Wizard displays a dialog box that you use to specify the fields.

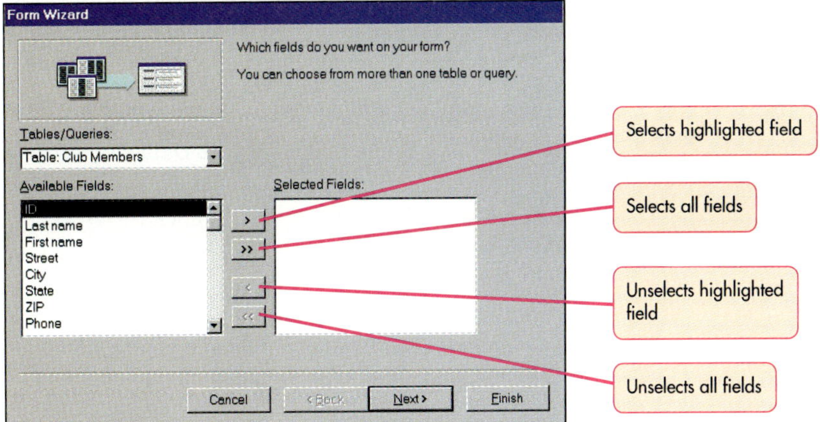

The **Available Fields** are listed at the left. Those that you have selected are listed at the right in the **Selected Fields** box. To move a field from one list to the other, click it to select it and then click the > or < buttons. Keep in mind that you don't have to move them in the same order in which they are listed. However, the order in which you move them determines their order on the finished form. To move all fields from one list to the other, click the » or « buttons.

☐ **4-1 CONCEPTS.** Forms are a great way to enter and view data in a database. In this concepts section you are introduced to creating forms.

☐ **4-1 TUTORIAL.** In this tutorial you create and save AutoForms for the *Club Members* table in the *Ever Hopeful Health Club* database. Then you use Form Wizard to guide you through the creation of a custom form. As you use this and other Wizards, be sure to read what is on each screen as you proceed through the steps. This way you will be acquainted with other paths or branches that we do not have time in this text to pursue.

☐ **4-1 DRILL.** In this drill you create and save AutoForms based on the *Publisher Sales* database's *Titles and Publishers* and *Quarterly Sales* tables.

4-2 USING A FORM TO VIEW, ENTER, AND EDIT RECORDS

Once you have created a form, you can open it at any time to view, enter, edit, and delete records in the table. To do so, you must first find the record you want to display in the form.

Opening and Closing Forms

To use a form that you have created and saved, you must open it if it isn't already open. When finished with a form, you can close it or click its **Minimize** button to reduce it to an icon if you'll need it again.

Q U I C K S T E P S

Opening and Closing a Form

Opening a Form

1. Click the **Forms** tab in the Database window to display a list of saved forms.

2. Double-click the name of the form you want to open, or click the name of the form to select it and then click the **Open** button on the Database window.

Closing a Form

▶ Pull down the **File** menu and click the **Close** command, or click the form's **Close** button (☒).

Finding Records in Form View

To edit a record in Form view, you must first display it in the form. You can do this by scrolling through the records one at a time and jumping directly to a record based on its position, its number, or its contents. The procedure you use depends on the type of form you are using. A form that displays just one record is much different from one that looks like the table on which it is based.

Finding Records in Form View

Scrolling Through Records

▶ Click the navigation buttons in the lower-left corner of the window.

▶ Press PgUp and PgDn to display the previous or next record when only one record is displayed on the screen at a time.

▶ Press Tab when the insertion point is in the last field.

Jumping to a Specific Record Number

▶ Pull down the **Edit** menu and point to the **Go To** command to cascade the menu so you can select the record to move to.

▶ Double-click the current record number in the record number box at the bottom of the window to select it (or press F5), type a new record number, and then press Enter.

Finding Records Based on Their Contents

▶ Click the **Find** button on the toolbar and enter data that identifies the record you want to find.

▶ Use the **Filter By Selection** or **Filter By Form** buttons on the toolbar so you only scroll through selected records.

Other Procedures

▶ When working with forms, it's often faster to move about to enter and edit records with the keyboard than with the mouse. Use any of the keyboard commands listed and described in the table "Moving Commands in Form View."

Moving Commands in Form View	
To	**Press**
Move Within a Record	
Move to the next field	Tab, →, ↓, or Enter
Move to the previous field	Shift+Tab or ↑
Move up or down one page when the form has more than one page	PgUp or PgDn
Move to the first or last field in the current record	Home or End
Move Between Records	
Move to the first or last field in the first or last record	Ctrl+Home or Ctrl+End
Move to the current field in the previous or next record	Ctrl+PgUp or Ctrl+PgDn
Move to the top of the previous or next record when the form has only one page	PgUp or PgDn

Editing Records in Form View

Once a record is displayed in the form, you can edit it just as you edited records displayed in Datasheet view. Just as in tables, changes are saved automatically when you move to another record. To save a record before you leave it, just click the **Save** button on the toolbar.

QUICKSTEPS

Editing Records in Form View

1. Display the record you want to edit.
2. Click in any field you want to change and edit the entry. If you press Tab to move to a field, the entire contents of the field is selected. Any character you type deletes the previous entry and replaces it with the new one. To edit the entry instead, press F2 to remove the highlight and display the insertion point. You can also use any of the commands described in the table "Editing Commands in Form View."
3. Close the form, and all records are saved automatically.

LOOKING BACK
Record Selector Symbols

Record selector symbols in the upper-left corner of the form indicate the status of the current record.

▶ A pencil symbol record selector ( ) indicates the record's contents have been changed but not saved.

▶ A triangle record selector symbol ( ) means the record's contents haven't been changed.

Editing Commands in Form View	
To	**Press**
Select or unselect all data in the current field	F2
Move insertion point to the beginning or end of the current line in a text box	Home or End
Move insertion point to the beginning of the previous or next word	Ctrl+← or Ctrl+→
Move insertion point to the beginning or end of the last line in a text box	Ctrl+Home or Ctrl+End
Undo changes to the current field	Esc
Insert the same value as the same field in the previous record	Ctrl+'
Enter the default value assigned to a field (see Section 2-3.)	Ctrl+Alt+Spacebar

TIP
Undoing Changes

To undo changes as you edit fields and records, click the **Undo** button on the toolbar, or pull down the **Edit** menu and click the **Undo** command. These commands undo changes made to a record until you begin editing a second record.

Adding Records in Form View

When a form is displayed, you can add new records. Any new records are added to the end of the table in the order in which you enter them. New records are saved automatically when you move to another record or close the table. To save a record before you leave it, just click the **Save** button on the toolbar.

QUICKSTEPS

Adding Records in Form View

1. Click the **New Record** button on the toolbar, or pull down the **Insert** menu and click the **Record** command to insert a blank record at the end of the table.
2. Type in data, pressing `Tab⇆` or `⇧Shift`+`Tab⇆` to move between fields. The description of the field containing the insertion point is displayed on the status bar.

Deleting Records in Form View

When a form is displayed, you can delete any record that you can see. If the form displays only a single record, that is the one that will be deleted. If the form displays many records, you have to click the record selector for the record you want to delete.

QUICKSTEPS

Deleting Records in Form View

1. Display the record you want to delete or click its record selector.
2. Click the **Delete Record** button on the toolbar, or pull down the **Edit** menu and click the **Delete Record** command to display a dialog box warning you that you are about to delete a record.
3. Click the **Yes** button to delete it, or the **No** button to cancel the deletion.

Printing Forms

When you print the form from Form or Design view, the detail section (the fields) prints the data much as it appears on the screen. (If you print it from Datasheet view, it prints like a datasheet.) To save paper, you should always click the **Print Preview** button on the toolbar to catch any layout errors before printing the document.

☐ **4-2 CONCEPTS.** Once a form has been created, you can use it to view, enter, and edit records in a table. In this concepts section you are introduced to these procedures.

☐ **4-2 TUTORIAL.** In this tutorial you use the *Club Members-AutoForm* form in the *Ever Hopeful Health Club* database to enter and edit records into the *Club Members* table.

☐ **4-2 DRILL.** In this drill you use the *Quarterly Sales-AutoForm Tabular* form to enter new records into the *Quarterly Sales* table.

Quarterly Sales Records to Add			
Field	Record 17	Record 18	Record 19
ISBN	96109	96110	96111
Sales Period	winter	winter	winter
Trade Sales	1000	750	300
Educational Sales	500	100	3
Mail Order Sales	25	35	1
International Sales	125	12	1

4-3 MODIFYING A FORM

Rather than create a form from scratch, it's often better to use the Form Wizard and then modify the form to suit your needs. To modify a form, you display it in Design view. In this view, the form is displayed with up to three sections:

▸ The *Detail* section appears in every form and displays the records from the table the form was based on. In Design view, each of the text boxes is called a *control*. Each control initially has a label to its left.

▸ The optional *Form Header/Footer* sections display information at the top or bottom of every form and print it at the beginning and end of every printout. Normally the header is used for such things as the form's title, instructions, or even command buttons. You display this section of the form with the **Form Header/Footer** command on the **View** menu.

▸ The optional *Page Header/Footer* sections print data at the top and bottom of every page. The page header can be used for title or column headings that you want to appear on every page. The page footer can be used to display the date or page number on every page. You display this section of the form with the **Page Header/Footer** command on the **View** menu.

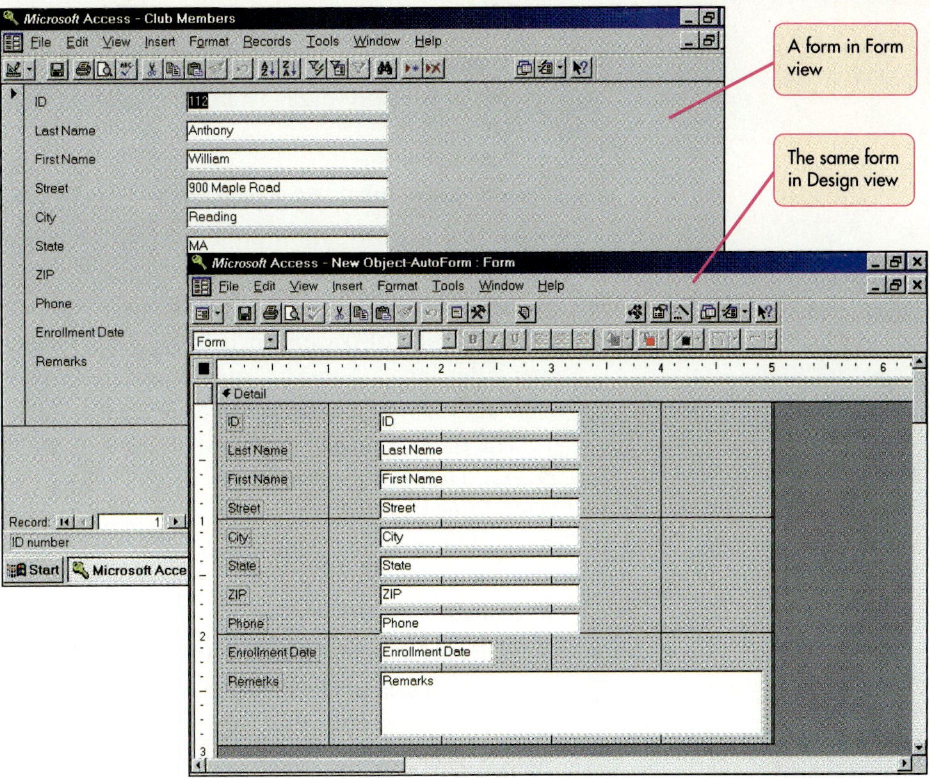

Parts of a form in Design view

You can resize any of the sections in the form's Design view by dragging its border. To do so, point to the border so the mouse pointer turns into a split vertical arrow. Hold down the left mouse button, drag the border to its new position, then release the mouse button. Have patience; it takes practice to get it just right.

QUICKSTEPS

Displaying a Form in Design View

1. Click the **Forms** tab in the Database window to display a list of forms.
2. Click the name of the form you want to modify and click the **Design** button on the Database window. (Or you can open the form and then click the **View** button on the toolbar.)
3. Customize the form as described in the following sections. If you make any mistakes, click the **Undo** button on the toolbar.
4. Click the **Save** button on the toolbar to save your changes.
5. Click the **View** button on the toolbar to see the changes.

Understanding Controls

All of the information displayed on a form is contained in *controls*—objects that display or identify data. There are three types of controls: bound, unbound, and calculated.

Bound and Unbound Controls

Most of the information on a form usually comes from a table or a query. Other information, such as the form's title, doesn't.

Information on a form that comes from an underlying table or query is called a bound control because it is linked—or bound—to the table or query. Any data you enter into a bound control is entered into the underlying table. Bound controls are most often displayed as text boxes with labels to their left.

The data that isn't linked to an underlying table or query is called an *unbound control*. Unbound controls are used for such things as a labels, titles, calculated fields, instructions, captions, and graphic design elements such as lines and boxes. Unbound controls are part of the form's design, not the underlying table.

Calculated Controls

A *calculated control* contains an expression that contains numbers and/or field names. Calculated controls are discussed in Section 4-4.

Manipulating Controls

When modifying a form in Design view, the most common approach is to move controls into better positions on the form and change their size, alignment, or format. Doing this allows you to make the form look more like a printed form and can ease data entry if the fields are arranged in the same order that data is entered into the form. To modify a form in this way, you need to know how to select controls and then move, size, or delete them.

Selecting Controls

To select a control you click it (and not its contents). When you do so, small squares called sizing handles and a larger square called a move handle are displayed. To unselect a control, click anywhere outside of it. If the control is a bound control, it has an attached label. You can click either the control or the label. The one you click will have sizing handles and a move handle; the other will have just the move handle. If you click the other element, the effect is reversed.

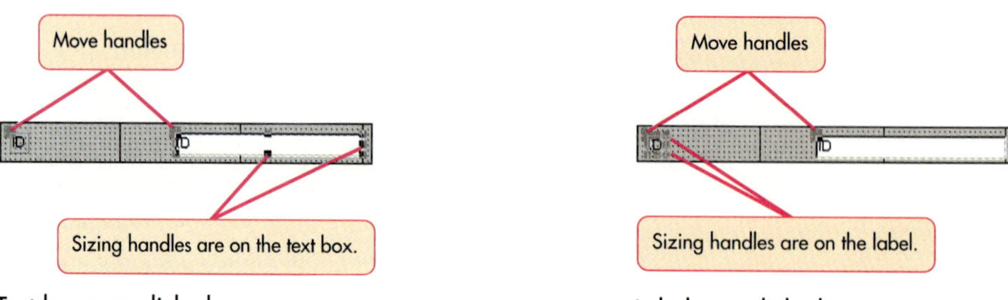

Text box was clicked   Label was clicked

You can move or align groups of controls at the same time. To select a group of adjacent controls, point beside but not on the first control in the group, hold down the left mouse button and drag the mouse. As you do so, a rectangle expands around the selected controls. When you release the mouse button, the controls in or touched by the rectangle remain selected.

To select nonadjacent controls, hold down ⇧Shift while you click each control. You can also hold down ⇧Shift and click individual controls to remove them from a previously selected group.

One final way to select controls is to click on the ruler above or to the left of those you want to select. You can also drag along the ruler to select all of those touched or enclosed by the box that is shown as you drag.

Deleting Controls

To delete a control with its attached label from the form, select the control (not the label) and press Del. To delete just the attached label, select it and press Del. If you delete a control or label by mistake, immediately click the **Undo** button on the toolbar. To delete a label without deleting a text box or other control, just select the label.

UNDERSTANDING
The Edit Menu

After selecting a control, you can pull down the **Edit** menu and use any of the following commands:

Undo undoes the previous command.

Cut deletes the selected control from the form and moves it to the clipboard.

Copy copies the selected control from the form to the clipboard.

Paste copies whatever is on the clipboard back into the form.

Delete deletes the selected control.

Duplicate makes a copy of the selected control.

Moving Controls

When you want to change the way fields are laid out on a form, you have to drag them into new positions. In Design view, you can drag a control and its label as a single unit, or you can drag each part independently. (To undo a move, click the **Undo** button on the toolbar.)

QUICKSTEPS

Moving Controls

▶ To move a control and its label together, click the part you want to drag by, then drag it by the border to its new position. The mouse pointer changes into an open hand on the border of the part you clicked to select the control. For example, if you clicked the label, you have to drag the control and label by the label's border. If you clicked the control itself, you have to drag it by the control.

▶ To move the control or its attached label separately, click either one to select the control and then drag the part you want to move using the move handle. (When on a move handle, the pointer changes to a hand with a pointing finger.)

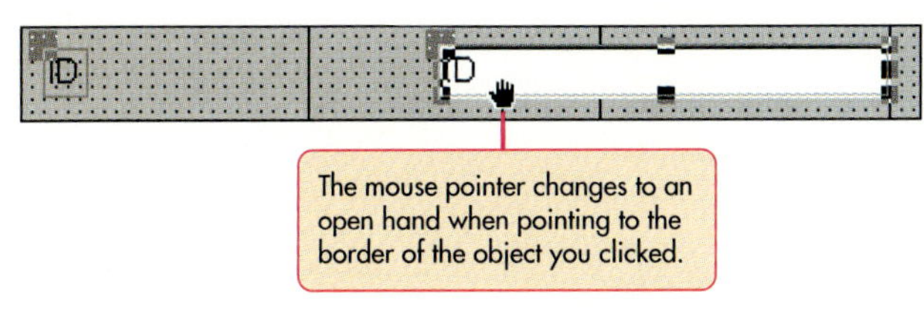

The mouse pointer changes to an open hand when pointing to the border of the object you clicked.

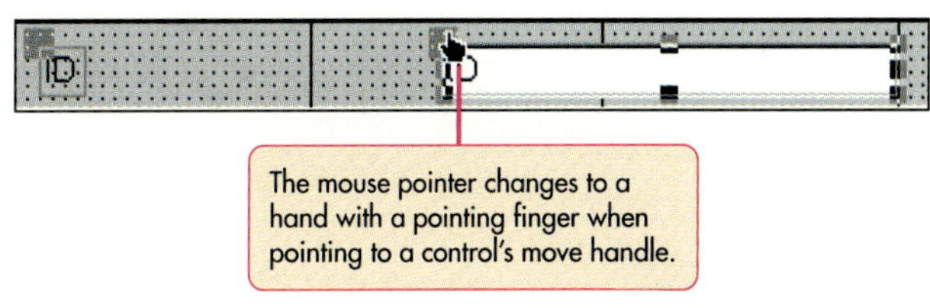

The mouse pointer changes to a hand with a pointing finger when pointing to a control's move handle.

Sizing Controls

After you have selected a control, you can drag the displayed sizing handles to resize it. When you point to the sizing handles, the pointer changes to a double-headed arrow that indicates the direction in which you can drag it.

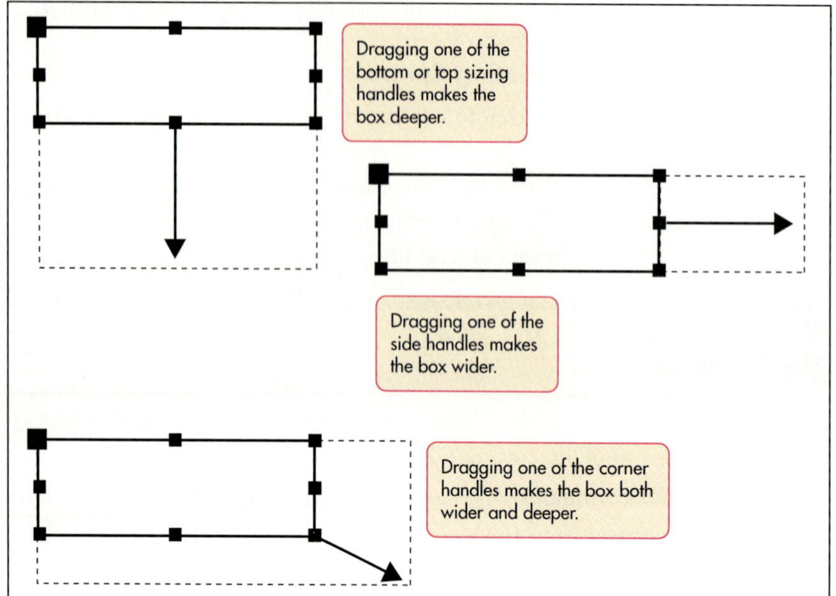

QUICKSTEPS

Sizing Controls

▶ Point to the top and bottom handles so the pointer is a vertical arrow, and drag to resize the control vertically.

▶ Point to the left and right handles so the pointer is a horizontal double-headed arrow, and drag to resize the control horizontally.

▶ Point to the corner handles so the pointer is a diagonal double-headed arrow, and drag to change both height and width at the same time.

▶ To size a control to fit the text it contains, select it, pull down the **Format** menu, point to the **Size** command to cascade the menu, and click the **to Fit** command.

▶ To size a group of controls relative to one another, select them, pull down the **Format** menu, and point to the **Size** command to cascade the menu. Click the **to Tallest**, **to Shortest**, **to Widest**, or **to Narrowest** command to set the width of all controls to the width or height of the one you specify.

Aligning and Spacing Controls

The alignment and spacing of controls on the form determine to a large extent how neat and professional the form looks. To ensure they align and space correctly, Access provides many tools and procedures as you move or size them.

PAL ON-LINE ACTIVITIES CHECKLIST

☐ **4-3 CONCEPTS**. Access will automatically create forms with just a few keystrokes. After creating one in this way, you can modify it to better suit your needs. In this concepts section you are introduced to this procedure.

☐ **4-3 TUTORIAL**. In this tutorial you modify the *New Object-AutoForm* form in the *Club Members* table in the *Ever Hopeful Health Club* database. When finished, your design should look like the one shown in the figure "The modified AutoForm design." Use this figure as a guide when following the steps in the tutorial. (Hint: Pull down the **Format** menu and be sure the **Snap to Grid** command is on.)

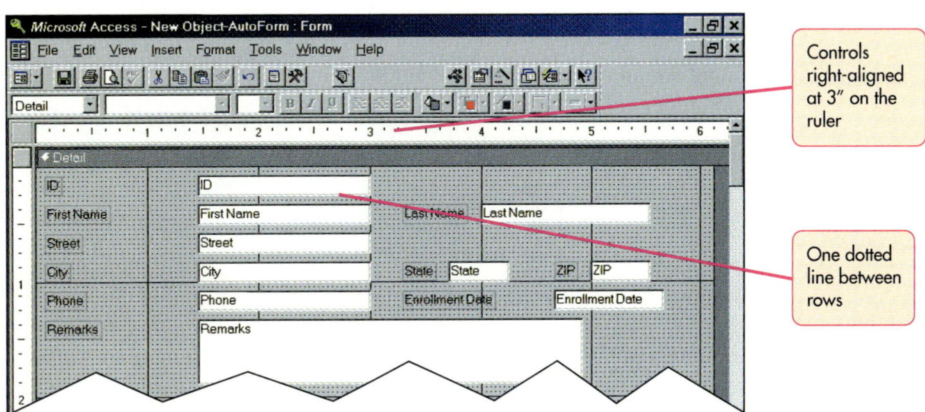

The modified AutoForm design

☐ **4-3 DRILL.** In this drill you modify the layout of the *Titles and Publishers-AutoForm: Columnar* form to match the figure "The modified *Titles and Publishers-AutoForm: Columnar* form." Your results should be close to those in the figure but needn't match exactly.

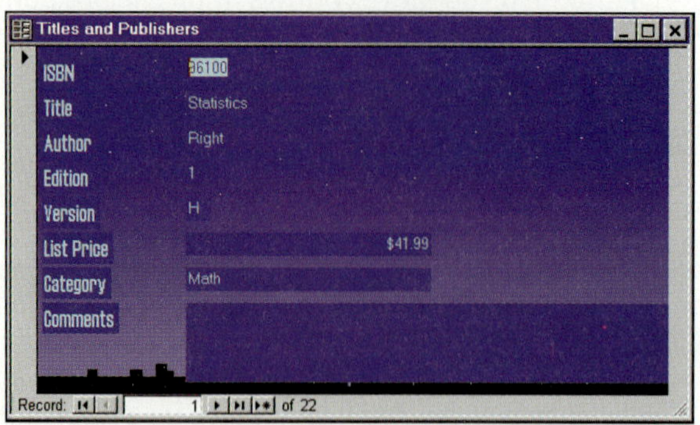

The modified *Titles and Publishers-AutoForm: Columnar* form

4-4 DESIGNING A FORM

Moving and sizing the controls on a form are not the only things you can do to make it more effective. You can also add new controls and graphic elements that make it more attractive and useful. There are so many things you can do, we don't have space to cover them all. In this section, we discuss those that are used most frequently.

The Toolbox

When you display a form in Design view, a floating toolbox is displayed. You use the buttons on this toolbox to design a form or a report. For example, when the **Select Objects** button at the top of the toolbox is on, the mouse pointer takes the shape of an arrow so you can click controls to select them. You can move the toolbox by dragging it by the title bar. Point to a tool to see its name displayed as a ToolTip, and its description is displayed on the status bar.

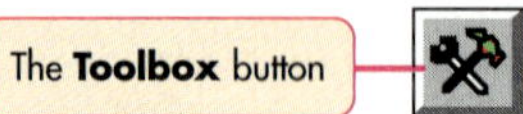

The **Toolbox** button

Displaying and Hiding the Toolbox

1. Display the form in Design view.
2. Click the **Toolbox** button on the toolbar, or pull down the **View** menu and click the **Toolbox** command to show or hide it.

When the toolbox is displayed, it normally floats in the Access window. However, if you drag the toolbox to the left, right, or bottom of the screen or onto the existing toolbar, you'll see its outline change shape. Release it and it becomes "docked." You can also dock it or float it by double-clicking its background.

The toolbox contains a set of buttons you click to add controls to the form. Most of the buttons, when clicked, display the mouse pointer as a crosshair with an attached icon. You click with this pointer on the form to indicate the placement of the item. Other clicked buttons display a Wizard that guides you through the process of creating the item. The toolbox has the following buttons:

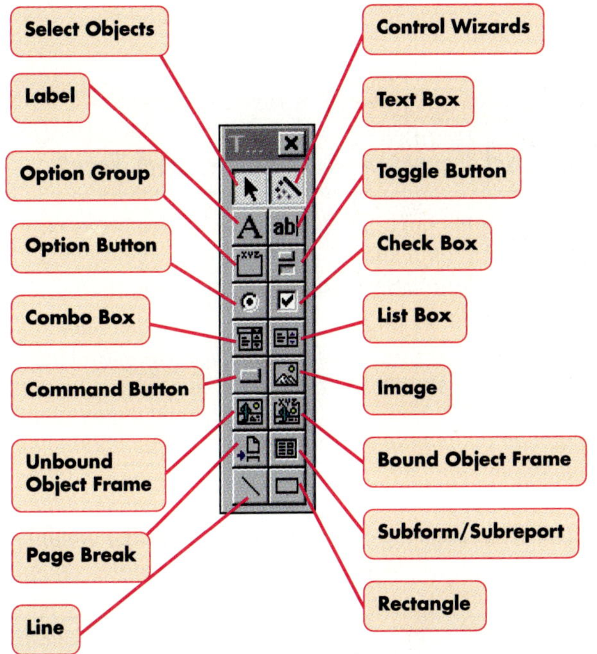

▶ **Select Objects** displays the mouse pointer as an arrow ($\searrow$) so you can click controls to select them.

▶ **Control Wizards** turns on and off the Wizards that guide you through creating a line box, combo box, option group, command button, or subform.

▶ **Label** adds an unbound label to the form. Just click where you want it to appear and type it in.

▶ **Text Box** adds an unbound text box with an attached label.

▶ **Option Group** displays the Option Group Wizard. An option group can contain either a set of toggle buttons or check boxes.

▶ **Toggle Button** adds a toggle button that acts like an option button or a check box. You click (depress) it to indicate something is true (for example, a check has cleared), or leave it unclicked to indicate it's false.

▶ **Option Button** adds an option button (◉) to the form.

▶ **Check Box** adds a check box (☑) to the form.

▶ **Combo Box** displays the Combo Box Wizard that adds a combination text and list box. This is like a list box but it allows you to enter data that isn't on the list.

▶ **List Box** displays the List Box Wizard that adds a list box. The box lists choices you can click to enter that choice into the table.

▶ **Command Button** adds a button to which you can assign a procedure that takes place when the button is clicked.

▶ **Image** creates a frame for a static picture on a form or report.

▶ **Unbound Object Frame** displays the Insert Object dialog box so you can select the type of object, such as a graphic, to be inserted.

▶ **Bound Object Frame** adds a bound object frame to the form.

▶ **Page Break** inserts a break that start a new screen in a form or a new page on a printed form or report.

▶ **Subform/Subreport** inserts a subform into the form.

▶ **Line** allows you to hold down the left mouse button and draw a line on the form.

▶ **Rectangle** allows you to hold down the left mouse button and draw a rectangle on the form.

Adding a Bound Text Box

When you base a form on a query, not all of the fields you want may be included on the form. However, you can easily add them to the form. You can also add back any bound fields that were inadvertently deleted.

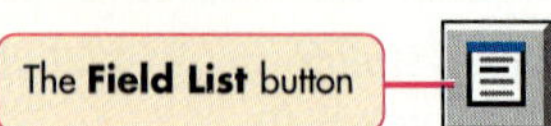
The **Field List** button

Adding a Bound Text Box

1. Display the form in Design view.
2. Click the **Field List** button on the toolbar, or pull down the **View** menu and click the **Field List** command to display a list of the fields in the table or query.
3. Drag the desired field from the list into the form and release it where you want it positioned. (To select an adjacent series of names, click the first, then hold down ⇧ Shift when you click the last. To select nonadjacent fields, hold down Ctrl as you click each.)

Adding, Editing, and Formatting Unbound Text

You can add descriptive text to a form, or edit and format text that is already there. You might want to do this to add identifying information to the form or to provide instructions to other users.

Adding, Editing, and Formatting Unbound Text

▸ To add an unbound label to the form, click the **Label** tool in the toolbox, click where you want the label, and type it in.

▸ To edit text in an existing label, click the label to select it, then click it again to move the insertion point into it.

▸ To format a label or control, select it and then use formatting buttons on the toolbar to format it. These buttons are shown in the figure "Formatting buttons on the toolbar."

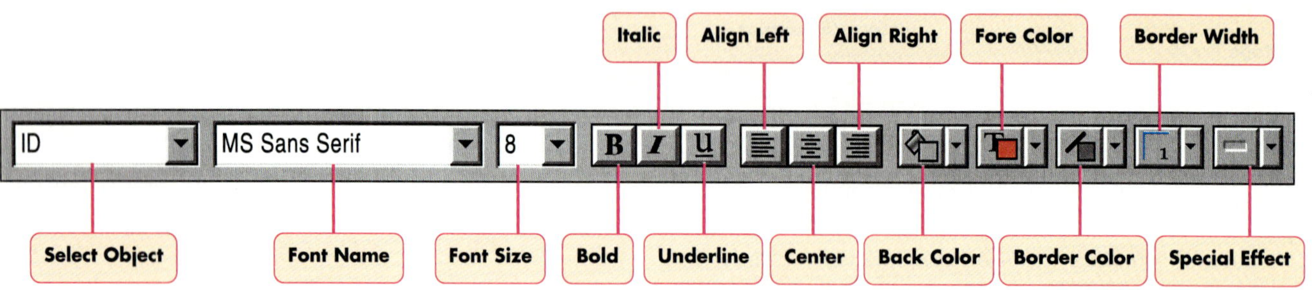

Formatting buttons on the toolbar

Adding Calculated Controls

You can add controls to a form that make calculations. The calculations are performed by an expression using operators such as + (for addition), - (for subtraction), * (for multiplication), and / (for division) or functions such as =Date(). Some of the most common forms of expressions are listed in the table "Expressions for Calculated Fields."

QUICKSTEPS

Adding Calculated Controls

1. Display the form in Design view.
2. Click the **Text Box** tool in the toolbox, then click on the form where you want the calculated field to appear.
3. Enter the expression into the text box.
4. Edit the label to identify the contents of the calculated control.

Expressions for Calculated Fields	
Expression	**Calculates**
=Date()	Today's date
=Now()	Today's date and time
=[Amount]*0.05	Contents of *Amount* field times 5%
=[Quantity]*[Price]	Contents of *Quantity* field times contents of *Price* field

Setting Properties

Normally a control's properties are inherited from the underlying table or query on which they are based. However, you can change these properties in the form, or add properties to controls that are not bound to an underlying table or query. For example, you can hide fields on the form or printouts, change the way records print, or have text displayed on the status bar when the insertion point is in the field.

QUICKSTEPS

Displaying and Changing Properties

1. Display the form in Design view.
2. Click the **Properties** button on the toolbar, or pull down the <u>View</u> menu and click the **Properties** command to display the property sheet.
3. Click any control to display or edit its properties. Clicking in some of the boxes displays a drop-down arrow (▼) you can click to select choices.
4. Click the **View** button on the toolbar to see the changes.

PAL ON-LINE ACTIVITIES CHECKLIST

☐ **4-4 CONCEPTS.** Forms can be plain or fancy depending on how much effort you want to put into them. In this concepts section you are introduced to procedures for making them easier to use and more attractive.

☐ **4-4 TUTORIAL.** In this tutorial you design the *Club Members-AutoForm* form in the *Club Members* table in the *Ever Hopeful Health Club* database to make it look professional.

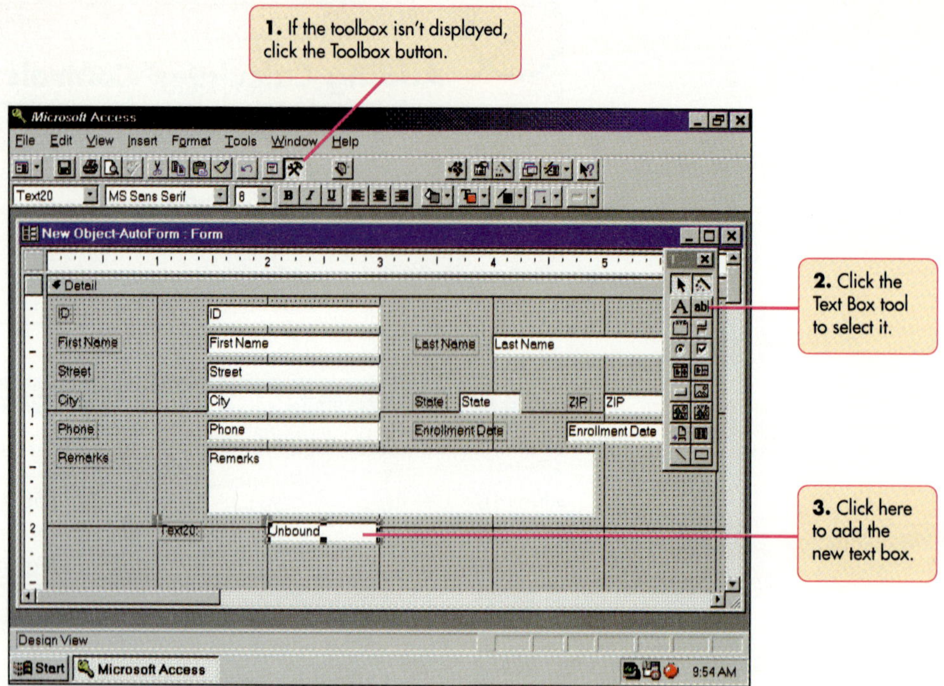

The first added text box

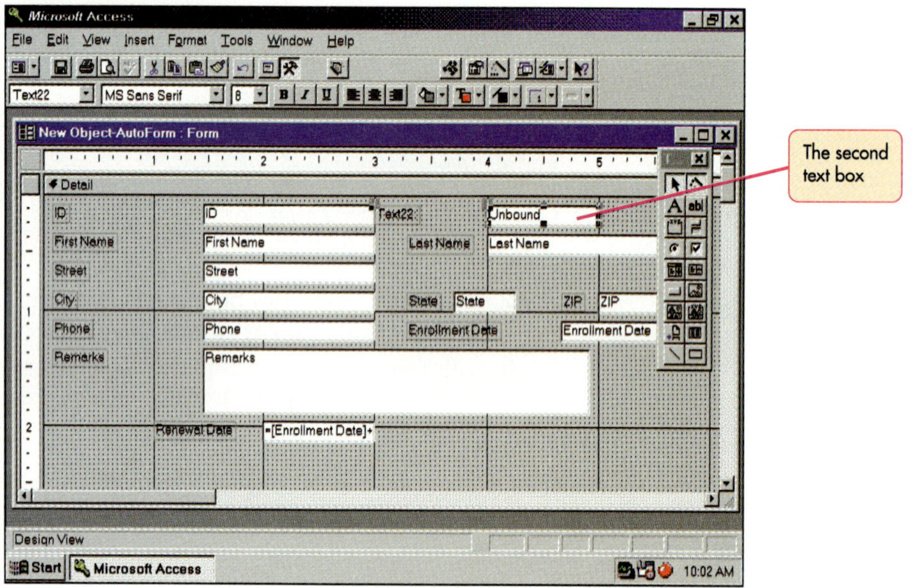

Another added text box

☐ **4-4 DRILL.** In this drill you add a calculated control to the *Quarterly Sales-AutoForm Tabular* form that calculates total sales for each record. When finished, your modifications to the form should look like those shown in the figure "The modified Quarterly Sales-AutoForm: Tabular form."

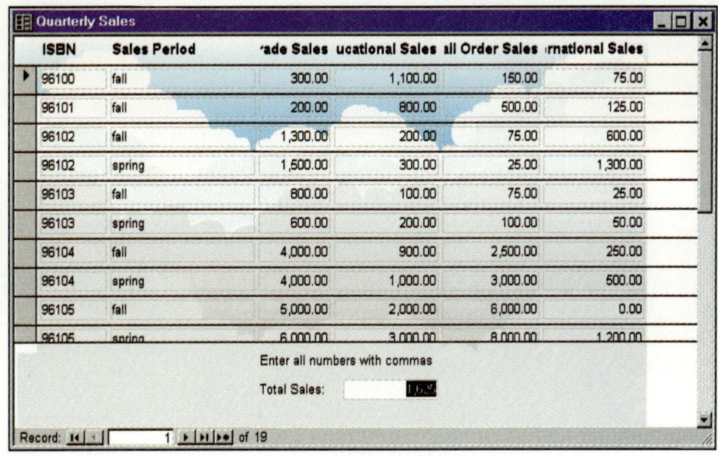

The modified *Quarterly Sales-AutoForm: Tabular* form

4-5 CREATING REPORTS

Most people in a business do not actually use the database itself. Generally, they use reports created from all or part of the information stored in the database. The database might contain information about all aspects of the business. Reports are designed to organize specific information needed by different people such as the sales manager, the president, or the finance department. Each report provides only the information needed by the person for whom it is printed. Reports consist of selected fields from selected records.

After you have created a report, you have control over how it presents data. You can use filters and criteria to govern the order of the records, specify which fields are to be included, and specify if totals and subtotals are to be calculated for numeric fields.

Access includes AutoReports and the Report Wizard that help you design reports much as AutoForm and the Form Wizard helped you with forms.

AutoReports

The easiest way to create a report is to select one of the three predesigned AutoReports and then modify the report as needed. The Report Wizard allows you to easily create columnar or tabular reports.

- *Columnar* reports list each field on its own row. Because of this layout, the report can be quite long, even for a small table.

- *Tabular* reports look much like polished versions of the tables they are based on. They have a number of columns, one for each field in the report, and each record is printed on a row by itself.

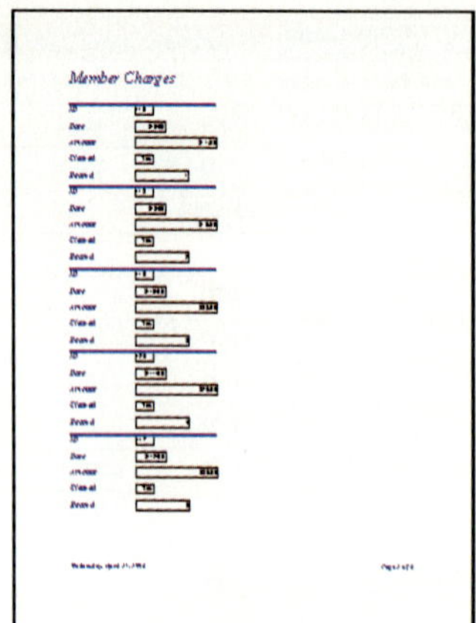

A columnar AutoReport

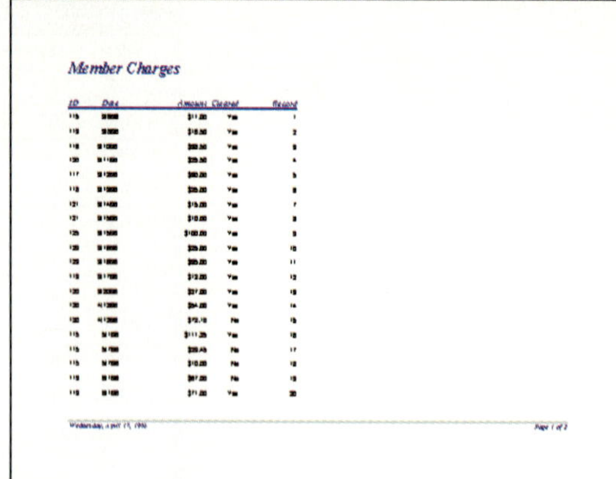

A tabular AutoReport

After creating or modifying a report, you have to save it. Saved reports are listed on the Database window's **Reports** tab.

QUICKSTEPS

Creating AutoReports

1. Click the **Reports** tab in the Database window.
2. Click the **New** button on the Database window, or pull down the **Insert** menu and click the **Report** command to display the New Report dialog box.
3. Click one of the two **AutoReport** choices to select it and click the drop-down arrow (⏷) to select the table or query you want to base the report on.
4. Click the **OK** button and in a few moments the finished report appears on your screen in Print Preview mode.
5. Click the **Close** button on the toolbar to close the Print Preview window.
6. Click the **Save** button on the toolbar, or pull down the **File** menu and click the **Save** command, enter a name for the report in the **Report Name** text box, and then click the **OK** button.

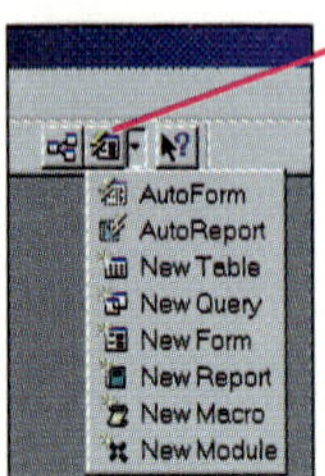

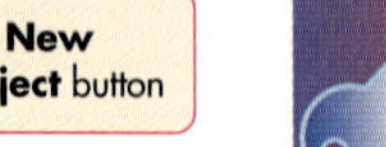

TIP
AutoReports

When a table is displayed in Datasheet view, you can quickly create an AutoReport by clicking the **New Object** button's drop-down arrow on the toolbar and clicking the **AutoReport** command.

Using Report Wizard

Using Report Wizard gives you more control over what is in your report and how it looks. As with AutoReports, you can create columnar and tabular reports, and specify a "look" for the report by choosing from a list of styles.

PAL ON-LINE ACTIVITIES CHECKLIST

☐ **4-5 CONCEPTS.** Reports are what you use to view, analyze, and share the data in a database. In this concepts section you are introduced to the procedures you use to create reports.

☐ **4-5 TUTORIAL.** In this tutorial you create and save AutoReports for the *Club Members* table in the *Ever Hopeful Health Club* database. Then you use Report Wizard to guide you through the creation of a custom report. As you use this and other Wizards, be sure to read what is on each screen as you proceed through the steps. This way you will be acquainted with other paths or branches that we do not have time in this text to pursue.

☐ **4-5 DRILL.** In this drill you create a columnar AutoReport for the *Titles and Publishers* table in the *Publisher Sales* database.

4-6 CREATING A REPORT WITH TOTALS

To have totals and subtotals calculated in a report, you specify which field the records are to be grouped by—the field you want a total for. This field is not the field that contains the numbers to be totaled but any field that contains duplicate data that you want subtotaled. For example, in a report that contains a field named *State* and a field named *Amount*, the *State* field would be specified as the field to group by to generate a report that totaled amounts by state.

You create a report with totals using the Report Wizard. The only difference between it and a regular report is that you specify the field to group by on the second screen and a function to total with.

TIP
Modifying Reports

Reports, like forms, can be displayed in Design view and modified by adding, deleting, moving, sizing, and formatting controls. Also like a form, a report in Design view is divided into sections, each of which prints in a specific place on the page.

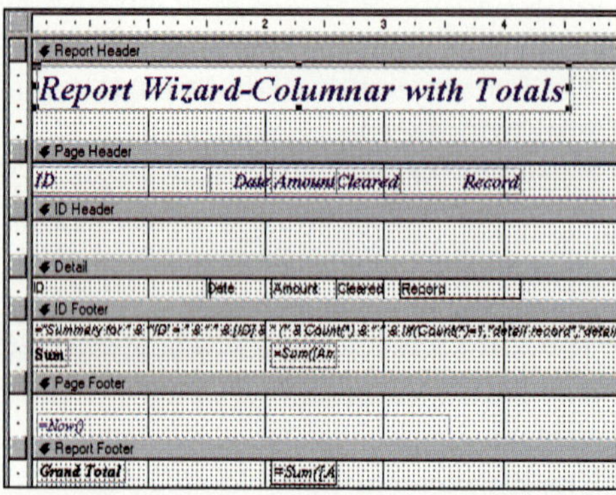

- ▶ The *Detail* section appears in every report and displays the records from the table the form was based on. In Design view, each of the text boxes is called a *control*. Some controls have attached labels.

- ▶ The optional *Report Header/Footer* section prints information only at the beginning or end of a report. Normally the header is used for such things as the report's title, date, or introduction. You hide or display this section of the report with the **Report Header/Footer** command on the **View** menu.

- ▶ The optional *Page Header/Footer* section prints information at the top or bottom of every page. The page header or footer can be used for column headings, page numbers, or dates. You display or hide this section of the report with the **Page Header/Footer** command on the **View** menu.

You can resize any of the sections in the form's Design view by dragging its border. To do so, point to the border so the mouse pointer turns into a split vertical arrow. Hold down the left mouse button, drag the border to its new position, then release the mouse button. Have patience; it takes practice to get it just right.

PAL ON-LINE ACTIVITIES CHECKLIST

☐ **4-6 CONCEPTS.** Reports can contain calculations such as totals and averages. In this concepts section you are introduced to the procedures you use to add these calculations.

☐ **4-6 TUTORIAL.** In this tutorial you create and save a report that calculates totals for the *Member Charges* table in the *Ever Hopeful Health Club* database.

☐ **4-6 DRILL.** In this drill you create a report with totals for the *Quarterly Sales* table in the *Publisher Sales* database.

4-7 PRINTING MAILING LABELS

Once a database has been created for one use, it's easy to use it for other purposes. For example, a database used to keep track of club member enrollments can also be used to print mailing labels for letters, bills, and announcements sent to members. This is easy to do with Access because mailing labels can be created by its Report Wizard.

☐ **4-7 CONCEPTS.** Any database that contains names and addresses can be used to print mailing labels. Other databases may contain data that can be used to print shelf, box, or even disk labels. In this concepts section you are introduced to the procedures you use to print such labels.

☐ **4-7 TUTORIAL.** In this tutorial you create a report that prints mailing labels using data from the *Club Members* table in the *Ever Hopeful Health Club* database.

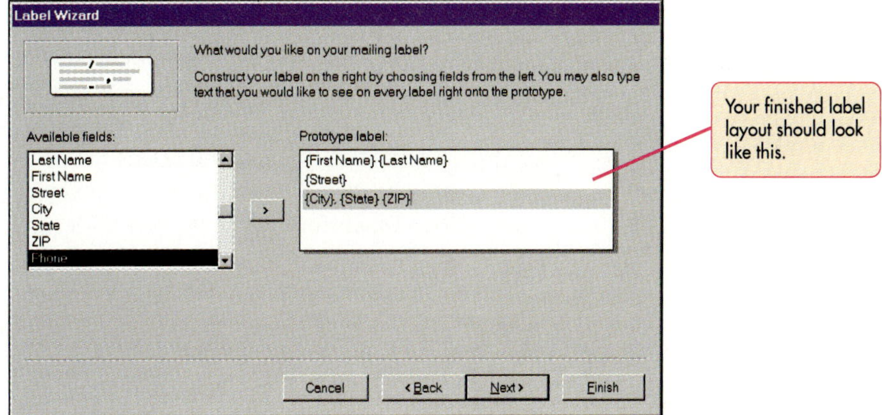

The label layout

☐ **4-7 DRILL.** In this drill you use Label Wizard to create shelf labels for each of the books.

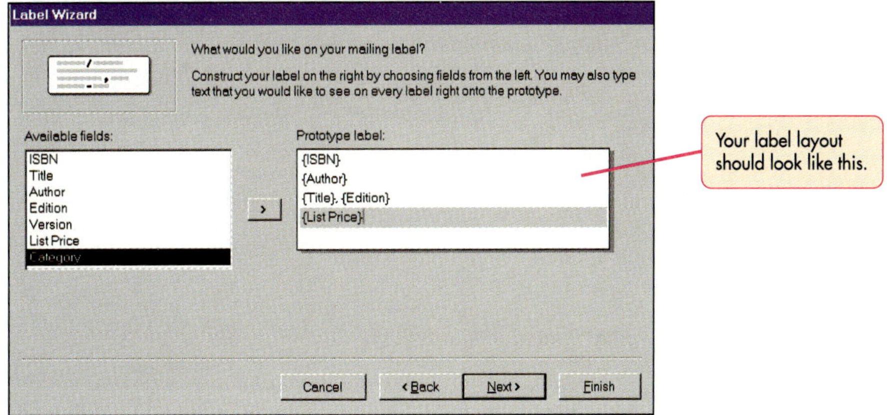

Book labels

Although Access's reporting and analyzing features are powerful, there may be times when you need more. In these cases, you can easily use Microsoft Word's word processing or desktop publishing features or Excel's spreadsheet or analytical features to enhance your work. You do so by selecting any table, query, form, or report and exporting it to Word or Excel.

When you select a table and execute the OfficeLinks command, the table is converted to a format that Word or Excel can work with and then stored in the same folder the database is stored in. You can use the Save As command to save the documents elsewhere, or move them to another folder.

The **OfficeLinks** button and drop-down list

QUICKSTEPS

Transferring Data to Microsoft Word or Excel

1. Select the table, query, form, or report that you want to desktop publish or analyze.

2. Click the **OfficeLinks** button's drop-down arrow on the toolbar and click the **Publish It with MS Word** or **Analyze It with MS Excel** commands. (**Chart Wizard** and **Merge It** are beyond the scope of this text.)

   ▶ If you choose **Publish It with MS Word**, the document is saved in an RTF (Rich Text Format) format in the same folder as the database. Word automatically starts and opens the document.

   ▶ If you choose **Analyze It with MS Excel**, the document is saved in Excel's .xls format in the same folder as the database. Excel automatically starts and opens the document.

3. Use the commands offered by those two applications.

PAL ON-LINE ACTIVITIES CHECKLIST

☐ **4-8 CONCEPTS.** Access is just one of the Microsoft Office applications. In this concepts section you are introduced to the procedures you use to publish Access data with Microsoft word or analyze it with Microsoft Excel.

☐ **4-8 TUTORIAL.** In this tutorial you publish a table from the *Ever Hopeful Health Club* database using Microsoft Word, and analyze it using Microsoft Excel. The tables are. One or both of those applications must be on your system to do this tutorial.

☐ **4-8 DRILL.** In this drill you export a table to both Microsoft Word and Excel.

LAB ACTIVITIES

EXERCISE

4-1 The General Store Database

In this exercise you create forms and reports for the tables in the *General Store* database.

Opening the Database

1. Open the database named *General Store* stored in the *Exercise Databases* folder of the *Access Student Resource Disk*.

Creating an AutoForm with the Form Wizard

2. On the **Forms** tab, click the **New** button, then select the *AutoForm: Columnar* choice and base the report on the *Employees* table. Save the finished form as **Employees-AutoForm: Columnar**.

Modifying the AutoForm

3. Use the **View** button on the toolbar to display the form in Design view. Use the **AutoFormat** button on the toolbar to select **Colorful 2**.

4. Still in Design view, select, drag, and size controls to make the form look something like the one shown in the figure "The modified employee form."

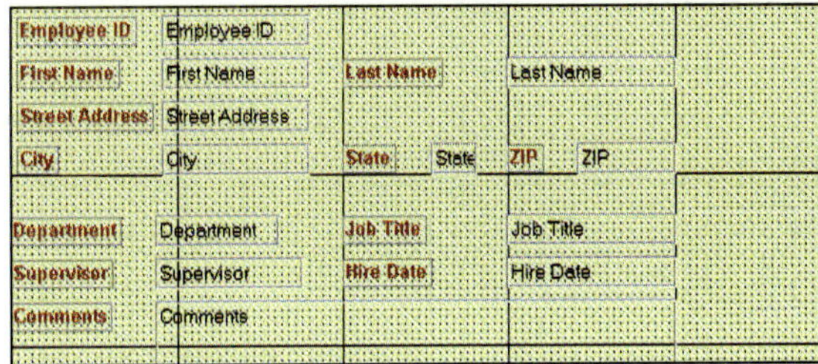

The modified employee form

Adding Calculated Controls

5. On the **Forms** tab, use the **New** button to select the *AutoForm: Columnar* choice and base the report on the *Daily Sales* table. Save the finished form as **Daily Sales-AutoForm: Columnar**.

6. In Design view, use the **Text Box** tool to add a new field labeled *Markup* on the same line as the *Selling Price* control and enter into it the expression =[Selling Price]*.5.

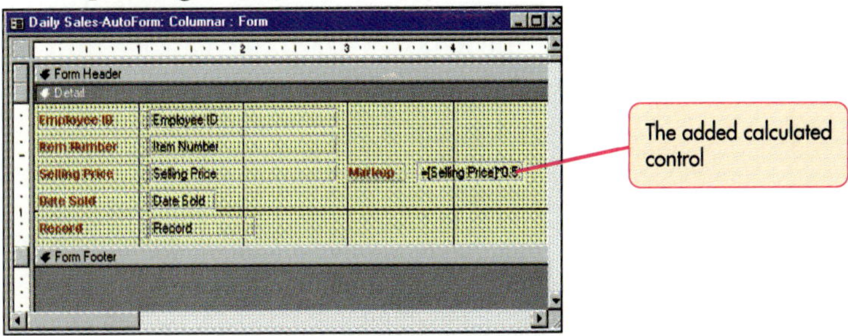

7. With the new control still selected, click the **Properties** button on the toolbar and set its format to *Currency*. Use the **Save** button on the toolbar to save your changes.

Creating a Totals Report

8. On the **Reports** tab, use the <u>N</u>ew button to select the *Report Wizard* choice and base the report on the *Daily Sales* table. When moving through the report Wizard's screens, make the following choices:

   ▶ Include all fields

   ▶ Group by *Employee ID*

   ▶ Sort by *Item Number* and use the **Summary <u>O</u>ptions** button to turn on *Avg* for the *Selling Price* Field

   ▶ Lay out as *Block* and *Portrait* orientation

   ▶ Style as *Casual*

   ▶ Save the report as **Daily Sales**

9. View the report, print it, and then close it.

Finishing Up

10. Close all open windows including the Database window.

4-1 The College Database

In this project you create forms and reports for the tables in the *College Courses* database.

1. Open the database named *College Courses* stored in the *Project Databases* folder of the *Access Student Resource Disk*.

2. Create an *AutoForm: Columnar* for the *Master Course List* table and save it as **Master Course List-AutoForm: Columnar**.

3. Modify the *Master Course List-AutoForm: Columnar* to look something like the one shown in the figure "The modified *Master Course List* form."

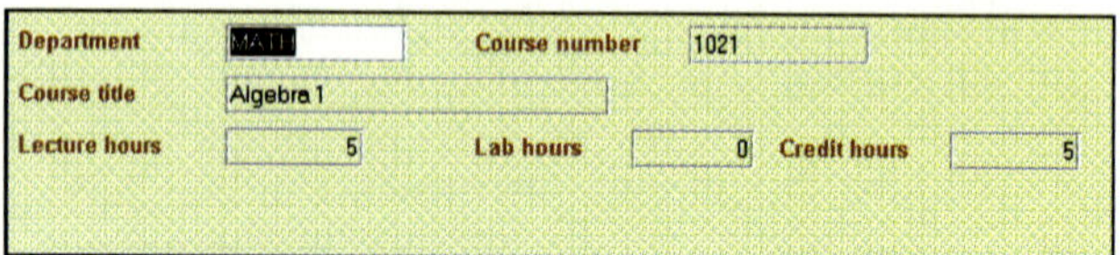

The modified *Master Course List* form

4. Add a new Text box named *Total Hours* on the line below the *Lecture hours* control and enter into it an expression that will add lecture hours and lab hours; then save your changes. Figure out how to use a toolbar button to right-align the data in the text box when it's displayed in Form view.

5. Use the Report Wizard to create a report for the *Master Course List* table with the following choices:

   ▶ Include all fields

   ▶ Grouped by *Department*

   ▶ Sorted by *Course Number* and summed by *Credit Hours*

   ▶ Any layout and style

   ▶ Saved as **Master Course List-Totals**

6. Print the report, and then close all windows including the Database window.

PicTorial FIVE

USING RELATIONAL DATABASES

After completing this PicTorial, you will be able to:

▸ **Describe the differences between record management and database management programs**

▸ **Relate tables**

▸ **Describe the difference between one-to-many and other types of relationships**

▸ **Create queries for multiple tables**

▸ **Create reports for multiple tables**

THE terms *database* and *database management program* are often used loosely. In fact, two types of programs are used to manage files of highly structured data: record management programs and database management programs.

Record Management Programs

Record management programs, sometimes called *file management* or *flat file database programs*, include those that are integrated into word processing and spreadsheet programs. They almost always store, maintain, and use data in single files. Until now, you have been using Access as you would use a record management program. If you tried to use a record management program to store data on various aspects of a business, you would have to store the data for different applications in separate files. To make changes, you would have to make them in each file when information is duplicated. Let's say you have one file for employee names, addresses, and phone numbers, and another file for payroll information. If a person's name occurs in both files, the name must be separately entered into each file. If the name must be changed or deleted later, it must be separately changed in or deleted from each file.

Database Management Programs

As the amount of information being processed increases, the record management method of using separate files to store information becomes cumbersome because information must be extensively duplicated. An employee's name might appear in several different files—for example, payroll, vacation, and expense accounts. There are disadvantages to this duplication:

▸ It increases the amount of data entry.

▸ It increases the risk of errors in the information. Because a person's name would have to be entered more than once, any changes in status would have to be made in different files, perhaps by different people. Over time, the data's accuracy deteriorates. Changes might be made in some files and not in others, or some data might be entered correctly into one file and incorrectly into another.

▸ It requires more storage space, which causes problems when the database is large.

Using a database management program such as Access eliminates these problems. With a database management program, each piece of information only needs to be stored once because the program can use related data stored in more than one table. Database management programs, therefore, have a major advantage over record management programs since many applications require more than one table. For example, if you stored data on your inventory, you might want to store the name, address, and phone number of the supplier to make it easier to reorder. In a record management program, this same information would have to be entered for each item from the same supplier, greatly enlarging the file and time it takes to enter data. If the supplier changed its address, each record that referred to one of its products would also have to be updated. Using a database management program such as Access, you could have one table store information on products and another store information on suppliers. The supplier's name, address, and phone number would only be entered or updated once.

Almost all microcomputer database management programs are *relational databases*. A relational database organizes its data into tables that can be related, or linked, to one another. You can then manipulate the data in these related tables to enter, update, and find information stored in the database.

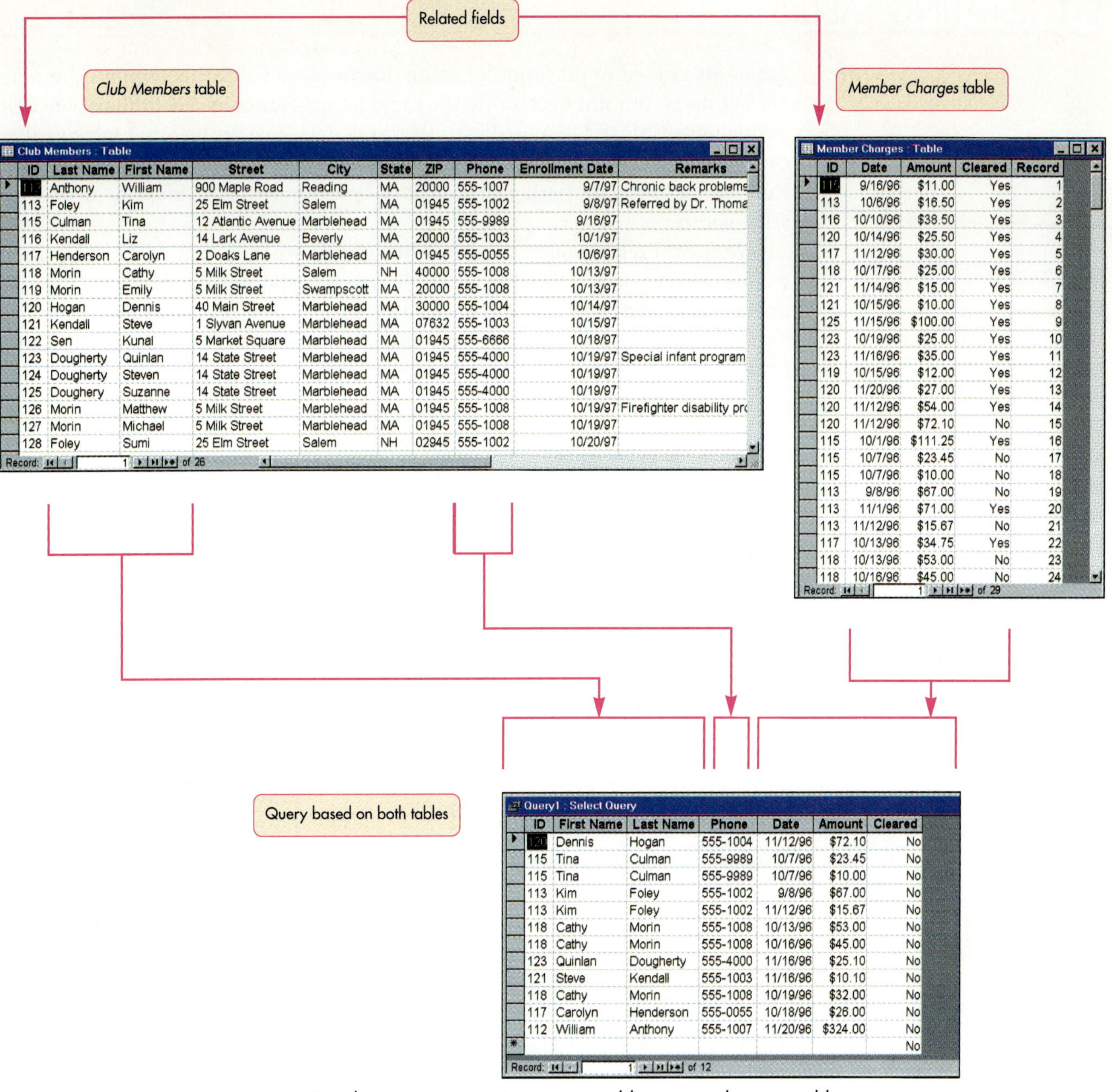

Database management programs address more than one table

Designing a relational database requires very careful planning because more than one table is involved. Not only does each table need to be well planned, but the relationships between files must also be carefully thought through. Since a relational database such as Access can store data in separate tables, the first step is to decide what data to keep in what tables. Then you define the relationships between these tables so Access can use the relationships for a variety of purposes, including the following:

▶ To automatically connect the tables for queries.

▶ To relate records in a Main/Subform form where the Main form is displayed as a Single-Column form and a second table, the Subform, is displayed as a datasheet.

▶ To enforce referential integrity (explained below)—ensuring that you don't add or delete records in ways that cause trouble.

Tables are related to one another using one or more fields that contain the same kind of data—but not necessarily the same name. Normally the primary key field in one table is linked to a field with the same data type in the other table—called the *foreign key*. In most cases the two fields must have only the same data type. However, if they are both Number data types, both fields must be set to the same width.

When you relate tables, you must first decide what kind of relationship there will be between them. The three possible types of relationships between tables are one-to-many, many-to-many, and one-to-one.

One-to-many relationships, by far the most common type, must meet two conditions:

▸ A single record in one table, called the *primary table*, can match many records in a second table, called the *related table*.

▸ No record in the related table can match more than one record in the primary table.

The field in the primary table used to relate it to the related table is usually its primary key, which by definition has no duplicate entries. Our *Ever Hopeful Health Club* database has a table listing members, with member ID as its primary key. It has a second table of charges incurred by members, where members are identified by their ID. In the *Club Members* table, member ID is the *primary key field*, and in the *Member Charges* table member ID is the *related field*. A one-to-many relationship exists between the two tables, in that each member can make many charges, but each charge can be made by only one member.

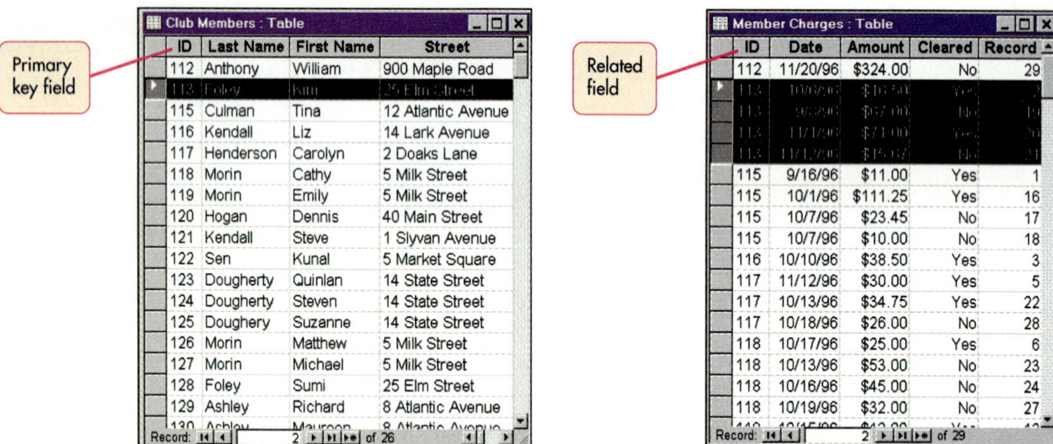

Tables with a one-to-many relationship, showing charges for the member with ID 113

Many-to-many relationships can have more than one matching record in both directions. For example, two tables used to match farm produce might list farmers in one table and farm products in another. Each farmer can grow many products and each product may be obtained from many farmers. These types of relationships can become very complex and are beyond the scope of this text.

One-to-one relationships can only have one matching record in both tables. For example, one table might contain each employee's name and address and another each employee's salary information. These relationships are rarely used because the information could all be stored in the same table.

A primary key field is used to link tables in a one-to-many relationship because that way you know there are no duplicate entries on the "one" side of the relationship. There is another way to do this, however. You can display a table in Design view and set a field's *Indexed* property to *Yes (No Duplicates)*. Either approach will ensure the field has no duplicates.

Enforcing Referential Integrity

When creating or editing a relationship between tables, you can specify that *referential integrity* be enforced. This simply ensures that you don't add or delete records in one table if it will adversely affect the data in another table. When you do so, you can only add and delete records under certain conditions.

▶ When you add a record to a related table, the data you enter in the matching field must have a matching record in the primary table. For example, you cannot enter a charge in the *Member Charges* table against a member ID that doesn't exist in the *Club Members* table.

▶ You cannot delete a record from the primary table if there are matching records in the related table. For example, you can't delete a member from the *Club Members* table when there are charges entered against the member's ID in the *Member Charges* table.

 If you violate these rules, the change is prevented and a message is displayed. Referential integrity can only be enforced when the following conditions exist:

▶ The matching field in the primary table is a primary key.

▶ The related fields share the same data type.

▶ Both tables are in the same database.

 When you specify that referential integrity be enforced, heavy bars on the relationship line indicate that it is.

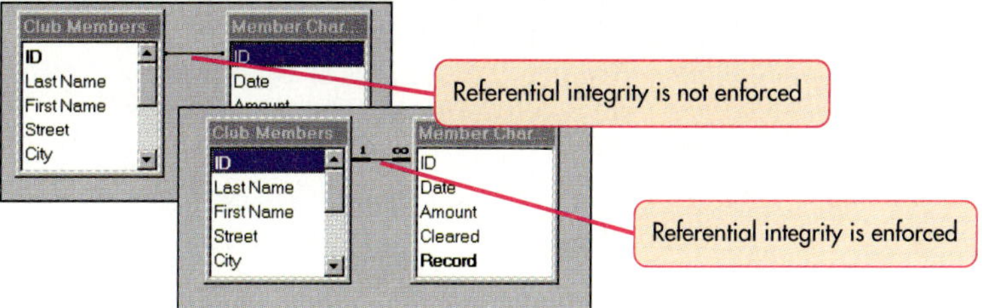

Heavy bars indicate referential integrity is enforced

Specifying Relationships

To specify relationships, you display the Relationships window. In this window, you can display any of the tables in the database with a list of their fields. To relate the tables, you then drag a field from the primary table's field list (the "one" table) and drop it on a field with the same data type in the related table's field list (the "many" table).

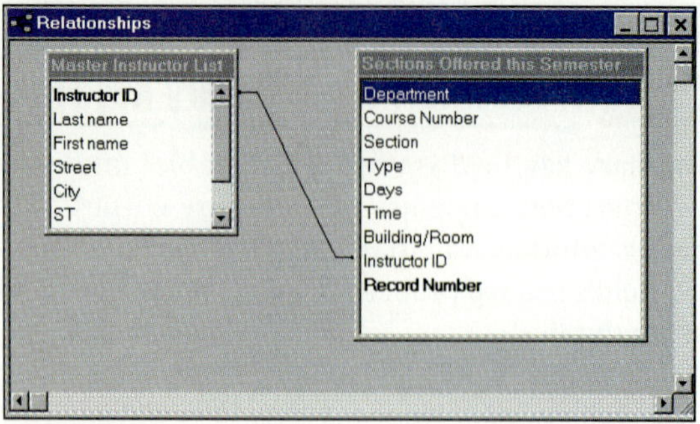

The Relationships window

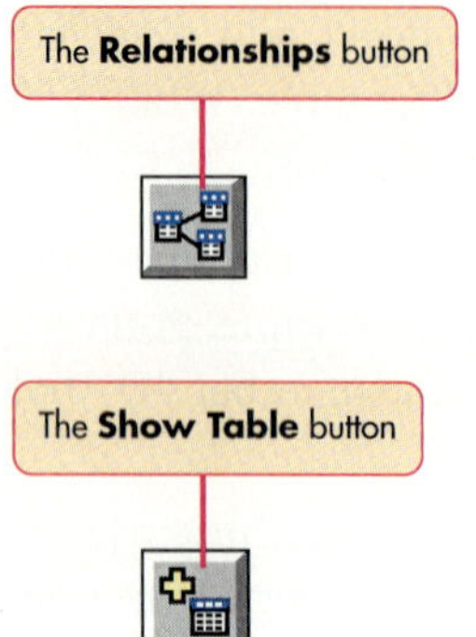
The **Relationships** button

The **Show Table** button

Creating New Relationships

1. Click the **Relationships** button on the toolbar, or pull down the **Tools** menu and click the **Relationships** command to display the Relationships window. (If you have previously established relationships, they appear as you last saved them—see the QuickSteps box "Editing Relationships" later in this section.)

2. Click the **Show Table** button on the toolbar, or pull down the **Relationships** menu and click the **Show Table** command to display the Show Table dialog box.

3. Click the name of each table you want to create a relationship for in the Show Table dialog box and then click the **Add** button to display them in the window. Each added table has a title and list of its fields. Click the **Close** button to close the Show Table dialog box.

4. Drag the primary key field (displayed in bold) from the primary table (the "one" table) and drop it on a field with the same data type in the related table (the "many" table). When you release the mouse button to drop the field, the Relationships dialog box is displayed.

5. Create relationships as described in the box "Understanding the Relationships Dialog Box."

6. Click the **Create** button to close the Relationships dialog box and lines appear in the Relationships window linking the tables. A bold line indicates that referential integrity will be enforced, while a light one indicates it won't be. A symbol at each end of the line indicates the type of relationship—either one ("1") or many ("∞").

7. Close the Relationships window and you are asked if you want to save changes to the layout. Your choice affects only the layout (the arrangement of tables you added or moved), not the relationships you set.

UNDERSTANDING
The Relationships Dialog Box

When you specify a relationship, the Relationships dialog box appears with the following options:

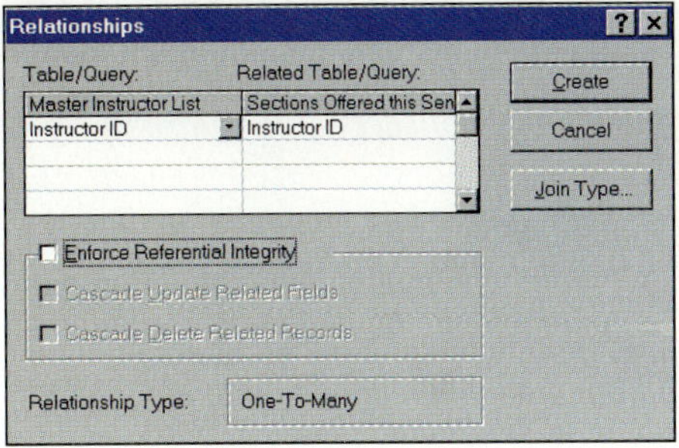

Table/Query lists the name of the field being related in the primary table. This field is often the table's primary key.

Related Table/Query lists the name of the field being related in the related table. This field is sometimes called the foreign key.

Enforce Referential Integrity check box, when on (☑), ensures that you don't inadvertently delete data (see the section "Referential Integrity").

Cascade Update Related Fields and **Cascade Delete Related Records** check boxes, when on (☑), allow additions and deletions that would otherwise break referential integrity rules. Access will then make the changes in the related table to preserve referential integrity. For example, if you delete a record in the primary table that has matching records in the related table, those records in the related table are also deleted.

Create button closes the dialog box and establishes the relationship based on the settings you have made.

Join Type button displays the Join Properties dialog box where you can specify inner joins (the default) or outer joins (which we don't use in this text).

Editing Relationships

After specifying a relationship between tables, you can edit it at any time to add tables, change the related fields, or change the properties of the relationship.

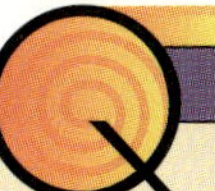

QUICKSTEPS
Editing Relationships

1. Click the **Relationships** button on the toolbar, or pull down the **Tools** menu and click the **Relationships** command to display the relationships as you last saved them.
2. Click the **Show All Relationships** button on the toolbar, or pull down the **Relationships** menu and click the **Show All** command.
3. Edit the relationships using the procedures discussed in the box "Understanding Relationship Editing Procedures."

UNDERSTANDING
Relationship Editing Procedures

When the Relationships window is open, you can use the following procedures to edit existing relationships:

▸ To edit a relationship, double-click the relationship line to display the Relationships dialog box. (See the box "Understanding the Relationships Dialog Box.")

▸ To delete a relationship, click the relationship line to select it and then press Del.

▸ To remove a table from the Relationships window, click anywhere in it to select it and press Del, or pull down the **Edit** menu and click the **Delete** command.

▸ To add a table to the Relationships window, click the **Show Table** button on the toolbar, or pull down the **Relationships** menu and click the **Show Table** command.

To remove all tables from the Relationships window, pull down the **Edit** menu and click the **Clear Layout** command.

☐ **5-1 CONCEPTS.** When you want to use more than one table to create queries, forms, or reports, the first step is to indicate how the tables are related. In this concepts section you are introduced to this procedure.

☐ **5-1 TUTORIAL.** In this tutorial you relate the *Club Members* and *Member Charges* tables in the *Ever Hopeful Health Club* database.

☐ **5-1 DRILL.** In this drill you relate the *Titles and Publishers* and *Quarterly Sales* tables in the *Publisher Sales* database.

5-2 CREATING QUERIES FOR RELATED TABLES

Querying a single table, as you have seen, is a powerful way to locate information in a database. This power is extended when you query more than one table at the same time. To query more than one table, you specify the tables to be queried by adding them to the Select Query window and then join, or connect, the tables to one another. Joining the tables is just like creating a relationship between them. In fact, if the tables are already related, they are already joined. When tables are joined, a *join line* connects a field in one table to a field in another to show how the tables are joined. These are called the *join fields*, and Access uses them to establish the connection between the two tables.

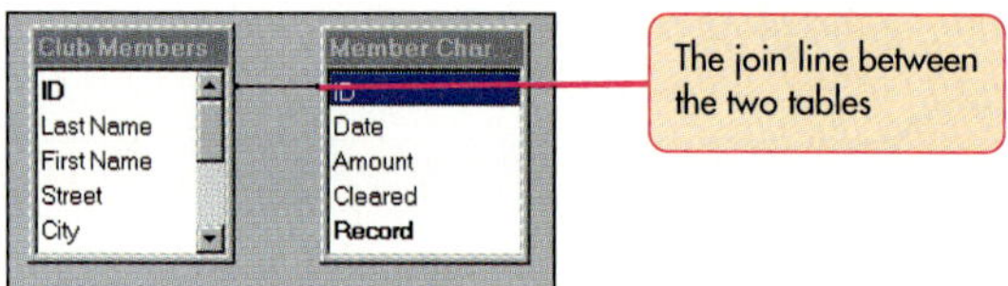

The fields that you use to join two tables must meet the same conditions you saw when establishing a relationship between tables. Basically they must have the same data type. (Additionally, if they are both Number data types, both must be set to the same width. And if one is an AutoNumber data type, the other must be a Number data type set to Long Integer format.) Tables can be joined in the Select Query window in any one of three ways:

▶ You can specify a relationship between the tables in the Relationships window before creating a query (see Section 5-1). If this has been done, when the tables are added to the Select Query window, a join line shows that established relationship. If referential integrity is being enforced, the "1" and "∞" symbols are displayed. As you've seen, the "1" indicates the "one" table in a one-to-many relationship and the "∞" symbol indicates the "many" table.

▶ The join line will be added automatically if two tables each have a field with the same name and data type and one of those fields is a primary key. The "1" and "∞" symbols are not displayed for this type of join because referential integrity is not enforced.

▶ You can specify the relationship between tables in a Select Query window by dragging a field from one table to another. If you do so, the relationship applies only to that query and again referential integrity is not enforced. To use the same table in another query, you will have to specify it again when you create that query.

If you include fields from two tables in a query that are not properly joined, Access cannot determine how to associate the data and the resulting dynaset may have data combined in such a way that it's meaningless. This can also take a long time and create a very large file. This type of dynaset created from an improper join is sometimes called a cross-product or Cartesian product.

When you query tables that have a one-to-many relationship you can usually update data in all fields but the one used on the "one" side to join the tables. However, you may have problems using the query to update the underlying tables. For example, if you update a record on the "one" side, you can't update the join field on the many side until you have first saved your changes to the "one" side. When specifying how the tables are related or joined, be sure the table on the "one" side is a primary key field or has its *Indexed* property set to *Yes (No Duplicates)*. Then design the query and use it to display the dynaset. When you try entering data, you may see a message on the status bar that explains why you can't do so. Use Help to search for the message's meaning under the topic "queries: updating underlying tables."

When you delete a record in a query based on two tables with a one-to-many relationship, it is deleted only from the "many" table. The entire record is deleted even if all of the fields are not displayed in the dynaset.

QUICKSTEPS

Querying Related Tables

1. Click the **Queries** tab in the Database window.

2. Click the **New** button on the Database window, or pull down the **Insert** menu and click the **Query** command to display the New Query dialog box.

3. Click the *Design View* choice and then click the **OK** button to display the Show Table dialog box.

4. Click the names of each table in the Show Table dialog box that you want to query and then click the **Add** button to list its fields in the top part of the Select Query window. (To add more than one table at the same time, hold down Ctrl as you click each of them.)

5. Click the **Close** button to close the Show Table dialog box.

6. If need be, specify how the tables are joined by dragging a field from the primary table (the "one" table) and dropping it on a field with the same data type in the related table (the "many" table). (If the tables have been related, the relationship line automatically becomes the join line in the Select Query window.)

7. Drag fields from any of the tables to the QBE grid and specify criteria just as you did for creating filters.

8. Click the **Save** button on the toolbar, or pull down the **File** menu and click the **Save** command, enter the query's name in the **Query Name** text box and click the **OK** button. The query is then listed on the **Queries** tab in the Database window.

QUICKSTEPS

Creating and Editing Joins

▶ To add tables to the top half of the Select Query window, click the **Show Table** button on the toolbar. Select the table you want to add and click the **Add** button. (To add more than one table, hold down [Ctrl] while clicking each.)

▶ To draw a join line, drag the name of a field in one table and drop it on the name of a field in another table when the pointer is displayed as a field symbol.

▶ To delete an existing join, click the join line to select it and press [Del].

▶ To display a join line's properties, double-click it, or select it, pull down the **View** menu, and click the **Join Properties** command.

▶ To delete a table from a query, click it to select it and then press [Del].

PAL ON-LINE ACTIVITIES CHECKLIST

☐ **5-2 CONCEPTS.** Once tables have been related, you create queries for them the same way you create them for a single table. In this concepts section you are introduced to this procedure.

☐ **5-2 TUTORIAL.** In this tutorial you create and save a query for the already related *Club Members* and *Member Charges* tables in the *Ever Hopeful Health Club* database.

☐ **5-2 DRILL.** In this drill you create a query using the related *Titles and Publishers* and *Quarterly Sales* tables in the *Publisher Sales* database.

Order	Table	Field
1	Titles and Publishers	ISBN
2	Titles and Publishers	Title
3	Titles and Publishers	Author
4	Quarterly Sales	Sales Period
5	Quarterly Sales	Trade Sales
6	Quarterly Sales	Educational Sales
7	Quarterly Sales	Mail Order Sales
8	Quarterly Sales	International Sales

5-3 CREATING FORMS FOR RELATED TABLES

To create a form for multiple tables that have been related, you base it on a query. The query's dynaset is displayed in the form just as if it were a single table. Any changes made to the data in the form are carried to the underlying tables. Using a query in this manner allows you to specify which fields appear in the form, what their order is, and how they are sorted. Criteria can also be used in the query to control which records are displayed as you use the form to scroll through the records.

You can design a query on which a form is based so that when you enter something like a customer's ID number, all of the information about that customer is automatically looked up in the appropriate table and entered into the form for you. This is the way many mail-order companies handle your order when you give them a customer ID or when your telephone number is looked up automatically after caller-ID identifies it for the database.

AutoLookup works in queries where the two tables have a one-to-many relationship. In addition, the join field (for example, the customer's ID) from the "many" table must be included in the query. When you enter the customer ID in the query, it looks up information from the "one" table. To see how to do this, search "AutoLookup" in Access Help.

PAL ON-LINE ACTIVITIES CHECKLIST

☐ **5-3 CONCEPTS.** Once tables have been related, you create forms for them the same way you create them for a single table. In this concepts section you are introduced to this procedure.

☐ **5-3 TUTORIAL.** In this tutorial you create and save a form designed to work with the related *Club Members* and *Member Charges* table in the *Ever Hopeful Health Club* database. To do so, you'll use the *Uncleared Charges* query that draws fields from both tables.

☐ **5-3 DRILL.** In this drill you create an AutoForm for the *Sales by Title* query you created earlier.

5-4 CREATING REPORTS FOR RELATED TABLES

Once you have related tables, you can not only create queries for them but also generate reports based on those queries. The report can then contain fields from more than one table.

Another way to create reports using more than one table is to use Report Wizard to design a custom report. When specifying fields to be included, you can click the **Tables/Queries** drop-down arrow on the first Report Wizard screen and select another table to draw fields from. Using a query in this manner allows you to specify which fields appear in the report, what their order is, and how they are sorted. You can also use criteria in the query to control which records are included in the report.

PAL ON-LINE ACTIVITIES CHECKLIST

☐ **5-4 CONCEPTS.** Once tables have been related, you create reports for them the same way you create them for a single table. In this concepts section you are introduced to this procedure.

☐ **5-4 TUTORIAL.** In this tutorial you create and save a report based on the *Uncleared Charges* query in the *Ever Hopeful Health Club* database. This query contains fields from both the *Club Members* and *Member Charges* tables.

☐ **5-4 DRILL.** In this drill you create an AutoReport for the *Sales by Title* query you created earlier.

LAB ACTIVITIES

EXERCISE

5-1 The General Store Database

In this exercise you relate the tables in the *General Store* database and then use that relationship for queries, forms, and reports.

Opening the Database

1. Open the database named *General Store* stored in the *Exercise Databases* folder of the *Access Student Resource Disk*.

Creating New Relationships

2. Use the **Relationships** button on the toolbar to display the empty Relationships window, then click the **Show Table** button on the toolbar to list the tables in the database.

3. Add all three listed tables to the Relationships window, then close the Show Table dialog box.

4. Drag the *Employee ID* field in the *Employees* table and drop it on the *Employee ID* in the *Daily Sales* table. When the Relationships dialog box is displayed, enforce referential integrity, then create the relationship.

5. Drag the *Item Number* field in the *Inventory* table and drop it on the *Item Number* field in the *Daily Sales* table. When the Relationships dialog box is displayed, enforce referential integrity, then create the relationship.

6. Drag the tables to better show the relationships, then close the Relationships window and save your changes to the layout.

Querying Multiple Tables

7. On the **Queries** tab, click the **New** button to display the New Query dialog box and select *Design View* and click the **OK** button.

8. Add all three tables to the top part of the Select Query window, then close
   the Show Table dialog box. (To add more than one table at the same time,
   hold down [Ctrl] as you click each of them.)

9. Drag the following fields to the QBE grid in the order shown:

Order	Table	Field
1	*Employees*	*Employee ID*
2	*Employees*	*Last Name*
3	*Daily Sales*	*Item Number*
4	*Inventory*	*Description*
5	*Inventory*	*Selling Price*

10. Save the query as **Sales by Employee**.

11. Use the **Run** button on the toolbar to display the query's dynaset. (The result
    here is meager because daily sales has only 1 employee and 5 items.) Close
    the dynaset's window.

Creating Forms for Related Tables

12. On the **Forms** tab, click the **New** button to display the New Form dialog box.

13. Select *AutoForm: Columnar* and use the drop-down arrow ([▼]) to select the
    query *Sales by Employee* to base the form on.

14. Save the form as **Sales by Employee** and close the form's window.

Creating Reports for Related Tables

15. Use the **Reports** tab to display the Report objects, and click the **New** button
    on the Database window to display the New Report dialog box.

16. Select *AutoReport: Tabular* and use the drop-down arrow ([▼]) to select the
    Sales by Employee query to base the report on. Click **OK** to create the report.

17. Close the Print Preview window then use the **Save As/Export** command on
    the **File** menu to save the report as **Sales by Employee**.

18. Close all open windows including the Database window.

PROJECT

5-1 The College Database

In this project you join tables in the *College Courses* database while using select
queries to list information in various pairs of tables.

1. Open the database named *College Courses* stored in the *Project Databases*
   folder of the *Access Student Resource Disk*.

2. Create a new select query in Design view as follows:

   ▶ Add the *Master Course List* and *Sections Offered this Semester* tables to the
     Query window.

▶ Join the *Course number* field in the *Master Course List* table to the same field in the *Sections Offered this Semester* table.

▶ Move the following field names to the QBE grid:

Number	Table	Field
1	Master Course List	Department
2	Master Course List	Course number
3	Master Course List	Course title
4	Sections Offered this Semester	Section
5	Sections Offered this Semester	Type
6	Sections Offered this Semester	Days
7	Sections Offered this Semester	Time

▶ Save the query as **Section Log**.

▶ Display the query's dynaset and then print it.

▶ Close the Select Query window.

3. Create a new select query in Design View as follows:

▶ Add the *Sections Offered this Semester* and *Master Instructor List* tables to the Select Query window. (Notice how identical fields are automatically joined.)

▶ Move the following field names to the QBE grid:

Number	Table	Field
1	Sections Offered this Semester	Department
2	Sections Offered this Semester	Course Number
3	Sections Offered this Semester	Days
4	Sections Offered this Semester	Time
5	Master Instructor List	Last name
6	Master Instructor List	First name

▶ Save the query as **Instructor Log**.

▶ Display the query's dynaset and then print it.

▶ Close the Select Query window.

4. Create an *AutoForm: Columnar* form based on the *Section Log* query. Save it as **Section Log-AutoForm: Columnar**.

5. Create an *AutoForm: Tabular* form based on the *Section Log* query. Save it as **Section Log-AutoForm: Tabular**.

6. Create an *AutoReport: Columnar* form based on the *Instructor Log* query. Save it as **Instructor Log-AutoReport: Columnar**.

7. Create an *AutoReport: Tabular* form based on the *Instructor Log* query. Save it as **Instructor Log-AutoReport: Tabular**.

8. Close all open windows including the Database window.

LICENSE AGREEMENT

YOU SHOULD CAREFULLY READ THE FOLLOWING TERMS AND CONDITIONS BEFORE BREAKING THE SEAL ON THE PACKAGE. AMONG OTHER THINGS, THIS AGREEMENT LICENSES THE ENCLOSED SOFTWARE TO YOU AND CONTAINS WARRANTY AND LIABILITY DISCLAIMERS. BY BREAKING THE SEAL ON THE PACKAGE, YOU ARE ACCEPTING AND AGREEING TO THE TERMS AND CONDITIONS OF THIS AGREEMENT. IF YOU DO NOT AGREE TO THE TERMS OF THIS AGREEMENT, DO NOT BREAK THE SEAL. YOU SHOULD PROMPTLY RETURN THE PACKAGE UNOPENED.

LICENSE.
Subject to the provisions contained herein, Prentice-Hall, Inc. ("PH") hereby grants to you a non-exclusive, non-transferable license to use the object code version of the computer software product ("Software") contained in the package on a single computer of the type identified on the package.

SOFTWARE AND DOCUMENTATION.
PH shall furnish the Software to you on media in machine-readable object code form and may also provide the standard documentation ("Documentation") containing instructions for operation and use of the Software.

LICENSE TERM AND CHARGES.
The term of this license commences upon delivery of the Software to you and is perpetual unless earlier terminated upon default or as otherwise set forth herein.

TITLE.
Title, and ownership right, and intellectual property rights in and to the Software and Documentation shall remain in PH and/or in suppliers to PH of programs contained in the Software. The Software is provided for your own internal use under this license. This license does not include the right to sublicense and is personal to you and therefore may not be assigned (by operation of law or otherwise) or transferred without the prior written consent of PH. You acknowledge that the Software in source code form remains a confidential trade secret of PH and/or its suppliers and therefore you agree not to attempt to decipher or decompile, modify, disassemble, reverse engineer or prepare derivative works of the Software or develop source code for the Software or knowingly allow others to do so.   Further, you may not copy the Documentation or other written materials accompanying the Software.

UPDATES.
This license does not grant you any right, license, or interest in and to any improvements, modifications, enhancements, or updates to the Software and Documentation. Updates, if available, may be obtained by you at PH's then current standard pricing, terms, and conditions.

LIMITED WARRANTY AND DISCLAIMER.
PH warrants that the media containing the Software, if provided by PH, is free from defects in material and workmanship under normal use for a period of sixty (60) days from the date you purchased a license to it.

THIS IS A LIMITED WARRANTY AND IT IS THE ONLY WARRANTY MADE BY PH. THE SOFTWARE IS PROVIDED 'AS IS' AND PH SPECIFICALLY DISCLAIMS ALL WARRANTIES OF ANY KIND, EITHER EXPRESS OR IMPLIED, INCLUDING, BUT NOT LIMITED TO, THE IMPLIED WARRANTY OF MERCHANTABILITY AND FITNESS FOR A PARTICULAR PURPOSE.   FURTHER, PH DOES NOT WARRANT, GUARANTY OR MAKE ANY REPRESENTATIONS REGARDING THE USE, OR THE RESULTS OF THE USE, OF THE SOFTWARE IN TERMS OF CORRECTNESS, ACCURACY, RELIABILITY, CURRENTNESS, OR OTHERWISE AND DOES NOT WARRANT THAT THE OPERATION OF ANY SOFTWARE WILL BE UNINTERRUPTED OR ERROR FREE. PH EXPRESSLY DISCLAIMS ANY WARRANTIES NOT STATED HEREIN. NO ORAL OR WRITTEN INFORMATION OR ADVICE GIVEN BY PH, OR ANY PH DEALER, AGENT, EMPLOYEE OR OTHERS SHALL CREATE, MODIFY OR EXTEND A WARRANTY OR IN ANY WAY INCREASE THE SCOPE OF THE FOREGOING WARRANTY, AND NEITHER SUBLICENSEE OR PURCHASER MAY RELY ON ANY SUCH INFORMATION OR ADVICE. If the media is subjected to accident, abuse, or improper use; or if you violate the terms of this Agreement, then this warranty shall immediately be terminated. This warranty shall not apply if the Software is used on or in conjunction with hardware or programs other than the unmodified version of hardware and programs with which the Software was designed to be used as described in the Documentation.

LIMITATION OF LIABILITY.
Your sole and exclusive remedies for any damage or loss in any way connected with the Software are set forth below. UNDER NO CIRCUMSTANCES AND UNDER NO LEGAL THEORY, TORT, CONTRACT, OR OTHERWISE, SHALL PH BE LIABLE TO YOU OR ANY OTHER PERSON FOR ANY INDIRECT, SPECIAL, INCIDENTAL, OR CONSEQUENTIAL DAMAGES OF ANY CHARACTER INCLUDING, WITHOUT LIMITATION, DAMAGES FOR LOSS OF GOODWILL, LOSS OF PROFIT, WORK STOPPAGE, COMPUTER FAILURE OR MALFUNCTION, OR ANY AND ALL OTHER COMMERCIAL DAMAGES OR LOSSES, OR FOR ANY OTHER DAMAGES EVEN IF PH SHALL HAVE BEEN INFORMED OF THE POSSIBILITY OF SUCH DAMAGES, OR FOR ANY CLAIM BY ANY OTHER PARTY. PH'S THIRD PARTY PROGRAM SUPPLIERS MAKE NO WARRANTY, AND HAVE NO LIABILITY WHATSOEVER, TO YOU. PH's sole and exclusive obligation and liability and your exclusive remedy shall be: upon PH's election, (i) the replacement of your defective media; or. (ii) the repair or correction of your defective media if PH is able, so that it will conform to the above warranty; or (iii) if PH is unable to replace or repair, you may terminate this license by returning the Software. Only if you inform PH of your problem during the applicable warranty period will PH be obligated to honor this warranty. You may contact PH to inform PH of the problem by writing: Application Software Editor, Prentice Hall Business Publishing Division, One Lake Street, Upper Saddle River, NJ 07458

SOME STATES OR JURISDICTIONS DO NOT ALLOW THE EXCLUSION OF IMPLIED WARRANTIES OR LIMITATION OR EXCLUSION OF CONSEQUENTIAL DAMAGES, SO THE ABOVE LIMITATIONS OR EXCLUSIONS MAY NOT APPLY TO YOU. THIS WARRANTY GIVES YOU SPECIFIC LEGAL RIGHTS AND YOU MAY ALSO HAVE OTHER RIGHTS WHICH VARY BY STATE OR JURISDICTION.

MISCELLANEOUS.
If any provision of this Agreement is held to be ineffective, unenforceable, or illegal under certain circumstances for any reason, such decision shall not affect the validity or enforceability (i) of such provision under other circumstances or (ii) of the remaining provisions hereof under all circumstances and such provision shall be reformed to and only to the extent necessary to make it effective, enforceable, and legal under such circumstances. All headings are solely for convenience and shall not be considered in interpreting this Agreement. This Agreement shall be governed by and construed under New York law as such law applies to agreements between New York residents entered into and to be performed entirely within New York, except as required by U.S. Government rules and regulations to be governed by Federal law.

YOU ACKNOWLEDGE THAT YOU HAVE READ THIS AGREEMENT, UNDERSTAND IT, AND AGREE TO BE BOUND BY ITS TERMS AND CONDITIONS. YOU FURTHER AGREE THAT IT IS THE COMPLETE AND EXCLUSIVE STATEMENT OF THE AGREEMENT BETWEEN US THAT SUPERSEDES ANY PROPOSAL OR PRIOR AGREEMENT, ORAL OR WRITTEN, AND ANY OTHER COMMUNICATIONS BETWEEN US RELATING TO THE SUBJECT MATTER OF THIS AGREEMENT.

U.S. GOVERNMENT RESTRICTED RIGHTS.
Use, duplication or disclosure by the Government is subject to restrictions set forth in subparagraphs (a) through (d) of the Commercial Computer-Restricted Rights clause at FAR 52.227-19 when applicable, or in subparagraph (c) (1) (ii) of the Rights in Technical Data and Computer Software clause at DFARS 252.227-7013, and in similar clauses in the NASA FAR Supplement.